Praise for *Force of Nature*

"George Fell, an unsung conservationist and founder of the Nature Conservancy, finally receives his just due in this extremely detailed biography. . . . Highly comprehensive, this biography not only does justice to an environmental hero but also serves as a credit to the concept that successful activism requires both perseverance and practicality."

ForeWord Reviews

"The inspiring story of the innovative conservation institutions and legislation instigated by George Fell and his wife, Barbara, highlighted by the Nature Conservancy, arguably the largest environmental organization in the world."

Stephen Laubach,
author of *Living a Land Ethic*

"George Fell sparred with fellow naturalists and politicians to bring into being organizations that are models for today's worldwide conservation efforts. Pearson documents this extraordinary life with a wide range of sources, including interviews over two decades with both Fell's partners and his doubters."

James Ballowe,
author of *A Man of Salt and Tree*

Force *of* Nature

George Fell,
Founder of the Natural Areas Movement

Arthur Melville Pearson

The University of Wisconsin Press

The University of Wisconsin Press
728 State Street, Suite 443
Madison, Wisconsin 53706
uwpress.wisc.edu

Gray's Inn House, 127 Clerkenwell Road
London EC1R 5DB, United Kingdom
eurospanbookstore.com

Printed in the United States of America

This book may be available in a digital edition.

Library of Congress Cataloging-in-Publication Data

Names: Pearson, Arthur Melville, author. | Crane, Peter R., author of foreword.
Title: Force of nature: George Fell, founder of the natural areas movement
| Arthur Melville Pearson; [Foreword by Peter R. Crane].
Description: Madison, Wisconsin: The University of Wisconsin Press, [2017]
| Includes bibliographical references and index.
Identifiers: LCCN 2016041570 | ISBN 9780299312305 (cloth: alk. paper)
Subjects: LCSH: Fell, George B. | Nature Conservancy (U.S.) – History.
| Natural Areas Association (U.S.) History.
| Illinois Nature Preserves Commission History.
| Natural Land Institute (Rockford, Ill.) – History.
| Natural areas Illinois History.
| Nature conservation Illinois History.
| Conservationists Illinois Biography.
| Natural areas United States History.
| Nature conservation United States History.
Classification: LCC QH76.5.I5 P43 2017 | DDC 333.7209773 dc23
LC record available at https://lccn.loc.gov/2016041570

ISBN 9780299312343 (pbk.: alk. paper)

conserved with a grant

Figure Foundation

by goodness termination

For

Barbara Fell

Contents

Illustrations

following page 80

Foreword

Looking today at the many organizations dedicated to the preservation of open space, the stewardship of landscapes, and the conservation of nature, it is a field of human endeavor that perhaps seems overly crowded. It was not always this way. Within the lifetimes of many who are still active in the environmental movement, these kinds of organizations have proliferated. The ways in which they operate have diversified and their missions have also become more nuanced. It is easy to conclude, with some justification, that the current complexity is less than efficient, and bedeviled not only by insufficient coordination and cooperation but also in some cases by outright competition. This wonderful book by Arthur Pearson shows us how, and also points to why, we have arrived at this point. And of course, our current complexity can all be traced back to people, and the different ways in which they react to the circumstances in which they find themselves.

Pearson details the life and accomplishments of George Fell, an influential iconoclast who dedicated his life to the cause of nature conservation. Fell was the right person, in the right place, at the right time, but through his tenacity and resilience he also made the most of his moment. As the title of this book makes clear, he was a true force of nature. He had a deep-seated dedication to the natural world, and in the two decades after World War II he left an indelible mark on land conservation in North America. Through the part he played in the creation of The Nature Conservancy and the Natural Land Institute, Fell also helped democratize nature conservation in North America and set it on a new course. As the postwar economy boomed, nature needed assistance. Fell stepped up. And the organizations that he advanced in the United States influenced conservation action around the world. Fell's efforts provided impetus for new levels of environmental awareness that began to coalesce through the late 1960s. He was one of the great early visionaries of the environmental movement but never sought the limelight. Pearson's book brings Fell out of the shadows and provides richly deserved and long overdue recognition.

George Fell was one of a kind. He was introverted and soft-spoken, even awkward, but once he found his purpose in life his dedication was unrelenting. Fell's cause was caring for nature and "striving for beauty," and he is a shining example of how individuals can make a difference. Fell's background was far from privileged; quite the contrary, he was a quintessential outsider, but he made good things happen through strength of will, force of effort, and personal sacrifice. George Fell was, as they say, a "doer" with a special kind of entrepreneurial flair for building organizations.

George Fell was also driven. His passion for nature was his life, and with his devoted partner Barbara, his commitment never wavered. He was a leader. But leaders come in many different flavors, and Fell, for all his strengths, was also complicated, uncompromising, and single-minded to a fault. As Pearson demonstrates by recounting the twists and turns in a remarkable life, Fell illustrates the general rule that an individual's greatest strength is so often also his greatest weakness. For George Fell, as with many who are driven by deep commitment and strong sense of purpose, compromise did not come easily. On more than one occasion, this led Fell to a parting of the ways with the very organizations he did so much to build.

George Fell, however, was nothing if not irrepressible. It was discord within the Ecological Society of America that led to the creation of the Ecologist's Union, which then evolved, with Fell at the helm, into The Nature Conservancy. Then, with his departure from The Nature Conservancy, Fell founded the Natural Land Institute. When that institution also reached a crisis point, Fell helped birth the Natural Areas Association. Pearson's insights into George Fell and his role in the genesis of The Nature Conservancy, the Natural Land Institute, and the Natural Areas Association are a case study of the creativity that can flow from individual passion but also how that can translate into organizational fission. This same process, played out with particular intensity over the past seventy-five years, is part of the reason why we have such a patchwork of environmental organizations today, all working broadly toward the same ends.

So should we be concerned? For me, the answer is no. Coordination and cooperation is always welcome, but here, as in many other areas, we should take care that the perfect does not become the enemy of the good. This book shows us that the complex organizational landscape we have today is a product of a particular history in which determined individuals like George Fell, often with their particular flaws and foibles, played a disproportionate role. There is even more work to be done now than when George Fell was at his zenith, and there ought to be room for any individual and any organization aligned with what he was trying to accomplish. George Fell and others like him found the right outlet for their passion and their own way to improve the long-term future of nature. Rather than dwell on their shortcomings, we should honor their strengths and be grateful for their accomplishments.

Sir Peter R. Crane FRS

President, Oak Spring Garden Foundation

Acknowledgments

I never met George Fell. I came to know him in a way that I am sure he would have appreciated: by immersing myself in his voluminous archive. Before and after the Natural Land Institute donated his papers to his undergraduate alma mater, the University of Illinois, I read through school records, journals, personal letters, professional correspondence, reports, pamphlets, newsletters, white papers, interview transcripts, news clippings, and complete sets of minutes from several conservation organizations, both large and small. My thanks to Anna Trammel and Emily Swain at the University of Illinois Archives and to the entire staff of the Natural Land Institute for their research help. Special thanks go to the institute's former executive director, Jerry Paulson, who first introduced me to Fell through the invitation to write a biographical treatment for the institute's fiftieth anniversary. Special thanks, too, to the institute's Jill Kennay for her exceptional research help, as well as for her devoted care of Barbara Fell during her final years.

For research assistance elsewhere, thank you to Sue Key of the Illinois Natural History Survey; Stacey Skeeters of the Illinois State Archives; Melissa Gottwald, collections archivist at Iowa State University; Chandler Robbins and Matthew C. Perry of Patuxent Wildlife Research Center; Janet Hinshaw, collection manager, Bird Division of the Museum of Zoology at the University of Michigan; Sandra Fritz, reference librarian at the Illinois State Library; Doug Staller, refuge manager, Necedah National Wildlife Refuge; Lisa Smith, executive director of the Natural Areas Association; Tom Clay, executive director of the Illinois Audubon Society; and the staffs of the Local History and Genealogy Department of the Rockford Public Library, the University of Michigan Bentley Historical Library, the Chicago Public Library, the Chicago Historical Society, and the Illinois State Academy of Science.

As scrupulous a documentarian as Fell was, the written record goes only so far in revealing who he was as a person. I was fortunate to get to know him by interviewing friends, family, and colleagues, who were generous in relating stories about a man who went out of his way not to call attention to himself. My thanks to Brian Anderson, John Alesandrini, Jill Allread, Steven Byers, Elizabeth Carter, Dale Birkenholz, Marlin Bowles, Gladys Campbell, Fran Harty, Kenneth Fiske, Roger Gustafson, Randy Heidorn, Max Hutchison, David Kenney, Edward M. Levin, Lee Johnson, Ruth Little, Don McFall, Gary McIntyre, Suzette Merchant, Stephen Packard, John Schwegman, Dorothy Wade, John Warnock, and Karen Witter; as well as the late Carl Becker, Frank Bellrose, Robert Betz, Edward Garst, Richard Goodwin, John Humke, and Richard Pough.

Thanks to Melody Herr, who provided encouragement and guidance in finding my voice to tell Fell's story. Thanks also to Jim Ballowe, Patty Berg, Carol Fisher Saller, and especially Gwen Walker and the entire University of Wisconsin Press team for their editorial insights, which provided the final polish to the manuscript.

Thanks to Susan, always and forever Susan, for her love and support.

Finally, my deepest thanks go to the late Barbara Fell. She spent countless hours talking to me about her husband. She hosted me in her home while I sorted through his papers at the Natural Land Institute. She cooked meals, took me out to dinner, and walked with me through landscapes that she and her husband had protected. Fierce in her opinions and a stickler for details, Barbara was an invaluable source of information except when it came to talking about herself: "I can't take credit for anything," she insisted repeatedly. "George was a genius. He would have done it all with or without me."

In spite of Barbara's protestations, the well-documented record is clear that she had more than a little to do with his success. As breadwinner, volunteer, and paid staff member; as editor, membership coordinator, and general factotum; as advocate and defender; as confidante, companion, and devoted spouse for forty-six years, Barbara was her husband's equal in passion, commitment, and tenacity when it came to advancing the cause of natural areas preservation. Therefore, it gives me great pleasure to acknowledge her own rightful place in conservation history by dedicating this book to her memory.

Chronology

1958	The Fells leave The Nature Conservancy and return to Rockford, Illinois. Fell establishes the Natural Land Institute and serves as its executive director into the last year of his life.
1960–62	Fell serves as secretary of the Illinois chapter of The Nature Conservancy.
1961	The first Illinois Natural Areas Preservation Act is vetoed.
1963	An alternate Illinois Natural Areas Preservation Act is signed into law.
1964	Passage of National Wilderness Act.
1964–70	Fell serves as secretary of the Illinois Nature Preserves Commission.
1970–82	Fell serves as executive secretary of the Illinois Nature Preserves Commission.
1972	Designation of the George B. Fell Nature Preserve. Federal Water Pollution Control Act, commonly known as the Clean Water Act, is amended.
1973	Passage of the Clean Air Act.
1979	Founding of the Natural Areas Association.
1979–90	Fell serves as secretary and executive financial officer of the Natural Areas Association.
1994	250th Illinois Nature Preserve is designated. George Fell dies.
2015	Barbara Fell dies.

Force of Nature

Prologue

An institution is the lengthened shadow of one man.
Ralph Waldo Emerson

To save land, George Fell built not just an institution but several of them, including The Nature Conservancy, the Illinois Nature Preserves Commission, and the Natural Land Institute. In doing so he sparked an entire movement to protect the most important natural lands left—no matter how small—from being destroyed. Although he never would have made the claim himself, in building these institutions he has had a guiding hand in protecting natural lands throughout Illinois, the rest of the United States, and the world: from the everglades of Florida to the Amazon Basin in Brazil; from barrier islands off the coast of New York to vast arid lands in Australia; from prairie chicken preserves in central Illinois to panda habitat in Sichuan Province, China.

Fell did not build these institutions alone, of course. Over the years, many individuals have made their own vital contributions. However, it was Fell who was the driving force in conceiving them. It was Fell who had the sheer persistence to turn concept into reality. It was Fell who took it upon himself to staff what he had structured to work through the critical start-up years. And it was Fell whose headstrong ways led to his dismissal from some of the very institutions he built.

All in all, Fell was the right man in the right place at the right time to set the path of conservation on a new course. In the United States, conservation began in the mid-nineteenth century to preserve scenic grandeur and ensure that there would be sufficient resources for a growing nation: think national parks and national forests. At the turn of the twentieth century, the study of natural history, fueled by the science of ecology, led to a deeper appreciation of natural lands for their irreplaceable biological value. By the time Fell came of age, following World War II, many of the obvious areas—large landscapes whose aesthetic, ecological, or recreational value was patently clear—had been protected. What natural lands remained were at grave risk of development in the building boom that followed the war. Fell was not the only one to recognize the need to protect the nation's remaining biological heritage, but he was the galvanizing force in transforming idea into action. Thus was born the natural areas movement.

That Fell is not more widely known for the transformative role he played in the nation's conservation history is not surprising. True, the highest annual award presented by the Natural Areas Association is named in his honor, as is one of the largest nature preserves in Illinois. Natural Areas practitioners who knew him speak reverentially of how Fell inspired them to enter a profession that he himself had pioneered. Yet Fell avoided the limelight. He cared little for attention and accolades. He published little beyond newsletters and a few journal articles. At the end of his career, slowed by illness, he intended to chronicle his nearly half century as a driving force in the natural areas movement. But his cancer proved both advanced and aggressive, and so he never set his own story to paper.

Colleagues, friends, and employees recall Fell as introverted, soft spoken, never one to call attention to himself. Without exception they also remember him as "a real bulldog," tenacious and uncompromising once he put his mind to something: a force of nature. "If one person is determined that something is going to be saved," Fell reflected in a 1989 documentary, "it can be done. It will be done. If there isn't that determination, it doesn't happen."[1]

The tenacity of a bulldog was precisely what was needed to launch major new initiatives, such as The Nature Conservancy and the Illinois Nature Preserves Commission. In both these cases, however, it was a quality that wore out its welcome over time. Less than a decade after Fell launched the conservancy, his adherence to a singular vision ultimately led to open conflict with the board to which he reported, which forced his departure. Fell lasted twice as long at the helm of the Illinois Nature Preserves Commission, but his self-acknowledged "worst shortcoming" of insisting upon his own way led to the same unfortunate fate. Despite such profound disappointments, he never quit. He never stopped devoting nearly every waking moment to coming up with new and creative ways to protect the natural lands he loved.

What made George Fell tick? What made him such an improbable success? The complex of reasons include a lonely childhood, a distant but passionate amateur botanist for a father, an education under some of the leading ecologists of the time, a devoted spouse who shared his passions, a willingness to buck convention and stand up for his convictions, an obsessive attention to detail, and a selflessness that allowed him to work for little or no money throughout his entire career.

Fell himself struggled to understand why he did what he did. A few months before he died, in what may have been intended as the introduction to a memoir, he composed a short piece, "We Strive for Beauty." Reflective, introspective, and with an uncharacteristic touch of the poet, he wrote, "Everywhere we look in the natural world we perceive beauty in form and color, whether in magnificent scenery or in the subtle patterns formed by bare branches against the winter sky, or the intricate mosaic of ground cover vegetation. Where did we get our perception of beauty? Is it essential to our survival? Do other creatures share it with us to some degree? I know nothing of this . . . to me it is a profound mystery."[2]

In the end, for all the facts and analysis, some mystery always remains. For Fell, it was enough to know that he and others working in the natural areas movement had a cause. "How many people have a cause—of any kind—a purpose in life?" he asked rhetorically in an article he wrote for the *Natural Areas Journal*. "What nobler cause can there possibly be? What we do is as important and selfless as feeding the hungry, healing the sick, teaching, and helping people in other ways. To us our work is among the most basic of charities. We fight a difficult and frustrating battle, with tragic losses, but we are making great accomplishments. What other cause can claim more?"[3]

1

From the Bend of a Beautiful River to the Alcatraz of Conscientious Objector Camps

The Rock River rises in Wisconsin's Horicon National Wildlife Refuge, the nation's largest freshwater cattail marsh. It flows south into Winnebago County, Illinois, through a gently rolling landscape sculpted by the outwash of its glacial-era forebear. About halfway along its southwestern course to the Mississippi River, its riverbed bites into limestone. This provided early pioneers a "rock ford" to cross the shallow river and, eventually, a name for the settlement they established astride its banks in 1835.

Less than a century after the founding of Rockford, a young boy named George Fell often stood with his bare toes in the water and looked west across the river at a rising tide of homes and businesses. Turning away, he let his feet follow his eyes across a landscape that still harbored large swaths of riparian forests dotted with gravel hill prairies. Thus, the Rock River afforded a sharp distinction between two worlds for the young Fell: on one side was intensive development, and on the other were the remnant natural lands he would devote his life to protecting.

Fell's passion for natural lands was sparked by his father's botanical passions, but his success as a preservationist was fueled by an uncompromising pursuit of his ideals. These twin spurs were born of a solitary childhood and tempered by the travails of his academic years and nearly half a decade as a conscript in a series of Civilian Public Service camps.

Finding Companionship in Nature

Like most preservationists, George Brady Fell developed his love for nature at an early age. Born on September 27, 1916, in Elgin, Illinois, he spent his formative years—from age seven through sixteen—some fifty miles to the northwest, in Rockford. There, he lived with his family at the Wilgus Sanitarium, where his father worked as a psychiatrist. Established in 1913, the sanitarium was located three miles by dirt road from downtown, "on a bend of the beautiful Rock [River] . . . in a virgin grove with living springs under great oaks, caressed by the sun and the breeze."[1] Beyond the sanitarium grounds, development on the leeward side of the river was spotty at the time, leaving lots of woods, wetlands, and prairies for a young boy to explore.

Why nature so captured the heart of only one of the three Fell children was likely the result of a young boy's loneliness. According to Fell's sister, Olive Elizabeth Carter, she and their older brother, William, were not particularly close to their little brother. Six and nine years older, respectively, Bessie and Bill preferred the company of friends their own age without the burden of a little brother tagging along. With few neighbors, Fell frequently turned to the sanitarium's maintenance staff, which indulged the young boy by teaching him how to repair and maintain various machinery, motors, and other equipment. Otherwise, as Bessie recalled, "George used to spend a lot of time on his own."[2] In an interview Fell gave a few months before he passed away, he confessed himself "a loner" as a child.[3]

Fell found some comfort in his mother, Olive Brady Fell, who cultivated in him a deep appreciation for the arts. An accomplished musician, for many years she was the organist and choir director at various Rockford-area churches. Fell recalled that she read Shakespeare aloud to him and was "a seeker of truth," who "spent a good deal of her life delving into religions" before converting late in life to Catholicism.[4] Bessie remembered their mother more for her mercurial temper. "I almost still resent it. Bill and I got whipped with sticks off the trees when we were naughty. The last time she switched me, I was starting into high school, and I had these welts all over my back." Years later, following a complaint from a neighbor whose son had been "knocked down" by Bill for not staying off the front lawn, Mrs. Fell lamented, "It seems a person can't lay hands on anyone's children no matter how big a nuisance they are."[5] As far as Bessie knew, however, their mother spared the rod with her youngest. "I don't think she ever [switched] George. He was her little darling. The apple of her eye."[6]

Fell may have been his mother's favorite, but it was his father's attention that he craved. Born and raised in Jacksonville, the county seat of Morgan County in west central Illinois, Egbert W. Fell graduated from Northwestern Medical School in 1903, specializing in nervous and mental diseases. In 1905 he married Olive Brady, also of Jacksonville, and thereafter spent nearly a decade as assistant superintendent of Eastern Washington State Hospital for the

Insane. During a brief stint at Elgin State Hospital in 1916, his third and last child, George, was born. Soon afterward, at the age of thirty-nine, Dr. Fell volunteered to serve his country in World War I and was appointed a major in the medical corps and chief of the neuropsychiatric section of Camp Grant Hospital in Rockford. He ended his military service in the neuropsychiatric section of Walter Reed Army Hospital in Washington, DC, and thereafter took a position as director of the Cincinnati Sanitarium.[7]

The year his youngest son turned seven, Dr. Fell moved his family back to Rockford, apparently with the intention of buying the thirty-five-bed Wilgus Sanitarium, whose naturalistic environs were thought to have a healing effect on those suffering from mild mental and nervous disorders related to drug and alcohol use.[8] For some reason, Dr. Fell did not acquire the facility. Instead, he hired on as a psychiatrist and moved his family into a house on the sanitarium grounds.

Although Dr. Fell provided a financially comfortable life for his family, Bessie remembered him as oppressively proper: "I always said I had everything I needed growing up, but when I got married I'd hoped we'd have fun. There was no fun in our family when I was a kid."[9] Fell echoed his sister's recollection of their home life, especially as it regarded his father, who was "very . . . formal or reserved. He was a silent person and not social. All my life I [never knew of] him ever going to a party or a function. He didn't pay too much attention to me, not in the early years. I didn't have a father that most people think of as the traditional father that plays with his kids."[10]

What Dr. Fell liked to do in his free time was botanize, or identify plants. Following in the tradition of previous generations of physicians who relied on plants for their medicinal properties, Dr. Fell was an avid amateur botanist. In a 1956 issue of the *Illinois Medical Journal*, he published an article titled "Illinois Physician-Botanists," in which he chronicled medical practitioners who had made valuable contributions to the knowledge of native Illinois flora. Never having learned to drive an automobile, Dr. Fell found kindred spirits in nineteenth-century physicians who traveled their rural routes by foot or by horse and buggy, modes of transportation "conducive to contemplation and to observation of what grew on the roadside." Identifying personally with his subjects, he opined, "Perhaps the basic reason for doctors being interested in plants is that they were nature lovers before they became medical students."[11]

Dr. Fell was modest in not appending his own biography to his article, recognition that would have been well deserved. Nearing retirement at the height of World War II, he began an earnest study of ferns in and around the Rockford area. This led to his self-appointed mission of cataloging the entire flora of Winnebago County. Over the course of fifteen years, he collected 3,500 different plant specimens, culminating in the publication of *Flora of Winnebago County, Illinois*. Beyond his home county, Dr. Fell botanized widely. In Rock County, Wisconsin, he collected specimens of blunt-leaved spurge, which the Botanical Club of Wisconsin declared the most significant vascular plant discovery of 1957. Once common in dry prairies throughout the Midwest, this distant relative of the Christmas poinsettia had become increasingly rare because of the widespread destruction of prairie habitat. For his many botanical accomplishments, Dr. Fell was named honorary curator of botany for both the Illinois State Museum and the Evelyn I. Fernald Memorial Herbarium of Rockford College.[12]

Dr. Fell was spurred in his collections quest in part by the loss of natural lands. From the time the Fells arrived at the Wilgus Sanitarium, in 1923, until the publication of *Flora of Winnebago County, Illinois*, in 1955, the population of Rockford more than doubled, to one hundred thousand persons.[13] As the natural areas he studied grew ever smaller and more fragmented in the face of development, Dr. Fell needed no crystal ball to foresee the fate of what remained of the region's native flora. "I'm looking into the future when all these species of plant life are gone," he said in a local newspaper feature, "Doctor's Hobby Becomes Area Plant Life Crusade."[14] In the preface to *Flora of Winnebago County, Illinois*, he wrote, "We are mindful of the rapid changes which must accompany the passing of time and we believe that those who will come tomorrow will be interested in the conditions of today, so we will try to picture the plant life of our county as it is now—we will attempt nothing more."

Dr. Fell's earliest efforts to interest future generations began with his own family. Bessie was ten years old when her father took her to the woods and taught her how to identify plants. Years later, he did the same with her daughters.[15] Fell recalled that his father had done the same with him, but he kept the details of those experiences to himself. One can easily imagine, however, how a young boy, with few friends and starved for his father's affections, might have relished the rare father-son outings and eagerly learned to love what his father loved.

In this, Fell shared a common bond with many other prominent conservationists, who "usually in childhood, often during a period of relative isolation from human contacts . . . began to love some aspect of the natural world."[16] A short list includes men like Theodore Roosevelt, T. Gilbert Pearson, Ansel Adams, and David Brower. Sickly and asthmatic as a child, Roosevelt found both inspiration and recuperation in his solitary pursuit of birds and other small creatures. Encouraged by family members who shared his passion for natural history, he enrolled at Harvard with the intention of making his avocation his vocation before switching to politics. As the twenty-sixth president of the United States, he signed into law the establishment of five national parks and 150 national forests.[17] Pearson, like Fell, was much younger than his siblings. Left to himself, he frequently skipped school to hunt for birds and bird eggs. When at last he realized he would need more education to pursue his interests in ornithology, he traded his collection of bird eggs for his first two years of tuition, room, and board at Guilford College in North Carolina. After founding the Audubon Society of North Carolina, he was among those who founded the National Association of Audubon Societies, serving as its "guiding genius" for nearly forty years.[18] In his youth, Ansel Adams was considered "unusual . . . not in his right mind" and "spent a lot of time by himself, walking on the beach and exploring the dunes near his home."[19] A family vacation to Yosemite National Park proved the spark that led to a storied career creating dramatic black-and-white photographs of Half Dome, El Capitan, and other rugged natural splendors. In their day, such images were instrumental in advancing numerous conservation causes, including the establishment of King's Canyon National Park. Today, Adams's photographs endure as timeless icons of our nation's wilderness beauty. In his youth, David Brower had his front teeth accidentally knocked out. He escaped childhood derision as a "toothless boob" by wandering the hills of Berkeley, California, alone, collecting butterflies, including a new species that was eventually named for him. Finding strength and confidence in nature, he transformed himself into a passionate activist: "Polite conservationists leave no mark save the scars on the Earth that could have been prevented had they stood their ground." As the first executive director of the Sierra Club, he transformed it into "the gangbusters of the conservation movement" during the 1950s and 1960s.[20]

Another bond Fell shared with his fellow conservationists was that his love of nature was tied to an acute awareness of its accelerating destruction. As a schoolmate, Alden C. Hayes, recalled, "One spring when I spent a Saturday with him out by Wilgus Sanitarium and we were prowling the meadows. I was imagining buffalo just over the horizon and wishing I was an Indian, and George was identifying each flower. I guess we were about 15, but even then he said, 'You know, this is one of the very few pieces of natural, unplowed prairie left in Winnebago County, and it ought to be preserved.'"[21]

There is no evidence that Fell immediately followed through on his youthful preservation instincts. Instead, he followed in his father's footsteps, collecting plants. Following the template in his *Manual and Workbook in Botany*, he skillfully collected and mounted more than one hundred species of native plants. This was more than was required during his two semesters of sophomore botany, a feat perhaps rewarded by his being elected vice president of the Botany Club at Rockford Senior High School. He made enlarged, competent sketches of each flower, correctly identifying each calyx cup, pappus, corolla, antler, style, and stigma. He recorded the common, scientific, and family names for each species, along with when and where he had collected it.[22]

Fell found many of his specimens literally in his own back yard. The riverside grounds of the Wilgus Sanitarium afforded a rich palette of native plant life, including columbines, shooting stars, May apples, bluebells, and red trilliums. Beyond the sanitarium, Fell searched for additional species at nearby sites, both pristine and disturbed. Between the train tracks and trolley line that ran in front of the sanitarium, he found saw-toothed sunflower. A vacant lot yielded blue-eyed grass. His old elementary school harbored Canada anemone. The swamp across from Rockford Country Club was where he found small-flowered buttercup, and a stretch of woods near Ingersoll Park allowed him to add Jack-in-the-pulpit to his school-project herbarium.

Among the richest sites he botanized was one of his father's favorites.[23] Harlem Hills, then known as Byron Easton Hill and located within hiking distance of the sanitarium, was the least disturbed among several gravel hill prairies that ran parallel to the Rock River from the Wisconsin border to the southern edge of Winnebago County. Unlike other kinds of hill prairies, most of which are composed of wind-borne sand or glacial-era soils known as loess, the hill prairies along the eastern side of the Rock River in Winnebago County are composed almost entirely of gravel left behind by the last retreating glacier. Rising up to 150 feet above the river valley, they boast a unique assemblage of native prairie plants. A poster child of these gravel hill prairies is the pasque flower, its common name deriving from the fact that it blooms around Easter ("pasque flower" being derived from the French word *passe-fleur*, which in turn is derived from the Latin *paschalis* or *pashalis*, which means "relating to Easter").

Years later, father and son would coauthor *The Gravel-Hill Prairies of Rock River Valley in Illinois*, in which they chronicled their findings and observations, including the extent to which most of the gravel hill prairies had been—and continued to be—lost to development. Yet Fell was first moved to write about Harlem Hills in a high school essay titled "A Hilltop": "Every spring this bare, desolate hill becomes a beautiful flower garden, equaling, in some respects, any ever made by man." After describing the seasonal parade of native prairie blossoms, from pasque flowers, which often push their lavender blossoms up through the last of winter snows, through deep-purple asters that last late into the fall, he concluded his essay, "Soon, however, there will be houses and streets, bordered with bushes and dried up flowers, which really belong in Europe, in place of the pleasant hilltop which is now there."[24]

Fell wrote another school essay that underscored his close and frequently adventurous connection to nature. In "A Storm on the Water," he grippingly related a rowing adventure on the Rock River. Ever pressing himself "to see what's around the next bend," he ended up being chased home by a sudden thunderstorm, and "in spite of all my years of rowing experience . . . it was only energy wasted." The rain whipped him, and the gale blew him "like a racing yacht" onto shore with such force that it ripped out the bottom of the boat. He survived the ordeal but wrote that—all wet and muddy—he was not well received at home by his mother.[25]

In 1932, after Fell's sophomore year in high school, his father left Wilgus Sanitarium and entered into private practice while continuing as psychiatrist for the Rockford Board of Education, the state attorney's office, and the county coroner. He moved his family to yet another home along the Rock River, a Victorian painted lady perched atop limestone bluffs with a commanding view of the water. Although the Fell family weathered the Great Depression better than most, the hard times were not lost on the impressionable youngest son. In yet another school essay, "The Depression and I," he described the suicides of businessmen and the Depression's effect on his father's psychiatric practice, "which, as with all other doctors, brings plenty of business but just the opposite amount of money." In his conclusion he proclaimed, "I believe that the depression has taught me the laws of economy, and I am glad it came, for that reason."[26]

Of all the essays Fell wrote during his high school years, the fact that an inveterate pack rat kept few beyond the three cited here is telling: one essay speaks to his eventual career as a preservationist, one to the fortitude that would serve him well in championing improbable quests, and the third to a Spartan frugality that would leave future colleagues wondering how he kept body and soul together. Along with his record from Keith Country Day School, a private, college preparatory elementary school, Fell's essays reveal him to be but an average student. Grades of B and C were the norm, even in his favorite subjects. However, neither his grades nor the Great Depression kept him from attending college. And if there was any place for a budding preservationist to study in the 1930s, it was the University of Illinois.

The University of Illinois

In 1867, in the heart of the largest expanse of tallgrass prairie east of the Mississippi River, the prairie sod was busted to establish the Illinois Industrial University. Like all of the thirty-seven original land-grant colleges, the Illinois Industrial University—later rechristened the University of Illinois—was charged with advancing the agricultural arts. In the same year the university was founded, the future first dean of the College of Agriculture, George E. Morrow, established ten half-acre experimental plots to help farmers increase their yields. Today, only three of the original Morrow Plots remain, but in 1968 they were designated a National Historic Landmark for being the oldest agronomic experimental fields in the United States and the oldest continuous experimental corn plot in the world.[27] The knowledge gleaned from the Morrow Plots helped the university help farmers to transform the "Prairie State" into, essentially, one big farm field: today about 75 percent of Illinois—twenty-seven million acres—is in active agricultural production.[28]

Early leaders of the university hardly mourned the passing of the prairie. Along with nearly everyone else who gazed across the vast sea of tall grasses and rainbow-hued wildflowers that once blanketed two-thirds of Illinois, for them the true beauty of the prairie lay not in what it was but in what it could be—a farm, a city, an institution of higher learning. David Kinley, who served as president of the university from 1920 to 1930, went so far as to regard the central Illinois landscape as "a desert of fertility" and the university that supplanted it as an "oasis of intellectuality."[29] About that same time, academics in the emerging field of ecology were beginning to understand and appreciate native landscapes—indeed, what was left of them—as astonishingly fecund, interconnected communities of plants and animals. Among those who championed this more enlightened view were two of the University of Illinois's own: Arthur G. Vestal and Victor E. Shelford. George B. Fell studied with both of them, but it was Shelford who proved a lynchpin in Fell's future career.

Vestal and Shelford were former students of Henry C. Cowles of the University of Chicago, one of the pioneers of modern ecology. In the two hundred years before Cowles made his mark, ecology had evolved from the mere classification of species to a dawning understanding of the complex relationships between plants and animals and their environments. Among Cowles's chief contributions at the turn of the twentieth century was his revelation that natural communities constantly evolve in more or less predictable and orderly ways. At the time he began his study of the dune and swale flora along the southern rim of Lake Michigan, it was assumed that it was impossible to observe how plant communities evolve because changes occur over hundreds, even thousands, of years. Yet, trained as a geologist, Cowles knew that the lake had expanded and receded several times in response to the advance and retreat of as many glaciers. He knew, too, that following the retreat of the last glacier, about fourteen thousand years ago, the lake had gradually shrunk to its current level, leaving behind a series of parallel beach ridges, akin to a series of bathtub rings. The intellectual leap that Cowles made was to conceive each beach ridge as a frame in a succession of time-lapse photos revealing how plant communities became increasingly diverse and complex over time. The youngest beach ridge, located at the current shoreline, represented the very first phase of succession, in which a few hardy plants, such as marram grass, established a tenuous toehold in the wind- and wave-swept sands. Moving inland, each successively older beach ridge boasted progressively more and different plants, eventually culminating in a mature, or "climax," forest of beeches and maples farthest from shore.[30] To test that his dynamic theory of plant community succession was not limited to the dunes area, Cowles published a second work in which he demonstrated the same theory of dynamic succession applied to plant communities throughout the entire Chicago region.

Vestal, having obtained his doctorate under Cowles, became the first to propose what he called a unified biotic concept, one in which both plants *and* animals existing within the same habitat were understood to constitute a single organic unit or biotic community (later called a biome, a term coined by one of Vestal's contemporaries, the ecologist Frederic Clements). In other words, every habitat—be it a woodland, wetland, prairie, or water body—contains many different individual kinds of plants and animals, but together they form a distinct, interactive whole. In this, a particular habitat is not unlike a car, which is made up of hundreds if not thousands of individual parts that, together and in specific relationships to one another, constitute a Model A Ford, a Toyota Prius, or one of hundreds of other vehicles.

While the idea of a biotic community might seem rather obvious today, at the time of its advancement it was quite radical. Since the dawn of scientific botany and zoology during the European Renaissance, "classical" zoologists had traditionally limited their studies to animals and "classical" botanists had focused on plants, with little or no acknowledgment of the interconnectedness between their respective fields. To extend the automotive metaphor, this kind of academic compartmentalization allowed for in-depth knowledge of particular steering wheels and engines without a sufficient understanding of how they relate to each other in order to make a car actually run.

Until Shelford came under the influence of Cowles, he was a classical zoologist-in-training. Betraying a bit of academic rivalry, he claimed that he "more or less independently . . . realized the significance of the biotic community" concept about the same time as Vestal, applying it to his study of a wide range of animal life, beginning with *Animal Communities in Temperate America as Illustrated in the Chicago Region: A Study in Animal Ecology*, published in 1913.[31]

Shelford had few rivals, however, in his conviction that scientists should be active preservationists. At the time, ecologists working in academia were inclined to restrict their efforts to pure rather than applied science, identifying, cataloging, describing, and theorizing about plants and animals rather than using their scientific knowledge themselves to preserve, restore, or manage the very subjects of their studies. Outside academia, the likes of William T. Hornaday, director of the Bronx Zoo, shared Shelford's convictions. A hunter turned "grand old man of wildlife conservation," Hornaday in 1914 delivered an address at the Yale University School of Forestry, in which he pulled no punches: "Dating as far back as 1898, fully 90 per cent of the zoologists of America stick closely to their desk-work, soaring after the infinite and diving after the unfathomable, but never spending a dollar or lifting an active finger on the firing-line in defense of wild life. I have talked to these men until I am tired; and most of them seem to be hopelessly sodden and apathetic."[32]

Shelford was prone to similar provocations as a land-hungry nation continued to develop, mine, timber, and otherwise exploit vital natural lands. "From 1600 right down to the present," he wrote in *Our Natural Resources and Their Conservation*, "the belief that all exploitable areas should be settled and developed has been almost a national religion."[33] Like many in the preservation field, he was particularly appalled when, in 1912, after a hotly contested legal and public relations battle, the federal government approved the damming of Hetch Hetchy, an exceptionally scenic and ecologically rich valley within Yosemite National Park, in order to create a reservoir to provide municipal drinking water for the city of San Francisco.

On the heels of the Hetch Hetchy defeat, which established the precedent that not even national parks were safe from the long arm of development, Shelford founded the Ecological Society of America. Established in 1915, its purpose was to employ sound scientific research to counterbalance exploitive interests and to do so in an influential and proactive way. For more than three decades, Shelford, along with his protégé and fellow University of Illinois professor S. Charles Kendeigh, would remain the driving force within the society. However, because of a nagging internal dispute between members who supported an activist role and others who preferred an old-school model of academic detachment, the society never achieved the level of success Shelford envisioned. Out of frustration, he eventually self-financed the start-up of a splinter group, but the accomplishments of the Ecologists' Union likewise remained limited until a former student of Shelford's—by the name of George Fell—seized the reins and set it on a course toward becoming The Nature Conservancy.

It is likely that neither Shelford nor Fell, who enrolled at the University of Illinois in 1934, foresaw their shared fate. Majoring in botany, Fell proved an unremarkable student, graduating with a grade point average of 2.7 out of a possible 4.0. He was a member of the Animal Ecology Club, a rigorous yet popular extracurricular ecological literature review and discussion group led by Shelford and Kendeigh, but took only one course with Shelford. Although Fell earned a B in Shelford's undergraduate-level animal ecology course, in return he graded Shelford, along with Vestal and Kendeigh, less generously. In a bit of youthful pluck that also provides the first hint of an inherently critical nature, among Fell's college papers is a handwritten report card, "What I Think of College Profs." He assigned an unfavorable letter grade to many of his professors, including Shelford and Vestal, who received a failing grade of D. Kendeigh fared only slightly better, with a grade of C.[34]

Shelford was not a polished lecturer, but he generally inspired great trust and loyalty among his students. Whatever Fell's reasons for disliking Shelford initially, in time he came to bear an uncanny resemblance to the man from whom he would accept the torch of natural areas preservation. Shelford, of average height, slim and wiry, was reserved, hardworking, even-tempered, dependable, and naturally serious in demeanor. Perpetually busy and of measured and thoughtful speech, he said and did what he believed. He was unfussy about his clothes. He enjoyed concerts and theater. Good with his hands, he did his own plumbing and electrical wiring. He built bookshelves, raised vegetables, resoled his own shoes, and did all the maintenance on his car. According to Shelford's daughter, his "most frequent lamentation was people's shortsightedness and unconcern for the damage being done to natural resources."[35] A stubborn individualist, "He chafed at regulations of any kind but did not hesitate in expecting adherence to his own. He was his own man, knew where he was going and never ever gave up."[36] Short of resoling shoes, the description would come to fit Fell to a T.

In time, Fell also came to manifest some of the best qualities of his father, but the correspondence between them during Fell's undergraduate years reveals a continued distance. The son's few letters to his father are brief and often relate little more than a strict accounting of expenditures: "Here are all the stubs to the checks. I have accounted for everything spent except about a dollar in sales-tax."[37] Dr. Fell's letters are equally few, short, and to the point: "The memo books are for you to keep track of your expenditures. If you so wish. I think it would be a good idea."[38] Even his response to his son's poor grade in an elective sociology course seems curiously detached: "'D' is passing I suppose. That is all that is necessary. Don't try to excel in side lines."[39] Over the course of four years, father and son exchanged hardly a word regarding the natural world, a curious omission given their shared passion for the subject and Fell's extensive plant-collecting experiences during class field trips. Fell ended every letter to his father, "Yours, George." Dr. Fell closed letters to his son even more dryly: "EWF."

In sharp contrast, Fell's letters to his mother number in the hundreds. They are chatty and always end "with love, George." They reveal his enjoyment of campus life. When not cracking the books, he went to Fighting Illini football games, where he cheered on a fellow Rockford native, John T. "Jack" Beynon, who quarterbacked the team. Fell attended theater productions, concerts, and movies. He got a particular kick out of the 1935 hit song "Yes, We Have No Bananas." He kept his lean, five-foot-ten, 135-pound frame trim with regular swimming—often twice a day—and ice skating. He eschewed the university's expansive fraternity system but did join the Men's Independent District Association, created to give nonfraternity men a "New Deal." Ever frugal, he no doubt appreciated the council's goals of "improved men's housing at reduced cost, low-cost eating [and] a non-profit book exchange."[40] He also may have had some interest in the council's sponsorship of mixers and annual dances. In fulfillment of a physical education requirement, he gave a dance class a try but confessed to his mother, "I don't know whether I'll ever learn enough clog dancing to pass the course or not."[41] No Fred Astaire, he squeaked by with a grade of C. Other letters home reveal that he preferred checking coats at Independent Council dances to cutting a rug.

By far his most enjoyable experiences during his undergraduate years were the many class field trips he took in his Model A Ford, which he had nicknamed "Juanita."[42] Having a car—especially a convertible with a rumble seat—was a rare luxury for students during the Depression and bolstered his popularity among his classmates, all of whom were expected to arrange their own transportation to field trip sites throughout the state and beyond. Well trained by the maintenance staff at the Wilgus Sanitarium and ever cost-conscious, Fell prided himself on performing his own automotive maintenance. "I saved five dollars by knowing how to take the generator apart. The Ford place tried to sell me a reconditioned one when mine quit working. There was just one little broken wire."[43] Classmates contributed money for gas and oil, which allowed Fell to report to his father that he operated the car virtually cost-free.

In letters home to "Mama," Fell raved about field trips to the Indiana Dunes, Cowles's source of inspiration in developing his pioneering theory of dynamic plant community succession. He was even more impressed with the tupelo and cypress swamps located at the far southern tip of Illinois in the Cache River basin: "I think [this place] is almost as pretty as anywhere I have been."[44] A quarter century later, he would preserve the first core natural areas in the basin, which today anchor a forty-five-thousand-acre conservation area designated as one of only thirty-eight "Wetlands of International Importance" in the United States by the Ramsar Convention, an international treaty signed in 1971 for the conservation and sustainable use of wetlands.[45]

In 1936 Fell's childhood friend Alden C. Hayes invited Fell to join him on a six-week summer archaeological excursion to Chihuahua, Mexico. Their original plan—cooked up during their days searching for turtles and birds from Fell's skiff on the Rock River—was to stuff the boat with camping gear and row all the way to the Gulf of Mexico.[46] Instead, they motored to Mexico in "Juanita" in search of pottery shards and other signs of early cultures. Hayes made particularly good use of the trip, preparing himself for a future career as a "failed farmer, bankrupt cattleman, sometime smoke-chaser, one-time park ranger, and would-be archaeologist"—a characteristically tongue-in-cheek self-assessment for a man who penned many scholarly archaeological publications and popular books about the southwest.[47] Fell's journal from the trip and postcards home to his mother reveal little beyond an accounting of automobile expenditures, lists of species encountered along the way, and passing mentions of his first taste of rattlesnake and a bout of intestinal disturbance caused by drinking water the color of "coffee with cream."[48]

Hayes thereafter lost touch with Fell until the 1950s, when they briefly corresponded by letter regarding Hayes's involvement in a conservation effort in the Chiricahua Mountains of Arizona. A few decades later, Hayes hoped to catch up with his childhood friend during a fiftieth anniversary high school class reunion but was not surprised when Fell proved a no-show: "[George] had little use for the social whirl."[49]

Fell's many letters home to his mother during his undergraduate years reveal that he enjoyed his field trips and campus life, but they also suggest he did not make many close personal attachments. Growing up isolated, being from the "wrong side of the river," as he described it years later, and being away from home for the first time were factors that may have conspired to make it difficult for Fell to make new friends.[50] Over the course of four years, he mentioned in his letters only a few acquaintances and not a single one by name. The few he mentioned at all he regarded even less favorably than his professors. The milder of his commentaries on a succession of dorm and boardinghouse mates underscored just how out of step he felt from his fellows: "Three of 'the boys' went out about midnight . . . (a nightly occurrence here.) All three had had about 10 or 15 beers and one of them just 'couldn't take it.' The next day the sinners started a purity campaign, which is now long forgotten. What will become of this younger generation?"[51]

The one individual with whom Fell did form a fast friendship was his classmate Frank Bellrose. Although Bellrose was interested in birds and Fell in plants, they enjoyed several canoeing and camping excursions together. Their longest was a three-week sojourn to the Great Smoky Mountains and Reelfoot Lake in Tennessee. Bellrose recalled that many nights the mosquitoes drove them into town, where they slept on the running boards of Fell's Model A to save money. But in their daylight exploration of the North Carolina and Tennessee territories, the student naturalists shared many thoughts, dreams, and ideas. Bellrose remembered, "We both had the same concept that we wanted to save natural areas from disappearing."[52]

The two talked especially about saving grassland or prairie habitat, a natural community that once covered much of the Midwest but had become increasingly rare because of the extensive amount of land that had been converted for agricultural use. Back at campus, Fell and Bellrose had the opportunity to study a rare prairie remnant that was monitored by one of their professors, Victor Shelford. Located just west of Champaign within a railroad right of way, the site not only had escaped the plow but also regularly caught fire from sparks from passing trains. Periodic fires—historically set by lightning or Native Americans—kept trees and shrubs from becoming established in prairie lands and also rejuvenated the indigenous grasses and wildflowers. A quarter century later, Fell would be among the earliest champions of using fire as a tool in the restoration and management of prairie habitat.

After graduating with a bachelor of science degree in botany in June 1938, Fell enrolled in four summer courses at the University of Minnesota—botany, limnology, and two field entomology courses. While there, uncertain as to his future career, he sought the advice of his closest friend regarding graduate schools. Confident in his own career direction, Bellrose recommended wildlife management, "as it is a new science and consequently easy to make a name for one's self. Then, too, there are quite a large number of positions available for those suitably trained."[53] As for which university to attend, Bellrose recommended Ohio State University, the University of Wisconsin, Cornell University, or the University of Michigan.

The University of Michigan

Why Fell chose the University of Michigan is unclear. Bellrose argued persuasively in favor of Ohio State, which had a cooperative relationship with the US Biological Survey, as well as for the University of Wisconsin, where Aldo Leopold had established himself as the country's leading wildlife management authority. Unclear, too, beyond his friend's suggestion, is why Fell actually did enroll in a wildlife management program. In its early years, wildlife management primarily focused on ensuring bountiful harvests of game animals for sportsmen. Unlike Leopold and nearly every other student or professional in the field, Fell was no sportsman. There is no evidence that he ever fished or hunted in his life. In fact, in the small woodland he would one day own, he would post no hunting signs and personally enforce the restriction during hunting season. Whatever his intentions may have been, by enrolling in the nonprofessional master's degree program Fell indicated that he did not plan to pursue wildlife management as a career. In any event, the shift from botany to wildlife management proved significant as it compelled him to think broadly and holistically, beyond the study of plants and ultimately toward systems for conserving land.

Although Fell opted not to attend the University of Wisconsin, he became a devotee of Leopold's philosophies and principles of wildlife management. Considered by many the most influential conservation thinker of the twentieth century, Leopold began his career in the US Forest Service, where he pushed past his classical training at the Yale School of Forestry to encourage the Forest Service to expand beyond its utilitarian approach to forest management. As a young forest ranger working in New Mexico, he convinced his superiors to dedicate the first wilderness area within the nation's national forests, sparing it from logging, permanent improvements, or other signs of human presence. Later, in launching the wildlife management program at the University of Wisconsin, Leopold made related inroads among farmers, game managers, and the general public, encouraging them to take it upon themselves to practice good husbandry, to manage public and private lands in a way that balanced human needs and the needs of wild nature.[54]

Among the hundreds of free conservation reports and pamphlets Fell amassed during his graduate years is a particularly well-thumbed reprint of Leopold's "The Farmer as Conservationist," published in 1939. It opens, as do many Leopold essays and articles, with a characteristically simple yet profound declaration: "Conservation means harmony between men and land." The article concludes that a farmer living in harmony with the land leaves unmanicured fencerows for the birds, snag-trees for raccoons and flying squirrels, and creeks unditched, unstraightened, and ungrazed for the health and benefit of fish and fowl and humans alike.[55]

There is little doubt that such words struck home with Fell. The management plans he drafted as part of his coursework closely adhere to models that Leopold piloted in Wisconsin, including the establishment of farmer cooperatives to improve and maintain game habitat in a way that would provide important residual benefits for native wildlife. In his thesis on the effect of electric fences on wildlife habitat along agricultural fencerows, Fell bolstered his own serviceable prose with several of Leopold's deceptively artful turns of phrase. What may have resonated most with Fell, whose critical nature led him to draw sharp distinctions between right and wrong, was Leopold's assertion that there was a right way and a wrong way for a landowner to manage his land. The wrong way, Leopold claimed in "The Farmer as Conservationist," ultimately depleted resources. Managed the right way, the "land does well for its owner and the owner does well by the land; when both end up better by reason of their partnership, we have conservation."[56]

The enthusiasm Fell felt as he pursued his new course of study did not much boost his grade-point average: a cumulative 2.85 out of a possible 4.0. Neither did it keep him from rendering an unfavorable critique of the school in which he was enrolled: "It is the consensus of opinion around here that the Forestry School is going to the dogs—at least it isn't as good as it used to be."[57] Letters to his father remained few in number and adhered to familiar subjects: "Check stubs enclosed," "I am working at the Wolverine for about half my board now."[58]

Fell still wrote to his mother about three times a week. His letters revealed little about his coursework but did include mention of a summer internship with the US Biological Survey at Necedah National Wildlife Refuge in Necedah, Wisconsin. Although he shared no details about his fieldwork, it must have been exciting to be present at the very start of a major new habitat recovery effort. The refuge had been established earlier that year on some forty-three-thousand acres of what had been the heart of the Great Central Wisconsin Swamp, the largest wetland bog in the state. Ill-fated efforts to drain the swamp for farming in the early 1900s had bankrupted most of the farmers and left the land, consisting mostly of peat and sand, unfit for cultivation.[59] In 1936, as part of President Franklin Delano Roosevelt's Rural Resettlement Administration program, the federal government bought out, for $3,200 each, ninety-eight families that had hung on in the hope of grubbing out a living.[60]

Fell's summer internship required him to collect plants and insects and to band waterfowl, work that had begun a few years earlier under the direction of Frederick and Frances Hamerstrom. Fell and his future wife would share many qualities with the Hamerstroms. Both couples would prove as devoted to each other as they were to their respective preservation efforts. Both would forgo convention and live frugally—but richly in other ways—according to their environmental values. Another thing both husband-wife teams shared, reflected in comments both Fell and the Hamerstroms made about their Necedah experiences, was an antipathy toward government. The Hamerstroms, who had left Necedah in 1937 to enroll in Aldo Leopold's graduate program in wildlife management at the University of Wisconsin, experienced numerous examples of the inefficiencies and outright failings of a large bureaucracy. "I grow daily more discouraged with the mess which the government insists upon making of this job," Hammy, as Frederick was called, wrote to his parents, "and see the chance of any worthwhile result becoming more and more remote."[61]

Fell, seven years Frederick Hamerstrom's junior, had a decidedly more self-interested take on dealing with the federal government during his brief time at Necedah: "Everything is going along fine here except that the gov't. moves as slow as ever," he wrote to his mother. "I should have got a pay-check yesterday but since one can't get paid until one takes the Oath of Office (which is supposed to keep out the communists, I guess) and since I didn't get the blanks for that and the other appointment declarations, etc. until Tuesday, I guess, it will be another week before the check gets here."[62] This marks the first of numerous complaints and criticisms he would level at government in the coming years, even as he sought to channel preservation efforts through the very state and federal agencies he distrusted.

After his return to Michigan for his final year in the fall of 1939, grim news of the war in Europe increasingly infiltrated the ivory tower walls of Ann Arbor, but Fell demonstrated little interest or worry. "About the only interesting thing which has happened here since I got back was the Peace Rally last Fri. morning. Somebody hoisted a Nazi flag up the flagpole and tied it with a slip-knot so they had quite a time getting it down."[63]

Due to receive his diploma in June 1940, he had more pressing matters on his mind, namely finding a job. He shared with his mother that he did not want to continue with his studies, which he would have had to do to pursue an academic career. The résumé he put together reflected that he still had no firm career direction in mind. His "Type of Employment Desired" listed wildlife manager, land use planner, field biologist, industrial biologist, museum biologist, teacher ("high school, jr. college, college, private school, etc."), photographer, park ranger, carpenter, machinist, and mechanic.[64] He twice took the federal civil service examination, scoring first a 78 and then an 88. His attempt to better his chances for a position with some agency such as the US Fish and Wildlife Service backfired when he scored a 68 on his third and final try at the test. With no particular criteria other than to work "in states with a relatively agreeable climate," he made applications to countless federal agencies, state agencies, park districts, and museums. The lack of a terminal degree did not keep him from applying for professorships at several colleges and universities. In the end, he received few encouraging replies.[65]

In spite of, or perhaps because of, his final civil service examination score, Fell landed a position correcting agricultural schedules in the Department of Commerce in Washington, DC. In letters home to his mother, he had nothing good to say about the experience: "The editing part is so hard now. The worst part is standing the noise that [fellow workers] make—they whistle & sing all day and make it rather difficult to work, especially when they can't stay on time."[66] Fell's discontent likely had as much to do with his own career equivocation as anything else. His close friend from his undergraduate days, Frank Bellrose, seemed to be thriving at the Illinois Natural History Survey, engaged in work he enjoyed. The dream the two of them shared about preserving natural areas remained just that—a dream, an especially remote one for Fell as day in and day out he found himself stuck in an office shuffling papers. Unhappy in his work, he lasted only two months in Washington before accepting a position teaching biology at West High School back in Rockford beginning in September 1940.

In that same month, President Roosevelt signed into law the Selective Service and Training Act, America's first peacetime conscription measure. With that law and a massive, unprecedented rearmament appropriation, the country was gearing up to join the Allied war effort against Adolf Hitler. In October 1940 Fell dutifully registered for the draft and was among the first to be called up. With his compulsory ROTC service in high school and at the University of Illinois, he might have been able to enter the military as an officer, as did his father. Instead, he filed papers as a conscientious objector and on June 26, 1941, reported to the first in a succession of Civilian Public Service camps.

The Conscientious Objector

The Selective Service and Training Act of 1940 authorized something new in American history: the first legal means for those opposed to war to perform alternative service under civilian command. Of the 34.5 million men who registered for the draft, nearly 73,000 applied for conscientious-objector status. More than a third of applicants failed to pass physical examinations and were exempted from serving in any capacity. Nearly as many opted to serve in noncombat roles such as battlefield medics. A relatively small number refused to serve under any condition and were sentenced to jail. The balance remained stateside to serve in the Civilian Public Service.[67]

Fell was among the twelve thousand conscientious objectors (COs) who, according to the enabling legislation, opted to perform alternative "work of national significance" in the Civilian Public Service (CPS). The service was modeled after the Civilian Conservation Corps, a New Deal program that was conceived and launched within the first thirty-seven days of President Roosevelt's first term in office. The CCC, as it was widely known, addressed two critical national issues. The first was the need to put young men to work at a time when 25 percent of the nation was unemployed because of the Great Depression; the second was to protect the nation's natural resources following the ravages of the Dust Bowl. Between 1933 and 1942, when the CCC was discontinued, about three million men between the ages of eighteen and twenty-six served at Civilian Conservation camps in all forty-eight states, plus the territories of Hawaii, Alaska, Puerto Rico, and the US Virgin Islands.[68]

Many of the CCC camps were reactivated for use by the Civilian Public Service. Under the control of the federal government, CPS camps were financed and operated by historic peace churches, mainly Mennonite, Quaker, and Church of the Brethren. Fell did not enroll in CPS for religious reasons. On his application to the National Service Board for Religious Objectors, he listed his religious affiliation as "none." Bessie Carter, Fell's sister, conjectured that her brother refused active duty simply because he held that killing human beings was wrong.[69]

Fell never explicitly stated his objections to the war, but the opportunity to use his skills to help address what Congress deemed the "national menace" of soil erosion was attractive. Although operated by religious bodies, CPS camps were affiliated with various agencies of government, including the US Forest Service, the National Park Service, the Farm Security Administration, the Puerto Rico Construction Administration, and the Office of Surgeon General. The first conscientious objector camp to which Fell was assigned—Camp Lagro, located about forty-five miles southwest of Fort Wayne, Indiana—was operated by the Brethren Service Committee in conjunction with the Soil Conservation Service. The establishment of the Soil Conservation Service in 1935 was driven by the crippling effects of the Dust Bowl. Severe drought, coupled with abusive agricultural practices, had led to as many as 850 million tons of topsoil a year being blown into massive dust clouds—known as black blizzards or black rollers—that darkened skies for days. As the United States entered World War II, many farmers, with help from the Soil Conservation Service, were still trying to recover from the loss of more than one hundred million acres of farmland that had been ruined and taking steps to avoid such catastrophes in the future.

In the first few months after his arrival at Camp Lagro, Fell engaged in a range of soil conservation efforts under the direction of Soil Conservation Service staff. He erected gully control works and terraces on farm fields, selectively thinned woodlots, cut brush along drainage ditches, and planted the first of eighty thousand trees on clear-cut land in the Salamonie River and Francis Slocum state forests. Living in barracks-style housing in a rustic setting, he wrote home that the camp was "really a very pleasant place to be. We get good food, have showers where we can cool off every day, etc. Also the fellows here are interesting."[70] Monday through Saturday, he rose at 5:30 a.m., ate breakfast at 6:00 a.m., and then worked from 7:00 a.m. until 3:00 p.m. with a half hour for lunch. The Brethren Service Committee provided additional programming and activities, both religious and nonreligious, but Fell and his fellow COs were free to spend the balance of their time in camp as they pleased. Some volunteered to help area farm families whose fathers and sons were serving overseas. Fell mostly kept to himself. He worked on his car, installing a new enclosed body, which he secured from a junkyard for a mere five dollars. He reported taking advantage of the camp library, which had been steadily increasing in size. He even managed to enroll in a course on Latin American relations at nearby Manchester College.

In spite of being promoted to assistant foreman of a work crew, Fell became restless after only a few months: "Every week is just like the week before except that it keeps getting duller all the time."[71] Fell's level of dissatisfaction only increased with the arrival of a new camp director, who abolished the camp government and assumed "the function of a dictator." Fell and some of his fellow COs took to "figuring up ways of showing our displeasure and of 'educating' him." In spite of what protests they may have lodged, the new director succeeded in lengthening the work schedule by two hours a day, requiring COs to work on Saturdays and restricting personal-time liberties. Such changes might have been better received had the federal government, following the Japanese invasion of Pearl Harbor on December 7, 1941, not extended the hitch for all COs from one year until the end of the war.

Fell was hardly alone in his complaints about how specific camps were run and about CPS in general. In spite of the professed goals of the program, the federal government was ultimately less concerned with providing meaningful work for COs than it was with keeping them out of sight. The public was strongly behind the war, enduring rationing and other hardships, and "conchies," as conscientious objectors were derisively called, were largely viewed as "damned yellow bellies" at best, traitors at worst. However, many COs were men of deep religious or moral conviction who desired to prove their bravery and patriotism in noncombat ways. Many were among the nation's first smoke jumpers, who battled wildfires. Others volunteered for a wide range of medical experiments, including—astonishingly—those that explored the effects of starvation, typhus, pneumonia, hepatitis, malaria, and DDT exposure on human test subjects.[72]

In an effort to provide more service opportunities that were meaningful yet out of the public eye, the National Service Board of Religious Objectors helped broker a compromise to allow COs to volunteer as attendants in state mental hospitals. Fell was among the first to apply for such a position, in part because it would afford him the opportunity to live close to home. Six months after first reporting to the Lagro camp, he applied for a transfer to Elgin State Hospital, about an hour's drive from Rockford. He cited his background in the sciences as well as his having spent the first sixteen years of his life "in the vicinity of insane asylums" as qualifications for working with the mentally ill.[73] Soon thereafter, the Elgin American Legion Post got wind of the proposal and drafted a resolution urging the national organization to oppose such transfers anywhere in the country, fearing they would "put a premium on religious objection as a means of keeping out of the armed services."[74] The local post was successful in stopping Fell and thirty-three others from relieving a severe labor shortage at the Elgin hospital. Eventually, however, hundreds of COs were assigned to other psychiatric hospitals, where they played a key role in setting a new, greatly improved standard in the quality of care.

Thwarted in his efforts to be transferred closer to home, Fell finally managed a transfer to Camp Walhalla, located within the Manistee National Forest in northwestern Michigan. The work at this camp consisted largely of fighting fires, building roads and trails, and reforesting burned-out areas within the national forest. But it was not the conservation work that attracted Fell to this particular camp. Fed up with the "dictatorship" of the Lagro camp director, he requested and received his transfer to Walhalla specifically to help set up and administer the operations at this newly established camp. "Walhalla is very wonderful compared with Lagro," he wrote to his mother. "The director used to administer a Brethren hospital in Chicago and he seems to know a little bit about administering compared with the others we've had. Looks like I've got a good chance to learn something here."[75] Within a week of arriving at Walhalla, however, Fell learned of yet another new camp, this one being established in Beltsville, Maryland, in association with the US Fish and Wildlife Service. Enticed by the prospect of being able to put his wildlife management degree to use, Fell put in for another transfer, offering to pay his own transportation expenses.

Camp Beltsville in many ways provided a dream opportunity for Fell, as it was affiliated with the nearby Patuxent Research Refuge. Established by an executive order of President Roosevelt in 1936, the refuge was created to advance the goals of the Migratory Bird Conservation Act of 1929.[76] Fell spent nearly a full year at Patuxent, now the largest wildlife research facility in the world, assisting Francis M. Uhler, an internationally recognized authority on waterfowl food plants and their ecology. While artillery guns boomed their practice rounds at adjacent Fort Meade, Fell enjoyed his job assisting with an investigation of ways to propagate different aquatic plants. "[Uhler] has a series of 24 experimental ponds with various kinds of plants in them. My job is to cut weeds around the ponds, build cages, identify stomach contents, etc. It is very interesting because there is so much variety. Also Uhler is a swell guy."[77]

Many of the seventy or so COs assigned to Patuxent were qualified foresters, biologists, and chemists with advanced degrees. After the war, a number of them remained at the refuge and spent their entire professional careers there. Fell, too, might have remained at Patuxent at least through the end of the war; he was happy in his work but could not keep himself from finding fault with the administration of the Beltsville camp. Rather than just complaining, he spent much of his free time in the camp library researching various management policies and techniques for the purpose of drafting a new set of camp government bylaws. Astonishingly, given the general lack of interest among supervisors in such matters, his revised bylaw document was adopted, but with so many changes, he lamented to his mother, that "they practically ruined it."[78]

Ultimately, what drove Fell to request a transfer from Camp Beltsville was neither the work nor the camp administration. Perhaps because of his mother's having spent much of her life experimenting with different faiths, Fell developed a deep antipathy toward organized religion. He did attend a few Quaker meetings during his early CPS years "to see what they were like" but came to resent the proselytizing of what he described as "soul savers and . . . other undesirables."[79] So strong were his feelings that he sought to be transferred to the only camp not operated by a religious group at that time. "I believe religion should be of a personal rather than an organized basis," he wrote in his transfer request, "and therefore feel that I should not be connected with any religious organization."[80]

The director of the Beltsville Camp thought highly of Fell, whom he insightfully described as "a philosophical objector, [who] has done well here in his work as a biologist. He has a high degree of social concern, which makes him an individualist. He makes no particular religious pretensions but is much interested in ethical implications. He is a clear thinker, frank, stimulating, unconventional."[81] Sorry to lose him, the director approved Fell's transfer to the government-run camp at Mancos, Colorado.

Fell arrived at Mancos, located just outside Durango, between the San Juan National Forest and Mesa Verde National Park, in August 1943. To his disappointment, he not only found the camp "padded with Witnesses, Mennonites and other fundamentalists" but also observed that the morale among COs was poor and degrading rapidly.[82] What work of national importance once might have been performed there had been largely replaced by mindless make-work, if any work at all. The cooperating agency for the camp was the Bureau of Land Management, which was to have organized crews to construct a dam, a reservoir, and irrigation systems to open thousands of acres to farming. Yet Fell's assigned duties ranged from sweeping floors to digging postholes to literally nothing. Constitutionally incapable of sitting idly by, he got nearly 70 percent of his fellow COs to sign a petition protesting the fact that most of the special projects at the government-run camp were church sponsored, leaving very few opportunities for those opposed to the principle of church sponsorship.

Across the country, many COs took to more radical means of protest. "Jerry Darrow, one of my pals in Lagro days," Fell wrote to his mother, "walked out of the Santa Barbara camp about a month ago. That's getting to be quite a common occurrence."[83] Those who went AWOL—absent without leave— were arrested and usually tried and sentenced to prison for the duration of the war. Other COs chose the route of noncooperation. As Fell observed, "There's a group called 'Tobacco Road' that doesn't bother to make their beds or keep cleaned up and periodically [they] tell the director and the foremen to go to hell."[84] Still others went on hunger strikes and were often force-fed.

Fell never resorted to such extreme measures, but his many letters, petitions, and legal challenges were underpinned by a burning indignation against the government: "It seems quite evident that the law [establishing CPS] is being misinterpreted if not ignored on a number of counts and the least we can do in place of fighting is to fight totalitarianism where it hits us."[85] In particular, he—like most other COs—strongly objected to being compelled to work for no pay, a condition the American Civil Liberties Union claimed placed them beneath some prisoners of war who were paid wages for their labor: up to $1.20 per day, in addition to a monthly allowance of $3.00. Adding insult to injury, prisoner of war officers were paid between $20.00 and $40.00 per month, depending on their rank.[86] COs, by comparison, received nothing but an allowance of between $2.50 and $5.00 a month for personal needs.[87] Arguing that their situation amounted to an unlawful detention—many would use the word "imprisonment"—Fell and a great many of his fellow COs petitioned to be released from CPS by filing a writ of habeas corpus. Generally, these petitions languished in the courts until they were summarily dismissed.

Fell also tried to be reclassified 4-F, a military classification meaning "unfit for active duty." Fell cited allergies, a history of recurring migraine headaches, and what he described on his Brethren Service Committee application as "slowness . . . both mentally and physically."[88] In several letters home during his CPS years, he made a point of mentioning his slow movements, speech, and reading. In an uncharacteristically lengthy and intimate letter to his father, he confessed, "I think the matter of my slowness is more important than you realize. I always tried to hide it before but now I don't see much sense in [it.]"[89] As a child, sister Bessie remembered her brother as "the slowest moving person you can imagine. My mother had to put his shoes on to get him to school on time because he was always so slow."[90] Toward the end of his life, Fell thought to record his memories about his conservation career but worried that "I talk so damn slow that . . . three quarters of the time, blank tape."[91]

Fell's well-credentialed psychiatrist father acknowledged his son's slowness but considered it no more than an "inconvenient peculiarity of makeup."[92] Certainly it was not enough to keep Fell from regular swimming and ice skating during his college years, or from hiking through countless prairies, woodlands, deserts, and mountains on his many field trips and camping excursions. However, the possibility that his "slowness" was symptomatic of some undiagnosed condition might help to explain his middling grades in spite of a great passion for his field of study. Even today, undiagnosed learning disabilities, for instance, are common. They were even more common in the early part of the twentieth century, when physicians and researchers still struggled to understand the causes, diagnosis, and treatment of what then were known as "invisible handicaps."[93]

Mindful of the effect if not the cause of whatever condition may have ailed him, Fell made up for it by being exceptionally orderly and methodical, qualities he self-identified as "strong points" on his Brethren Service Committee application. With all the things he could have been doing with his free time in the camps, for instance, it is hard to imagine anyone other than Fell spending so much of it in libraries seeking to improve the operation of camp governments. In later years, he would spend countless hours teaching himself to maintain and operate antiquated office equipment in order to minimize expenses, as well as researching the best way to structure and run nonprofit organizations, down to the most efficient ways to seal and stamp envelopes.

Fell ultimately failed in his efforts to be reclassified 4-F, but as a result of his letters, petitions, and other agitations he succeeded in being transferred to a camp where rebellious and other noncooperative COs were concentrated.[94] At Germfask, another government-run camp, located near the Hiawatha National Forest in the Upper Peninsula of Michigan, he anticipated a future generation's war protestors by growing a beard, letting his hair grow long, and lending his tenor voice to "a lot of new songs which we've sung at mealtimes to entertain the administration—words specially written by some of our literary geniuses."[95]

> Over there, over there
> You were born to be killed over there
> It's your patriotic duty
> To love each cootie
> That bites you when you're lying there
> Be a man!
> Join the band
> Dig those cold pork and beans from a can
> Be a hero
> Your pulse at zero
> But don't ask for a job
> When it's over over there[96]

About midway through his yearlong stint at Germfask, Fell vented his pent-up frustration to an unlikely audience: his father. A stateside veteran of World War I, Dr. Fell had considered re-enlisting when the United States entered World War II but upon reflection determined that a return to full-time duty was beyond his capacities at the age of sixty-two. Instead, he accepted an appointment to serve as a member of the US Medical Advisory Board. That he and his son held radically different opinions about war service is as clear as the fact that the habitual distance between them precluded their discussing the issue much, if at all. In the same letter in which he discussed his "slowness," Fell shared with his father: "I believe this whole [CPS] business is illegal from top to bottom. I realize your ideas about this sort of business are quite different from mine probably; and I haven't gone into much detail on the situation before because I didn't think you were especially interested."[97]

Fell may have felt able to open up to his father because they had re-established a common bond. Not long before receiving his son's heartfelt letter, Dr. Fell had begun collecting plant specimens in earnest. His son, meantime, when not idling through grunt-work assignments or railing against the injustices of the CPS, had taken to collecting live plant specimens in and around the camps, which were located in or near major natural areas. Within a quarter mile of the camp at Germfask ran the Manistique River, where Fell collected some ferns. Unable to identify one particular species, he wrote to his father, "Dear Papa . . . I was just about to dig up some of the roots to send you. However, the frond you sent in the letter seems to be exactly the same thing—*Aspidium cristatum!*"[98] Fell returned the favor by frequently sending home live plants for his father to transplant in an extensive backyard terrace turned mini–botanical garden overlooking the Rock River.

The renewed nature connection between father and son resulted in an increase in the amount of correspondence between them, and for the first time Fell even closed one letter "with love, George."[99] Nonetheless, Fell's written observations about nature remained as dry and unsentimental as ever. In many of his letters home, he made some passing mention of nature. But never once did he describe the thrill he must have felt in witnessing the mating flight of woodcocks, or how the wild blueberries he harvested fresh off the bush tasted, or why the sight of the northern lights held his attention for hours. He had no trouble venting his spleen about compromised bylaws, inept administrators, unjust government, and religious zealots. But when it came to nature, his was an introspective, deeply personal appreciation, not unlike his strongly held views on religion.

In June 1945—about a month after Nazi Germany surrendered—Fell was transferred to his final CPS camp, at Minersville, California. Another government-run camp for troublesome COs, Minersville was described in a local paper as the "Alcatraz of conscientious objectors camps."[100] By the time Fell arrived, however, the notorious institution seemed to him almost laughable, a disintegrating holding tank "where the inmates run the asylum."[101] He reported to his mother that "six fellows have 'gone to Chicago for the winter' during the last few days. They say 'they'll be back next spring when the works of national importance start again.' I expect there'll be more following them."[102] In spite of the fact the war was nearly over, Fell kept up his protests, but he never walked out. He also kept current with various court cases against conscientious objectors, including that of Corbett Bishop, a fellow CO at Mancos who had embraced what was known as "total noncooperation."

Bishop refused to eat, wash, or dress himself. During one stretch, he went without food for 426 days and had to be force-fed to keep him alive. Each time he appeared in court he had to be carried, as he refused even to walk. The government, in addition to force-feedings, fined him and sentenced him to various prison terms, to no avail. Thanks to considerable press coverage, the government eventually paroled him unconditionally with no admission of guilt on Bishop's part.[103]

Finally, within three months of Fell's arriving at Minersville, the Japanese government surrendered, bringing World War II to an end. Facing his imminent discharge, Fell remained undecided about what career path to follow. In November 1945 he took a vocational test and scored highest in the scientific category and second highest in the social service category. According to the test administrator, this combination qualified Fell for the following careers: explorer, inventor, plant physiologist, psychologist, or ecologist. After four and a half years, on December 16, 1945, he received his discharge papers and headed back home "to see if I can get my [teaching] job back in Rockford at least for next semester & then decide what to do from there."[104]

Over the course of his first three decades, Fell traveled a long way from the idyllic Rock River of his boyhood to the Alcatraz of conscientious-objector camps. Throughout an otherwise solitary childhood, his father instilled in him a passion for the native plants of Illinois. This sparked Fell's academic pursuit of botany and his exposure to some of the leading ecologists of the early twentieth century, including the activist-minded Victor Shelford. In declaring himself a conscientious objector to an overwhelmingly popular war, Fell demonstrated to his father and to others that he set his ethical compass by his own internal north star. And when his critical eye got the better of him, as it inevitably did, he backed up his criticisms with methodically researched actions to try to make matters better.

As Fell traveled back to Rockford in December 1945, he took with him skills, experiences, and convictions that did not subscribe to any conventional career path. Rather, they provided just the right mix to launch him on an entirely new course of preservation in the postwar boom that was to come.

2

Threatened Lands, Living Museums

The postwar years were a time of major change for George Fell, as indeed they were for the entire country. After his discharge from the Civilian Public Service, he returned home to find Rockford booming. The postwar euphoria fueled a population surge to ninety-three thousand by 1950.[1] New bridges spanned the Rock River. New suburbs incorporated, expanding the footprint of development ever further. The city opened its first municipal landfill. The buildings of Camp Grant, where Fell's father had treated patients suffering from psychological wounds during World War I, were torn down, and a new airport went up in their place.

In the midst of Rockford's sprawl, Winnebago County did manage to set aside a sixty-acre tract of land as Memorial Forest Preserve in honor of its men and women who had served in the armed forces during the war. For Fell and the woman who would become his wife, that was not nearly enough. They were deeply troubled by the accelerating destruction of remnant natural areas throughout the greater Rockford area and beyond.

Fell finally found his calling: pushing back against the powerful tide of postwar development by pursuing a state-sponsored system for preserving natural lands. Initially, with little more than a vague idea of what that system should be, he tapped into a network of like-minded individuals who had been wrestling with this idea for years. They were impressed with Fell's passion and persistence and with how quickly he pulled together a new and viable strategy for protecting what amounted to the state's orphaned natural land remnants. Fell's initial state-sponsored effort failed to materialize, but it set the stage for his advancing the nascent natural areas movement on the national stage.

Honeymoon on the Prairie

Following his discharge from the Civilian Public Service, Fell was no closer to deciding on a career than he had been at the time of his induction four years earlier. Just as he had following his graduation from the University of Michigan, he applied for a scattershot array of positions, this time ranging from researcher at Patuxent Research Refuge to director of a children's museum in Nashville, Kentucky, run by the William T. Hornaday Memorial Foundation. Into this mix he added the possibility of returning to the University of Illinois to obtain his doctorate, provided he could secure a teaching assistantship to offset the cost of tuition.[2]

Once again, Fell had little luck. There is no record that he received any response from Patuxent, where he had spent time as a disgruntled conscientious objector. In an ironic twist, his old undergraduate professor Arthur Vestal, whom Fell had "graded" poorly as a teacher, candidly informed Fell that his being accepted into the doctoral program at the University of Illinois was unlikely because "some of your past grades will not impress favorably."[3] Perhaps the most encouraging response came from the Hornaday Foundation. The foundation's director responded that Fell did not have sufficient experience to head up a children's museum. Having been a conscientious objector himself, however, and knowing how hard it could be for "conchies" to find work so soon after the war, the director offered Fell an entry-level position as a stepping stone toward advancement.[4] "A bit incensed" by the low pay offered, Fell refused the offer.[5]

As it turned out, the rejections and lack of suitable offers did not matter. Fell soon found his calling while wooing his future wife. On his return to Rockford following the war, Fell found a part-time job teaching botany at the University of Illinois Extension. To help make ends meet, he also hired on as a lab technician at the Rockford Public Health Department, filling the position of a young woman who had returned to the University of New Mexico to complete her undergraduate degree.[6] That woman was Barbara Garst. While on summer break in 1946, she stopped in to see her friends at the lab and met her replacement. Asked later if it was love at first sight, Barbara replied, "Oh, I think probably. We hit it off right away. I had taken courses in entomology, ornithology and field botany, and I was interested in field work, so we had lots to talk about."[7] Fell went further, recalling that at their first meeting "it became an alliance between the two of us."[8]

"Alliance" is the perfect word to describe the relationship between Fell and Barbara. Like that between Frederick and Frances Hamerstrom — contemporaries who became engaged on their third date and spent their entire married life jointly committed to the cause of prairie chicken conservation in Wisconsin—the relationship between Fell and Barbara was based on a shared determination to do whatever was necessary, as a team, to preserve the natural lands they both loved. But first Barbara returned to the University of New Mexico to complete her degree and to become an initiate of Phi Sigma, the biological sciences honor society. After graduation, the following year, she returned to Rockford and took up with her future husband. Their courtship consisted of driving around the state in search of remnant natural areas, with Fell helping to pass the travel time by serenading Barbara with songs he had learned during his Civilian Public Service years. During the course of their many scouting trips, they discovered that there remained a significant number of natural area remnants throughout Illinois but that they were at risk of being destroyed. Since no one was protecting those ecological orphans, they decided that they would assume the responsibility themselves. Although Barbara insisted that the man who became her husband would have taken up his preservation pursuits with or without her, the fact remains that his efforts acquired direction and focus only after he met his future wife. As Fell's sister recalled, "George was slow moving, methodical, indecisive, even, wanting to do everything right. Barbara got after him to get things done."[9]

Barbara descended from a long line of military officers, doctors, teachers, missionaries, merchants, land speculators, and politicians, including a governor of Iowa. Perhaps best known among the Garst clan is one who never graduated from college. Barbara's uncle Roswell "Bob" Garst was one of the leading purveyors of hybrid corn, fertilizers, and other pioneering agricultural advancements. A born booster, he played a pivotal role in the development of US agricultural policy during the New Deal years and later facilitated relations between the United States and the Soviet Union during the height of the Cold War. As part of an exchange program with Soviet agriculturalists in the mid-1950s, Garst gained the trust and friendship of Soviet Premier Nikita Khrushchev, who had established a corn institute in the Ukraine toward the goal of establishing a Corn Belt in the Soviet Union. In 1959 *Life* magazine and a host of other media covered Khrushchev's visit to Garst's Coon Rapids, Iowa, farm to see why "agriculture, America's biggest success, [was] communism's biggest failure."[10] Although Garst relished the opportunity to sell five thousand tons of seed corn behind the Iron Curtain, above all he hoped—albeit he had little success—to cultivate agricultural cooperation between the two super powers as a means to lessen the threat of nuclear war. "You know," Garst told Khrushchev during the tour, "we two farmers could settle the problems of the world faster than diplomats."[11]

Goodwin Garst, Barbara's father and Roswell's eldest brother by several years, abandoned his early interests in entomology and natural sciences while a student at Grinnell College to assume an active role in the Garst general store and the social life of Coon Rapids, Iowa, the historical province of the Garst family.[12] However, a few years after his marriage and the birth of his daughter, Barbara, on July 8, 1920, Goodwin sold his half interest in the Garst business and moved his family to the affluent suburban north shore of Chicago. Barbara recalled her father fondly. Long family trips, she recalled, were "much more instructive than going to school because [my father] knew so much. I mean, if he'd see a flying squirrel, boy, we stopped and looked. And . . . his sense of geology was perfection."[13] Like Fell's mother, Barbara's mother played the piano and was a fine musician. The Depression, however, hit the Garst family hard. Barbara's maternal grandparents moved in with the family to help make ends meet. According to Barbara's brother Edward, "One night there was a violent argument among the adults and my father left home. . . . I never saw him again."[14] Neither did Barbara. Nonetheless, she appears to have inherited his interest in the natural sciences along with the more general Garst clan value of civic responsibility, of trying to make the world a better place in her own way. But she was equally well known for her temper. "Whoa!!! Lawdey!!!" wrote a close friend with whom she had corresponded frequently throughout his wartime service, in response to some unintended slight. "That red hair came to the fore in that last letter! Lucky it got here when it did. The edges of the sheets were already charred and in some spots scorched so badly it was difficult to read!"[15]

In temperament George Fell and Barbara Garst may have been polar opposites, but in their shared passion for protecting natural areas they were two native partridge peas in a pod. And so, on May 21, 1948, they sealed their alliance in a civil marriage ceremony. Roswell Garst and his wife were among the small gathering of friends and family that attended. A modest reception followed at the home of Barbara's mother, Lovena, who had returned to Rockford and married a merchant, Dimitre Kovacheff.[16] The Fells spent their wedding night in a tent pitched on the gravel hill prairie Fell had written about in eleventh grade. Barbara maintained that they were simply "too Scotch" to spend money on a hotel, an unlikely explanation as the next few nights they paid for cabin lodging at White Pines Forest State Park, located further west along the Rock River near Oregon, Illinois. Whether they were conscious of it or not, spending the first night of their marriage on a bed of prairie grasses, surrounded by pasque flowers and the wispy blossoms of prairie smoke, served to consecrate not only their commitment to each other but also their mutual dedication to saving what was left of Illinois's natural lands.

Living Museums

Two weeks before the Fells were married, Harlow B. Mills, chief of the Illinois Natural History Survey, made a report to the Illinois State Academy of Science as chairman of its Conservation Committee: "The idea has been maturing in my mind that there may be areas in the state, very distinct for some reason, but too small for inclusion in the State Park System as now visualized. These areas may well deserve public ownership and protection in the public interest." Just how long the idea had been percolating in Mills's mind is unknown, but in his report he acknowledged that he brought the issue before the academy at the urging of Fell, "whose ideas coincided so closely with those outlined above that I requested him to list specific instances."[17] Two days after their initial meeting, on April 24, 1948, Fell delivered to Mills a brief report citing several small natural areas.[18] Included in the report was Harlem Hills Prairie, where soon he was to spend his honeymoon night. To press home the point that immediate action was needed to protect such areas, Fell listed a two-acre remnant of wet prairie that he and Barbara had discovered on one of their numerous scouting trips. Describing the site, located in Shirland, a little north-northwest of Rockford, he proclaimed that it was "the most beautiful flower garden we have ever seen." A year later, the Fells were saddened to report, its owner had plowed the site and planted it in rowcrops "in an effort to make it earn its keep."[19]

The academy—an independent body affiliated with the Illinois State Museum and composed of leading academics, museum professionals, and government agency staff—supported Fell with a resolution that charged its Conservation Committee to "(1) find some administrative state agency interested in the acquisition of such widely spaced areas, (2) propose some way of administering and protecting them, and (3) devise some method of selecting deserving sites, formulate specifications which the sites should meet, and assure that the purpose for which the sites are set aside be actually preserved."[20] Not surprisingly, Fell had taken it upon himself to author the resolution. This action betrayed not only his penchant for organizing and taking matters into his own hands but also—and more significantly—his conviction from the outset that the preservation of remnant natural areas required more than just buying the few odd parcels that might become available; what was required was a comprehensive strategic approach in selection, stewardship, and administration.

Buoyed by the resolution and his recent marriage, Fell rebuilt the engine of his prewar Plymouth and then took his new wife on an extended honeymoon tour of the East Coast, camping in natural areas all along the way. Soon after their return, he accepted a position with the Soil Conservation Service in Pekin, about 170 miles nearly straight south of Rockford in the heart of Illinois's

Corn Belt. Fell hired on to assist farmers address erosion issues, despite the fact that he had but minimal experience with soil erosion and none with farming. Nonetheless, he threw himself into his new position with his accustomed diligence.

His true work, however, as detailed in the journal he and Barbara began keeping the day they got married, was the establishment of a statewide system of nature preserves. In October 1948, once he had settled into his new job, Fell took up the Illinois State Academy of Science resolution in earnest. Since the passage of the resolution, six months earlier, the academy's Conservation Committee had taken little action. To get the ball rolling, Fell sent a letter over his own signature—he was neither a member of the academy nor empowered to correspond on its behalf—to conservation interests and educators throughout the state. Addressed to "Fellow Conservationists," the letter opened, "As you know, the job of conserving Illinois resources is far from complete. I am writing to ask your assistance in an attempt to do something about one phase of the conservation job—that of preservation of some of the remaining *Natural areas* of the state for educational and research purposes."[21]

Although he conducted a voluminous correspondence with his parents during a combined ten years at college and in the Civilian Public Service, Fell's writing about nature was never his strong suit. His letter to his fellow conservationists was no different. Beyond borrowing a former professor's call to protect "living museums" for future generations, Fell's rationale for preserving natural areas may have been sound but feels lifted from a particularly dry textbook of the time: "Unmolested natural areas are indispensible for an adequate understanding of the ecological processes of nature that have such a fundamental control over our lives. They are needed as scientific check areas by which to gauge our management research."[22]

More compelling were Fell's arguments about why traditional public preserves were insufficient to address the identified need. At the time, many of Illinois's state, county, and national forest preserves had been timbered, farmed, or otherwise heavily affected by human use before coming into public ownership, meaning that much of their native vegetation had been destroyed or greatly compromised. Adding insult to injury, state forests—following the lead of national forests—were managed in a utilitarian fashion, primarily to ensure a sustainable supply of lumber. To this day, a number of Illinois forests still harbor harvestable plantations of fast-growing pine trees planted in soldier-straight rows to the near exclusion of native canopy, understory, and ground cover species. State parks, too, had suffered because they were managed first and foremost for recreation. In his field trips with Barbara, Fell found that campgrounds, cabins, and trails were often sited in the most picturesque areas, which frequently contained—or had contained—the richest and rarest assemblages of native plants. Fell also noted that most of Illinois's publicly preserved lands were relatively large forested areas concentrated in the south and the northeast, leaving entirely unprotected the many smaller patches of other kinds of biotic communities—prairies, wetlands, bogs, and marshes, for instance—throughout the rest of the state.[23]

For the first time, and without going into any detail, Fell raised in his "Fellow Conservationists" letter the idea that enabling legislation might be necessary to establish a statewide system for preserving small natural areas. If he was to convince the state legislature to take up such a measure, "there must be ample evidence that such areas exist, and that there is sufficient interest in their protection." Fell therefore ended his letter with an appeal to his readers to let him know "(1) if you feel such areas would be of value in your field of interest, and (2) if you know any suitable natural areas, however small, that should be investigated for such a program. I will compile this material and see that it is presented to the proper State officials."[24]

Fell's call for the establishment of a statewide system to preserve natural areas was bold but not unprecedented. He had discovered in his research that some preliminary discussions along these lines were under way in Wisconsin and Michigan but that any formal action was then a few years away. More advanced were efforts in Iowa, where Ada Hayden—born on an Iowa farm and one of the first women to receive a PhD in biology—had been advocating for the preservation of prairie remnants since 1919. It took another fourteen years before prairie preservation was included in a statewide conservation plan and yet another thirteen years before the state of Iowa acquired its first prairie preserve, in 1946: a 199-acre parcel that would eventually expand to 240 acres and be named in honor of Hayden.[25]

Statewide natural areas preservation efforts in Illinois likewise had begun back in 1919 when The Friends of Our Native Landscape launched an effort to identify "in a comprehensive and scientific manner . . . scenic and historic lands in [Illinois] . . . worthy of preservation." The group included such luminaries as Henry C. Cowles, the pioneering dunes ecologist from the University of Chicago, and Jens Jensen, the headstrong landscape architect whose passion for the native Midwestern landscape was reflected in his enduring naturalistic landscape designs for the Chicago Park District. In its final report, *Proposed Park Areas in the State of Illinois*, the group identified several areas that in time became state parks. However, the group had limited its investigation to tracts of at least one thousand acres, leaving it up to individual counties to preserve "small areas which are of local interest only."[26] Courtesy of enabling legislation passed by the Illinois legislature in 1913, Cook County became, a year later, the first in the state—the first in the nation, in fact—to establish a forest preserve district, which carried the legal authority to acquire and hold natural lands. By the time Fell started exploring his natural areas preservation idea, the Forest Preserve District of Cook County had acquired nearly half of the sixty-nine thousand acres that it holds today.[27] As impressive as this accomplishment was, only a very small handful of Illinois's 102 other counties followed Cook County's lead in establishing their own forest preserve districts; the few that were established were concentrated within northeastern Illinois, leaving few if any viable options throughout the rest of the state to protect the kinds of remnant natural areas that Fell identified as needing to be saved.

Outside the Midwest, the most viable state-sanctioned preservation effort beyond state parks and forests was accomplished by the Massachusetts Trustees of Public Reservations. In response to the intensifying urbanization of Massachusetts in the late nineteenth century, Charles Eliot, a landscape architect, proposed setting aside "special bits of scenery [to] provide fresh air, scenic beauty, and opportunities for quiet repose—antidotes to the ills of urban life." In 1891 the Massachusetts legislature established the Trustees of Public Reservations, a private, nonprofit organization empowered to preserve places of both natural beauty and historic interest for the public to enjoy "just as a Public Library holds books and an Art Museum holds pictures."[28] At the time of Fell's investigation, the organization owned and managed twenty-four properties and had partnered with various agencies to preserve eighteen more.[29]

In spite of these precedents, Fell's idea of a statewide system of natural areas preservation remained a hard sell. True, he had in hand a supporting resolution from the Illinois State Academy of Science, but a leading member of the academy—Harry J. Fuller, professor of botany at the University of Illinois— was among those who strongly doubted that small natural areas could be preserved because of the challenges inherent in managing such small and widely scattered remnants.[30] Another factor that made Fell's idea challenging to advance was that he was an individual with no position of note. Added to that, he had little practical experience, limited professional contacts, and zero political connections.

What Fell lacked in credentials, however, he more than made up for in gumption. His "Fellow Conservationist" letter managed to spark the interest of several key environmental leaders. Among them was the chairman of the Ecologists' Union, Charles Kendeigh. Perceiving promise in his former undergraduate student's idea, Kendeigh invited Fell to join the union to help it be more effective nationally as well as on a state-by-state basis. Launched in 1946, the Ecologists' Union was a splinter group of the Ecological Society of America. Both organizations were founded by Victor Shelford, another of Fell's former

University of Illinois professors. The Ecological Society of America, established in 1915, was envisioned as an activist organization of professional ecologists, one that would utilize sound science to guide the preservation of the nation's ecological resources. Among the society's early achievements was the 1926 publication *The Naturalist's Guide to the Americas*, the first inventory of North America's natural areas. Over the course of the next twenty years, the society's Committee on Preservation of Natural Conditions in the United States, chaired by Shelford, utilized the guide to advocate for the preservation of numerous natural areas for scientific purposes.

While Fell was still working his way through a succession of Civilian Public Service camps, a contingent within the society questioned the activist role of Shelford's committee, which frequently advocated for the preservation of natural areas in opposition to powerful political and commercial interests. In an attempt to settle the nagging issue once and for all, Shelford circulated a questionnaire among the society's membership at his own expense. The response revealed continuing majority support for an activist role in preservation. However, a year later, those who favored less controversy managed to secure passage of a referendum that prevented any committee of the society from taking direct preservation action. To put the exclamation point on the mission shift, if not to rub salt in the founder's wound, the society voted to dissolve both Shelford's Committee on Preservation of Natural Conditions in the United States and its Canadian counterpart.

About the same time Fell was railing against a Civilian Public Service camp director who had assumed "the function of a dictator," Shelford decided to rebel against the society's "dictatorship of conservation activities" by providing three hundred dollars out of his own pocket to establish the Ecologists' Union. The essential purpose of this new organization was to provide a means for the two preservation committees disbanded by the society to continue their active preservation efforts.[31]

By the time Fell joined the Ecologists' Union, Shelford, at the age of seventy-one, was still active but had relegated himself to an emeritus position on the board of directors. Under Kendeigh's leadership as chairman, the union continued to advocate for the establishment of a national grassland preserve in the Great Plains and an international park on the Minnesota–Canada border and against the transfer of Western grazing lands from government to private control.[32] However, the union was unsuccessful in its efforts to establish local committees in Illinois, Iowa, North Dakota, Nebraska, Oklahoma, Texas, Arizona, and Saskatchewan for the purpose of designating in each state and province "a large prairie preserve as well as a small prairie research area near an educational institution."[33]

Kendeigh saw in Fell's proposal the opportunity for the Ecologists' Union finally to establish a strategic toehold in Illinois. Kendeigh went so far as to suggest not only that his former student join the union's Illinois subcommittee but that he be appointed its chairman. Curtis L. Newcombe, a zoologist at the University of Chicago and a member of the union's Illinois subcommittee, was equally enthusiastic if not prophetic: "Perhaps [Fell's effort] will constitute a model that may be followed in other states."[34]

Fell initially utilized his appointment to the Ecologists' Union's five-member Illinois subcommittee—in the end he was not offered the chairmanship—as little more than another endorsement of his statewide natural areas preservation idea. In addition to the union and the Illinois State Academy of Science, he had secured the backing of The Friends of Our Native Landscape; the Chicago Conservation Council, a preservation group notable for its eventual role in advocating for the establishment of the Indiana Dunes National Lakeshore along the southern rim of Lake Michigan; and the Illinois chapter of the Wild Flower Preservation Society, founded in 1925 to establish wildflower preserves and cultivate rare plants. With Barbara as his constant helpmate, Fell strove tirelessly to parlay the support of these organizations into ever-widening circles of support from other organizations and individuals. He spoke to countless garden clubs, nature clubs, and social clubs; he met with various government agency staff at multiple tiers of authority; he solicited the advice of additional colleagues and always asked for the names of yet more individuals who might be receptive to the idea of natural areas preservation.

Fell's tireless networking eventually led to a meeting on January 12, 1949, with Illinois state representative Robert H. Allison (R-30th District). An attorney from Pekin, Illinois, targeted because of his amateur interest in geology, Allison was enthusiastic enough about the concept of a state system of natural areas preservation not only to request that Fell flesh out his idea but also, astonishingly, to consider a state appropriation of $200,000 to launch the effort. Within a month, Fell presented to Representative Allison two documents: an outline, "A Proposal for a System of State Natural Area Preserves," and a companion white paper, "Living Museums for Illinois."

The outline was short and straightforward, proposing that "a state operated system shall be established to locate, acquire, and maintain natural areas as Natural Area Preserves." Fell defined natural areas as "tracts of land having distinctive natural features worthy of preservation for scientific, educational and esthetic reasons. These include areas that have unusual plant or animal life or geological features and areas having remnants of the original vegetation which has [sic] not been altered by the activities of man." Eligible areas could be of any community type, but a priority was placed on increasingly rare remnants of prairies and bogs. Eligible areas also could be of any size: "in many cases they would include only a few acres." Guided by a three-member advisory board of professional biologists appointed by the governor, the areas would be fenced off and "maintained in as primitive a condition possible."[35] In the accompanying white paper, Fell put an impassioned exclamation point on his proposal, reiterating the loss of the prairie remnant near Shirland and other natural area gems: "How many others must be disappearing? Here is an opportunity for Illinois to lead the way . . . to establish living museums of Illinois natural history."[36]

The white paper also raised the idea that the Illinois Department of Conservation—forerunner of the Illinois Department of Natural Resources—might be the best administering agency for his proposed statewide system of nature preserves. Correspondence between Fell and various members of the Ecologists' Union and the Illinois State Academy of Science reveals that there was extensive debate as to which entity was best positioned to assume such a responsibility. The Illinois Department of Conservation was a logical choice given its authorization to acquire, hold, and manage land. However, as Fell repeatedly pointed out, its main thrust was recreation, not natural areas preservation. Another option was the Illinois Natural History Survey, "guardian and recorder of the biological resources of Illinois," but it had no authority to acquire, hold, or manage land.[37]

Beyond conflicting statutory authorizations, Fell voiced strong reservations about housing a natural areas preservation program within *any* government agency. Because of his own experience—as a summer intern at Necedah National Wildlife Refuge, as a clerk in the US Department of Agriculture, and, most significant, as a conscript in the Civilian Public Service—Fell harbored a deep-seated antipathy toward government. In a letter to Barbara before they were married, he confessed, "My philosophy . . . is that the 'best government is the least government.' I would, if I were running things, throw out of Washington about ¾ of all the public employees to start with and then proceed to weed out the remainder of the crop. I am obviously very prejudiced about the matter, but it can't exactly be said I don't know what I'm talking about because I've worked under 3 departments of the federal government."[38] To this list he would later add a fourth: the Soil Conservation Service, an experience that would further cement his feelings about government.

Outside government, there were few viable options to serve as administering bodies for a system of protecting nature preserves. The short list included the Illinois State Museum and the University of Illinois. Even if such institutions could, by enabling legislation, be empowered to acquire, hold, and manage remnant natural areas throughout the state, there was concern about the potentially debilitating red tape inherent in any large bureaucracy, be it within academia, government, or the private sector. Of paramount concern, as voiced by Hurst H. Shoemaker, a zoologist at the University of Illinois and secretary of the Illinois State Academy of Science, was the need to identify "a necessary supporting institution without at the same time taking the initiative out of the hands of such enterprising persons as the Fells." In the end, Fell acceded to the fact that the Illinois Department of Conservation was the best of the existing candidates, but he qualified his support by stipulating in his outline to Representative Allison that natural area reserves "shall not be developed for recreational use or for the production of a crop such as timber or game."[39]

What no one anticipated was the extent to which the Illinois Department of Conservation would take umbrage at Fell's proposal. More than thirty years earlier, it had been no mean feat for Aldo Leopold to persuade the US Forest Service to relinquish its entrenched utilitarian approach to forest management by establishing a wilderness area—free from roads, logging, grazing, and other human impacts—within a national forest. The Illinois Department of Conservation proved even less receptive to the idea of altering its management approach—focused primarily on recreation—to lands under its authority. It took Leopold a couple of years to convince his own agency to establish the first wilderness area in the nation, the first in the world. Resistance from the Illinois Department of Conservation, on the other hand, would plague Fell's efforts to establish a system of state natural area reserves for the next fifteen years and beyond. In fact, it was likely because of opposition from the Department of Conservation that Representative Allison responded coolly to Fell's proposal. Deeming it merely "adequate," he advised Fell that legislators would be more inclined to support the establishment of a natural areas preservation program if the start-up costs were low.[40] Backing off the $200,000 he had originally proposed, Allison suggested a budget of between $15,000 and $20,000.

Meantime, Fell received a letter from a man whose fate was destined to coincide with his own. Richard H. Pough, an MIT-trained engineer turned conservationist, was chairman of the Department of Conservation and General Ecology at the American Museum of Natural History. With his election to the board of the Ecologists' Union, he hoped to get directly involved in the preservation of natural areas. In the February 1949 issue of *Nature* magazine, Pough read with interest editor Richard W. Westwood's supportive coverage of Fell's "Fellow Conservationist" appeal.[41] Pough and Fell exchanged several letters, and Fell twice traveled to New York for face-to-face meetings, finding the elder Pough businesslike, passionate, and eager to save select natural areas throughout the country "apparently despite cost."[42] Thus began a relationship between two men who, according to Charles Kendeigh, "would become very aggressive in the affairs of the [Ecologists'] Union" and later serve as competing forces in its transformation into The Nature Conservancy.[43]

By April 1949, Fell was on a roll. With his wife's dedicated assistance—typing correspondence, editing position papers, accompanying him to meetings and becoming a compelling spokesperson in her own right—he had conceived of a plan to protect the remnant natural areas of Illinois. To help advance the plan, he had cultivated the support of an esteemed group of academics and conservation leaders. Political support was thin and resistance by a state agency was bubbling in the background, but in his many speaking engagements he had persuaded a large number of people to write letters of support to their elected leaders. In addition to all of this and in spite of his lack of a typically requisite PhD, he was a rising star in an Ecologists' Union composed almost exclusively of highly credentialed academics. One month later, Fell received a notice of termination from the Soil Conservation Service.

The Soil Conservation Service

Near the end of Fell's standard nine-month probationary period with the Soil Conservation Service, his supervisors determined that that he was not progressing satisfactorily in his training and would not develop into a competent farm planner.[44] In his performance review, he received no "outstanding" ratings but was deemed "adequate" in fourteen of sixteen categories, including industriousness, dependability, and resourcefulness in the fulfillment of his responsibilities. Not surprisingly, one of his two "weak" ratings was in "practical knowledge of farming."[45] Although District Conservationist A. O. Potts acknowledged that Fell "displayed above average ability in analyzing and absorbing highly technical information," his limited field work while earning his graduate degree and serving in the Civilian Public Service proved no substitute for firsthand farming experience. His supervisors determined that "the lack of understanding of practical crop and livestock management and farm mechanics is a handicap to discussion of the farmer's conservation problems with him and arriving at practical solutions."[46]

More telling, Fell's other "weak" rating was in "effectiveness in meeting and dealing with others." As Potts explained in a lengthy interoffice transmittal, fundamental to success in this category, at least as far as the Soil Conservation Service was concerned, was "cooperativeness." The transmittal went on to define cooperativeness as "working for the group results . . . subordinating personal likes, dislikes or interests for the benefit of the organization—working unselfishly and generously . . . [being a] team worker." The transmittal went further still: "These elements [of cooperativeness] are based on attitude. The matter of attitude is extremely important and anyone who displays an attitude which will adversely affect his work can be recommended for termination during his probationary period even though his other performances may be satisfactory."[47]

Fell vehemently disagreed with his review. For the next couple of months, the journal that he and his wife kept to chronicle their natural area preservation efforts reflects little other than how far he went to keep his job. He protested up and down the chain of command, complaining of supervisors he claimed had provided insufficient training. He encouraged colleagues to contact various Soil Conservation Service personnel on his behalf. He even suggested that the real causes for his dismissal were that he had crossed out "so help me God" on the oath of allegiance then required for federal government employment and that he had been a conscientious objector to the war.[48] His fears regarding the latter were not unfounded. Sentiment against conscientious objectors continued to run high well after the war had ended. Several peace periodicals of the time closely followed an Illinois court case that challenged the rights of a lawyer to practice law in Illinois because of his views as a conscientious objector. In the case *In re Summers*, 325 US 561, the US Supreme Court upheld a lower court's decision barring the lawyer from practicing law in his home state.

To refute his weak ratings, Fell crafted a questionnaire and without the permission or knowledge of his supervisors sent it to those farmers with whom he had worked: "Because of my limited farm background, the question has been raised as to whether I can effectively meet and deal with the farmers. My supervisor has been too busy to spend much time with me in the field, and therefore is handicapped in judging me in this respect. I am therefore asking you to do me the favor of filling out the following statement concerning the work I did on your farm." Fell asked his farmer clients to rank him outstanding, adequate, or weak in five different areas: (1) ability to talk about farm problems, (2) ability to "speak the farmer's language," (3) ability to accomplish the objectives of farmers, (4) ability to create confidence and respect for himself and his employer, and (5) knowledge of practical farming.[49]

It is unknown how many surveys Fell distributed, but the half dozen or so responses he kept were positive, with farmers finding him adequate or outstanding in all areas without a single weak rating. This may have allowed Fell to refute one of his employer's criticisms, but in so doing he put a damning exclamation point on the other. There was a reason Fell's review went into such extended detail about attitude, subordinating personal biases, and being a team player. Certainly, Fell could get along with a wide range of people, as he ably demonstrated in cultivating broad-based support for his proposed system of natural areas preservation. Yet, in the same letter to Barbara in which he railed against government, he confessed to "his worst shortcoming": that when people disagreed with him, "my irritability is usually quite unreasonable, [I] even get bothered when people don't do things the way I suppose they should be done even though the other may be just as good."[50]

Tenacity and strength of conviction would be indispensable tools throughout Fell's long career. In fact, absent his single-minded determination, it is unlikely that The Nature Conservancy and the Illinois Nature Preserves Commission would have come into existence as they did, if at all. However, taken to an extreme—as Fell did not only in refuting his Soil Conservation Service review but later in attempting to wrest control of The Nature Conservancy board of directors and later still in challenging the Illinois Department of Conservation for primacy in administering the Illinois Nature Preserves Commission—his stubbornness and inflexibility had the effect of alienating even close friends and supporters.

In response to his final appeal, a Soil Conservation Service regional personnel officer affirmed the recommendation to terminate employment but offered words of encouragement as well: "You have so many other outstanding abilities that I feel certain that you will have little difficulty in developing into an outstanding individual in any line of work in which you may go where a knowledge of farming is not a prerequisite."[51]

Rather than suffer the ignominy of being fired, Fell resigned his position with the Soil Conservation Service on June 10, 1949. Newly married, with no job and no immediate prospects, what he most worried about was how to continue to pursue his nature preserves idea. Several colleagues advised him to abandon the effort for a while and concern himself with finding a job that suited him. Fell considered how he might continue his nature preserves idea in tandem with pursuing his doctoral degree. However, the GI Bill did not cover college tuition for conscientious objectors. Proud, frugal, and independent, the Fells refused to seek assistance from their families. Instead, Barbara, with her background as a bacteriologist, secured a position at the Rockford Hospital lab. Together, the couple decided that this would allow Fell to abandon what amounted to distracting efforts to find work in favor of using all his time and attention to secure a statewide system of nature preserves.

In October 1949 the Illinois State Academy of Science passed a second resolution in support of establishing a nature preserves system and voted its Conservation Committee—now chaired by Fell—an allocation of $150 to continue to advance the idea. By this time, Fell had identified a preliminary and admittedly incomplete list of fifty-three natural areas in need of protection. He had made a more detailed study of related natural area protection efforts in surrounding Midwestern states, as well as in New York, England, and the Netherlands. He had undertaken a keener analysis of the structure of Illinois government in search of an appropriate, more receptive agency in which to imbed a natural areas program, and even floated the idea of the academy embarking on a fund-raising campaign to acquire identified natural areas and then transfer them to the state. Impatient with how long it was taking to gain traction for his ideas, he concluded his report with a recurring refrain: "I cannot stress too strongly the urgency of this matter. The remaining natural areas in the State are disappearing very rapidly."[52]

In spite of Fell's dogged research, his repeated appeals for action, and the continued support of various organizations and individuals, it had become increasingly clear that there was little political will to pass enabling legislation. Given his recent experience with the Soil Conservation Service, which further fueled his misgivings about government, Fell needed little convincing to turn his focus elsewhere. At the suggestion of *Nature* magazine editor Richard Westwood, Fell began exploring the prospect of launching a nonprofit organization. One potential model, then making its way through Congress, was the National Trust for Historic Preservation, which was designed to provide protection for the nation's most important historic sites. Fell preferred the model of the Massachusetts Trustees of Public Reservations not only because it had an established track record but because it was supported entirely by private—nongovernment—dollars.

Because fund-raising perforce would be critical to the success of a new nonprofit organization with a mission to acquire land, Westwood further suggested that Fell cultivate a relationship with "the proper angel . . . somebody who is liberally endowed with worldly goods, and wants to leave some sort of a monument by way of contribution to posterity."[53] Fell managed to arrange a meeting with Mary Ann Leslie Walgreen, who, in addition to her skill as a nature photographer, was the wife of Charles R. Walgreen Jr., chairman of the Walgreen Company, which operated a major chain of pharmacies. She expressed support for Fell's idea but confessed that she was too busy to take on another cause. Fell's journal reveals that he attempted to meet with the investment mogul William McCormick Blair, the civic-minded Unitarian pastor the Reverend Dr. Preston Bradley, the utilities magnate Samuel Insull Jr., Colonel Robert R. McCormick of the Tribune Company, Edward and Joseph Ryerson of Ryerson Steel, Sterling Morton of the Morton Salt Company and the Morton Arboretum, John Beatty of Rand McNally, and several others. None were available or would agree to meet with him.

Through various channels, Fell did manage to arrange a meeting with Stanley Field, the venerable, long-time president of the Field Museum in Chicago. Fell recalled giving Field, also the nephew of the museum's founder, Marshall Field, his very best pitch. Stanley Field responded with "the worst put down [by] anybody I've ever talked to." Field railed against the natural areas idea, not to mention the notion of starting up yet another public charity, of which he felt there were too many. "It can't be done, there's no way to afford it, and so forth and so on."[54]

In the face of such flat-out rejections, Fell returned to the advice that "just kept echoing" in his mind.[55] Leon Urbain, an architect and avid amateur botanist who often accompanied Fell's father on his plant collection excursions, warned the younger Fell to beware of three things if he wanted to be successful in the realization of his nature preserves system idea: "1) other members [who] give lip service but [are] too jealous to allow anyone to do anything and too lazy to do it themselves. 2) The damn politicians. 3) The indifference of [the] general public." Urbain did, however, add a hopeful coda to his otherwise curmudgeonly perspective: once the public was on board, "nothing would stop them."[56]

In August 1949 the Fells attended a conference that revealed that a growing number of people were mobilizing around preservation in Europe. If in Europe, the Fells reasoned, why not in the United States? The conference, sponsored by the International Union for the Protection of Nature, was held in Lake Success, New York. To save expenses, the Fells packed enough sandwiches for the entire trip so that they would not have to eat at restaurants. To save on the cost of hotels, Fell jerry-rigged the front seats of his car to fold flat and installed removable curtains on the windows so that he and Barbara could sleep in their car. One night, they used the parking lot of the United Nations building as their urban campsite and were awakened at 2 a.m. by a guard with his sidearm drawn.[57]

The International Union for the Protection of Nature (today known as the International Union for the Conservation of Nature) had been established after the end of World War II in the belief that "an improvement in the well-being of humanity and nature could only be achieved through international solidarity." The conference the Fells attended was held in conjunction with the United Nations Science Conference on the Conservation and Utilization of Natural Resources. What impressed Fell most was the large membership numbers touted by the many European preservation organizations in attendance. Without citing specific examples, he marveled that some foreign membership roles were "in the thousands!" By comparison, he lamented that "in this country all there was were National Audubon and Wilderness Society and the National Parks Association . . . and sportsmen's groups and so forth . . . nothing dedicated to preserving nature."[58]

At the time of the conference, the organizations Fell mentioned in his journal, along with several others, did in fact have memberships numbering in the thousands, and each was playing some role in preserving natural lands. Incorporated in 1905, the National Audubon Society had grown its membership by 1947 to 8,400. Five years later, this number would increase by nearly 50 percent to twelve thousand. In its early years, Audubon focused on passing and enforcing laws that made it a crime to kill most native, nongame bird species. Drawing on the emerging science of ecology, the organization's leadership recognized that protecting birds necessarily entailed preserving their habitat and so played a critical role in the establishment of numerous wildlife refuges and related natural lands.[59]

The Wilderness Society—whose founders included Aldo Leopold and Robert Marshall, who greatly expanded on Leopold's wilderness areas idea on behalf of the US Forest Service—had five thousand members in 1952.[60] Although the society had adopted a policy of "supporting the preservation of small 'wildland patches,'" its efforts centered primarily on the protection of large-scale tracts, which usually involved policy issues that had a national profile.

At the time, organizations dedicated to hunting and fishing generally dwarfed nongame-conservation organizations in terms of membership. In 1945 the Izaak Walton League, for example, had more than forty thousand members. The league weighed in on select conservation issues, including, alongside the Ecologists' Union, its opposition to a bill that would have returned Western federal grazing lands to individual states. Its real strength, however, lay in localized, on-the-ground habitat improvements, which tended to benefit nontarget wildlife as well as game species.[61]

Fell knew of these organizations and their accomplishments. What really bothered him was that they were too small. If preservation organizations in comparatively small European nations had memberships in the thousands, he reasoned, their counterparts in a nation as large as the United States should have memberships in the tens or hundreds of thousands. He further reasoned that nothing short of such an overwhelming show of support was required to protect small, remnant natural areas that were overlooked by public and private interests because of their limited scenic, material resource, or recreational value but that collectively constituted an essential and irreplaceable portion of the country's biological heritage.

Stymied in his Illinois plans, Fell turned his attention to the Ecologists' Union. Thinking along the lines of larger memberships, a new private organization, and the need for preserving lands far beyond the boundaries of Illinois, in early December 1949 he crafted a "Memorandum Concerning Establishment of a Nature Protection 'Foundation,' 'Trust,' or 'Association.'" In this five-page, single-spaced memo—a significant expansion of his two-page outline "A Proposal for a System of State Natural Area Preserves"—he summarized his preservation efforts to date, the sum of which led him to propose that the Ecologists' Union consider transforming itself into, or establishing as a subsidiary, a private foundation for the purpose of acquiring and maintaining nature reserves throughout the country. He cited several potential organizational models but ultimately proffered the National Trust for Historic Preservation as the best: "This is an organization *identical in practically every respect* with what we need."[62]

In his memorandum, Fell premised his recommendations on ten "facts that had become quite clear" to him over the course of the two years he had spent bringing the natural areas preservation effort to this point:

1. People are . . . sold on "conservation" in general, and they want to do whatever needs to be done.
2. They do not know exactly what needs to be done or what they can do.
3. They expect *those who know* will lead the way.
4. They *expect to be told* by means of publicity what to do. They cannot dig the facts out themselves.
5. They expect *those who know* to do the organizing.
6. They will only support an *existing, active* organization.
7. They will only support an organization whose cause is identified in its name.
8. There are many organizations *capable* and *anxious* to help in nature protection, *if* they are provided with technical leadership.
9. Many people who own natural lands want to preserve them. They want advice—legal and technical. They want a dependable organization to which they can entrust their property, but they have a hard time finding one.
10. Starting an organization without funds is a slow, difficult job. It would be easier to start one national organization rather than a number of separate local organizations. Once this is done, the problems of local divisions are greatly simplified.[63]

The list reads less like objective facts than tenets in the manifesto of a born organizer. During his Civilian Public Service years, Fell spent an inordinate amount of time trying to reform camp governments. After the war, he ultimately worried less about finding a job than about developing a new statewide system for preserving natural lands. It mattered not at all that his organizing efforts as a conscientious objector had had little if any impact on the administration of CPS camps. It mattered not at all that he had negligible experience and that his effort to establish a system of nature preserves in Illinois had stalled. Undaunted, Fell counted himself among "those who know" how to lead and organize the preservation of natural lands on a national scale. Apparently, Charles Kendeigh, the chairman of the Ecologists' Union, agreed, because he placed Fell's proposal on the agenda for the union's next annual meeting. On December 24, 1949, while many celebrated Christmas Eve with friends and family, the Fells packed sandwiches for two days and set off for the union's annual meeting in New York City.

The meeting began auspiciously. At Kendeigh's recommendation, Fell was elected to the position of vice president. Richard Pough, with whom Fell had maintained an active correspondence, was appointed chair of the Conservation Committee. Together the two nonacademics urged the union to undergo fundamental changes in order to become more effective. The membership debated Fell's proposal, which included the recommendation to reorganize the union along the lines of the National Trust for Historic Preservation, which finally had won its congressional charter two months earlier, on October 26, 1949.[64] In addition to such a bold change of direction, union members also discussed the merits of reaffiliating with the Ecological Society of America, newly affiliating with the Wilderness Society or some other national environmental organization, or making no substantive changes at all.

To Fell's disappointment, the union took no formal action to decide which, if any, of these reorganization options to pursue. However, its members did agree to act on another, seemingly minor suggestion by Fell: to consider a new name for the Ecologists' Union. Fell, Pough, and Kendeigh were appointed to come up with suggestions. Kendeigh, for some reason, was unavailable to participate, leaving Fell and Pough to brainstorm alone. The two men could not have been more different. Pough was spontaneous, gregarious, and charming; few within his sphere failed to succumb to his ingratiating personality. A dozen years younger, Fell was methodical, reserved, introverted; he gained the confidence of people largely through the conviction of his arguments, seldom by the force of personality. Both men, however, shared a profound sense of urgency born of the increasingly rapid disappearance of natural areas and were equally frustrated with the union for not having directly preserved a single acre during its first four years of existence. Both agreed that advocacy efforts no longer were enough. Direct preservation of natural areas was all that mattered.

In fulfillment of their charge, Pough and Fell settled on the name "Nature Conservancy." Pough had recently returned from England, where he had become acquainted with the British Nature Conservancy, established by royal charter in 1949 to manage national nature preserves. Thinking it a "perfect name," Pough suggested simply Nature Conservancy for its American cousin.[65] Fell agreed, but their discussion did not end there. Although their fellow board members failed to come to any consensus on a future direction for the union, the two men took it upon themselves to pursue more than a mere cosmetic name change.

Pough recalled challenging Fell to go to Washington, DC, to open an office and establish a physical presence for the organization. Fell recalled the seminal moment differently: "[Barbara and I] didn't go [to Washington] specifically to set up an office, but rather we were seeking the means to go forward toward our goal. One might say our move there was part of a foreordained plan rather than due specifically to Dick Pough's persuasion."[66] Whether by persuasion or providence or a combination of the two, following the meeting the Fells drove directly from New York to Washington, DC, arriving at 8:00 p.m. on January 1, 1950, "with just the clothes on our back."[67] They bought a paper and managed to find a furnished room with bath for fourteen dollars a week. On January 2 they toured Great Falls Potomac Park. On January 3 they got to work and scarcely took a day off during the next eight years.

If nothing else, the two years that Fell spent trying to establish a statewide system to preserve natural areas revealed the seeming impossibility of the task. In spite of a groundswell of support from the environmental community, political will was too weak, the bureaucracy of government too intransigent, and money— from both public and private sources—too difficult to raise. If Fell had quit or merely taken a time-out at this point to concentrate on finding full-time employment, no one would have blamed him. But few counted on his single-mindedness, a quality that underscored an ill fit with the Soil Conservation Service but that would prove vital in the start-up of a national-scale effort to preserve natural areas.

In retrospect, the Fells' move to Washington indeed may have seemed part of some inevitable, foreordained plan. However, when they arrived in the nation's capital, nothing was certain except that neither of them had a job. They scarcely knew a soul. They had no office, no legislative experience, and no experience running a nonprofit organization, let alone starting one. What they had was conviction, tenacity, and, of course, each other. As it turned out, that was more than enough to get them started.

3

The Nature Conservancy

Setting Up the Necessary Structure Ourselves

In light of how formidable The Nature Conservancy is today, it may be tempting to think that it sprang effortlessly, even inevitably, from the Ecologists' Union. In truth, success was far from certain and the end result different from what was initially envisioned. George Fell took it upon himself to give form to chaos during the start-up years. Among many other things, he conceived and put into place the conservancy's vaunted chapter system, set the stage for its massive membership program, and inculcated an institutional commitment to conserving land systematically and strategically. To ensure that everything worked as he intended, he and Barbara staffed the organization for little or no pay.

Fell's insistence on laying the groundwork for a strong national organization put him at odds with another strong-willed leader of the conservancy. Richard Pough preferred a far more flexible, opportunistic approach to protecting land. Pough readily acknowledged that "were it not for George Fell, the Ecologists' Union might never have become The Nature Conservancy." On the other hand, he and other leaders eventually came to the conclusion that Fell, with his particular brand of tenacity, was "not the right man" to lead the conservancy long-term.[1] With his accustomed stubbornness, Fell fought to retain his position, even more aggressively than he had when faced with dismissal from the Soil Conservation Service. In both instances, Fell's actions only further reinforced the other side's decision to part ways. Nonetheless, the structure Fell conceived and instituted during the launch years of the conservancy anchored its growth as it became what is today the largest conservation organization in the world.

Setting Up the Necessary Structure

When the Fells arrived in Washington in 1950, they had no firm plan in mind. They had no idea how long they might stay. They had little money of their own and the organization they informally represented had only about three hundred dollars in the bank—the same amount Victor Shelford had provided out of his own pocket as seed money four years earlier. Prior to the Fells' arrival, the Ecologists' Union had not acted on any of the reorganizing ideas presented at its annual meeting, including Fell's own intriguing but vague assertion that *"those who know"* should lead and organize some kind of national organization to preserve remnant natural areas.[2] About the only direction they received came from the Ecologists' Union president, Charles Kendeigh, who, given the union's modest resources, reiterated his preference for affiliating with an existing organization or agency. "If we were to build up a large, effective organization of our own," Kendeigh wrote, "this [would] require a great deal of time and effort at merely organizational and administrative duties."[3]

Heeding Kendeigh's advice and following a course that had served him well while trying to advance a statewide system of natural areas preservation back home in Illinois, Fell met with anyone who would meet with him. Over the course of the first couple of weeks, he met with representatives from the National Parks Association, the National Park Service, the National Council for Historic Sites and Buildings, the US Department of the Interior, the US Fish and Wildlife Service, the US Forest Service, the Wild Flower Preservation Society, and the Wilderness Society. Most individuals with whom he met were supportive of the concept of a national natural areas preservation effort, some considerably more so than others. But no one was willing or able to take on the effort, for reasons no different from those Fell had encountered in Illinois. For some, preserving small, isolated natural areas was not specifically within their missions. For others, preserving such areas would have been impractical from a management perspective, besides which there was hardly enough money available to administer those lands already preserved. Yet others balked at Fell's idea merely because no one had ever suggested such a thing before.

In spite of encountering the same excuses that had plagued their state efforts, the Fells determined that the people they had met had been sufficiently "friendly and supportive" to warrant their remaining in Washington to explore additional options.[4] Staying, however, meant first finding a means of supporting themselves. In search of work, Fell paid calls on the personnel departments of several federal agencies, including, ironically, the very same Soil Conservation Service that a few years earlier had terminated his employment after an initial probationary period. He received no offers. With some experience as a lab technician, he applied at various hospitals but found no work. Fell recorded in his journal that his Illinois State Academy of Science colleague Hurst Shoemaker advised him to get a job in ecology, where he belonged, and forget about the natural areas idea for a while."[5] Barbara, meantime, falling back on her own lab skills, managed to secure a medical technician job in a private practice for two hundred dollars a month. This provided enough to cover their modest living expenses, liberating Fell to devote himself around the clock to promoting his national preservation idea, or, rather, *their* idea. According to Barbara, who helped her husband virtually every waking minute she was not at work, they neither discussed nor came to any kind of explicit understanding about how they would make ends meet. They were a team, she stated adamantly, each doing whatever was necessary to make their shared idea of a national preservation effort a reality.[6]

To relieve the burden of living and working in their tiny basement apartment, *Nature* magazine editor Richard W. Westwood offered the Fells a table in the library of the American Nature Association. From this first "office," Fell abandoned his efforts to affiliate with an existing organization. Instead, he seized on his earlier idea of establishing a congressionally chartered organization that would be to natural areas preservation what the recently established National Trust for Historic Preservation was to the preservation of historic places. In the postwar boom, just as Fell had observed an alarming increase in the destruction of natural areas, so, too, had a consortium of historic-preservation interests perceived an accelerating loss of historically significant buildings and sites. In 1947 nearly forty organizations, agencies, and institutions—among them the National Gallery of Art, the American Institute of Architects, and the National Park Service—had formed the National Council for Historic Sites and Buildings to coordinate their efforts. Following two years of an intense, coordinated campaign, on October 26, 1949, the council obtained a congressional charter for the National Trust for Historic Preservation in the United States.[7] As signed into law by President Harry S. Truman, the main purposes of the Trust were "to receive donations of sites, buildings, and objects significant in American history and culture [and] to preserve and administer them for public benefit."[8]

Taking his lead from the National Trust law, Fell crafted a draft bill to establish a new congressionally chartered organization "to facilitate the conservation of wildlife and the preservation of natural features by providing a Nature Conservancy of the United States." Fell stuck with the name "Nature Conservancy," first suggested by Pough during their brainstorming session at the December 1949 meeting of the Ecologists' Union. While in Britain to participate in discussions that eventually led to the establishment of the World Wildlife Fund, Pough had first learned about the British Nature Conservancy.[9]

Established by an act of Parliament in 1949, the British conservancy had as its mission to identify and establish National Nature Reserves in order to protect natural habitats and provide scientific research opportunities.[10]

Conceptually, Fell's vision for an American Nature Conservancy generally coincided with the goals of the British Nature Conservancy. Organizationally, he took his cue stateside, raising the question whether the Ecologists' Union and The Nature Conservancy should be one and the same or two distinct entities. As originally conceived, the National Council for Historic Sites and Buildings, an independent nonprofit organization incorporated in the District of Columbia in 1947, would serve as the membership, education, and outreach arm for the National Trust for Historic Preservation. The trust, also an independent nonprofit but one chartered by Congress, would serve as the legal entity through which historic properties could be acquired and operated.[11] Fell theorized that the Ecologists' Union and a congressionally chartered Nature Conservancy could function in the same interrelated way, but he worried about sustaining an entirely new entity on top of an existing one with a nonexistent track record for raising money.

Without resolving this issue, Fell pushed forward with his Nature Conservancy bill. Similar to the National Trust, the national Nature Conservancy, as conceived by Fell, was to be governed by a board of trustees composed of the Attorney General of the United States, the Secretaries of the Interior and of Agriculture, the secretary of the Smithsonian Institution, the president of the National Academy of Sciences, ex officio members, and no fewer than six general trustees chosen by the president of the United States. Seeking a broader mandate than that given to the trust, which originally was empowered to receive properties only through donation, Fell crafted a bill that would allow The Nature Conservancy to acquire property by outright acquisition. Indicative of the proactive role Fell envisioned for the conservancy, he included in the bill a provision empowering it to conduct surveys and to maintain "a register of nature reserves that it deems to be of national significance." Anticipating concerns of property rights advocates, however, Fell added that no nature reserve would be listed in the registry without the prior approval of its owner.[12]

Fell's pursuit of a congressionally chartered, national system of nature preserves, like his proposed statewide system, was inspired. It was also a nonstarter. It had taken two years for the members of a formidable coalition of forty organizations and agencies, working together, mining established contacts and cultivating new ones, to marshal the public, political, and financial support necessary to charter the National Trust. By contrast, Fell worked alone, representing a small and comparatively unknown union of scientists. The agencies he incorporated into his bill supported it but played no active role in its development. Neither did they advocate on its behalf. Furthermore, in the minds of many senators and representatives, there already existed national forests, national parks, and national monuments, as well as established mechanisms for designating more. Legislators expressed concern about taking yet more land off the tax rolls. Others, including some federal agency officials of a utilitarian bent, fundamentally disagreed with the idea of setting aside natural areas in an undisturbed condition. Reflecting the bias of his agency and an unfortunate misunderstanding—though not atypical at the time—of the critical differences between natural and human disturbances in relation to the health of native ecosystems, Edward H. Graham of the Soil Conservation Service told Fell, "Too many things . . . disturb them anyway (fire, hurricane, etc.) Therefore human modification [is] just another cog in a chain of modifications [such as] selective cutting."[13]

In spite of the fatal challenges facing it, The Nature Conservancy bill advanced farther than it would have without Fell's prodding it through the legislative process. Finding no sponsorship support from any senators—including Senator Paul Douglas of Illinois, who later would champion the establishment of the Indiana Dunes National Lakeshore—Fell poured over the House Public Lands Committee hearing minutes regarding the National Trust legislation to learn which representatives had supported it. One by one, he contacted each identified representative, including Charles Edward Bennett, a Florida Democrat. Having previously introduced a bill to protect the endangered Florida Key deer in his home state, Bennett was receptive to conservation issues and agreed not only to introduce The Nature Conservancy bill but also to work on its behalf.

True to his word, on May 15, 1950, Bennett introduced HR 8513, which immediately was referred to the Committee on Merchant Marine and Fisheries. Fell tracked the bill as it moved through review at the Departments of Justice, Agriculture, and Interior; the National Park Service; the Bureau of Indian Affairs; the Bureau of Land Management; and the Office of Land Utility. In June, Representative Bennett expressed confidence that the bill could be passed in the current session. Fell intensified his one-man lobbying efforts, paying multiple calls on every relevant agency and potential ally. As the summer wore on, however, the bill languished for lack of support.

The flagging prospects for a congressionally chartered Nature Conservancy compelled Fell to explore several alternative career opportunities. He inquired about a public health service position in Maryland writing pollution reports for various river basins.[14] He applied for the directorship of yet another children's museum, this one the Fernbank Children's Nature Museum in Rock Hill, South Carolina.[15] In the fall of 1950, he applied for a John Simon Guggenheim fellowship to locate and evaluate natural areas representing each grassland community type.[16] Fell's correspondence betrays sincerity in his several applications, but the widely disparate nature of the queries — not unlike his job searches following graduate school and his discharge from the Civilian Public Service — suggests that they were halfhearted fishing expeditions rather than efforts to achieve his heart's desire.

The September 1950 annual board meeting of the Ecologists' Union marked a turning point for the organization and for Fell. He reported the moribund status of The Nature Conservancy bill and "with prompting from Barbara . . . I suggested that this was evidence of our present dilemma that could be resolved only by our taking positive action and setting up the necessary structure ourselves."[17] Fell was not ready to abandon the idea of a congressionally chartered organization, but he was impatient enough to make some progress that he recommended incorporating the Ecologists' Union as a nonprofit organization in the District of Columbia. Pough made a motion to that effect, and the motion carried. Reiterating one of the "facts" from his December 1949 report to the Ecologists' Union that people would support only an organization "whose cause is identified in its name," Fell urged a formal name change for the organization. The board adopted the name The Nature Conservancy. (*The* Nature Conservancy, *the* Nature Conservancy, and simply Nature Conservancy would be used interchangeably throughout Fell's tenure with the organization.) The inaugural officers included Stanley A. Cain, of the University of Michigan, as president; Fell, as vice president; and Joseph J. Hickey, of the University of Wisconsin, as secretary-treasurer. Rounding out the founding board of governors were William Vogt, of Planned Parenthood Federation of America; Richard Pough; Charles Kendeigh, who continued as chair of the Committee on the Study of Plant and Animal Communities; and Victor Shelford, Fell's former undergraduate professor and the man who had sowed the seeds of the conservancy thirty-five years earlier with the founding of the Ecological Society of America.

The board placed great faith in Fell's organizational abilities, entrusting to him entirely the mechanics of transitioning the informal Ecologists' Union into the incorporated The Nature Conservancy. He certainly had a knack for this kind of thing, and — not incidentally — he was the only one to raise his hand for the unpaid privilege. Except for Fell, all of the board members had busy, full-time professional commitments and were unable or unwilling to put in the "great deal of time and effort at merely organizational and administrative duties" that Kendeigh knew too well would be required.

As Fell shouldered the responsibility for starting up the conservancy, his compensation came in the form of being able to set the agenda for what the conservancy would do, why, and how its operations would be structured. The agenda setting began with Fell's filing of the incorporation papers, which both echoed the fundamental tenets of his Illinois nature preserves proposal and reflected the even broader research, outreach, and education goals he envisioned for a national-scale organization. The purpose of The Nature Conservancy was "a) to preserve or aid in the preservation of all types of wild nature including natural areas, features, objects, flora and fauna and biotic communities; b) to establish nature reserves or other protected areas to be used for scientific, educational, and esthetic purposes; c) to promote the conservation and proper use of our natural resources; d) to engage in or promote the study of plant and animal communities and of other phases of ecology, natural history, and conservation; and e) to promote education in the fields of nature preservation and conservation."[18]

On October 22, 1951, The Nature Conservancy was formally incorporated as a nonprofit organization in the District of Columbia. About that same time, the Wilderness Society, which shared an office with the National Parks Association at 1840 Mintwood Place, NW, offered a sublease to the conservancy for the nominal rate of seven dollars per month. The Wilderness Society was led by Howard Zahniser. Widely respected within the conservation field and well-connected politically, he would prove the guiding hand for the multiyear campaign to pass the Wilderness Act, which was signed into law just a few months after his death, in 1964. He held no position with the conservancy beyond being a general member, but he strongly supported its mission and took a particular shine to the Fells. Sympathetic to the fact that neither of them was drawing a salary for the considerable time and effort they were pouring into the conservancy—Zahniser himself had taken a 50 percent pay cut to leave the US Biological Survey to head up the Wilderness Society—he offered them occasional part-time employment.[19] In the natural areas journal the Fells continued to keep, Barbara several times mentioned that "Zahnnie" and his wife helped the struggling couple further still, inviting them to dinner to ensure that they got a good meal every now and then.

More important, Zahniser offered access to the society's mailing list, which helped Fell work toward achieving his number one priority: building a large membership base for the conservancy. Still fresh in his mind was his 1949 trip to the International Union for the Protection of Nature conference, where he had learned of European conservation organizations that enjoyed membership rolls "in the thousands!" Neither had he forgotten the advice given to him by one of his father's botanizing companions, Leon Urbain: that once the public was brought on board, "nothing would stop them." Accordingly, Fell believed it was essential to expand membership far beyond professional ecologists and to foster a "grass-roots" organization "that would have the size and strength to take its rightful place in a country that does things on a gigantic scale."[20]

In launching the conservancy's membership campaign, Fell solicited primarily two-dollar memberships (five-dollar, ten-dollar, and twenty-five-dollar memberships also were available) that entitled members to a stream of informational materials. Principal among them was a semiregular newsletter titled *Nature Conservation News*, forerunner of the current *Nature Conservancy Magazine*. In the first issue of the newsletter, writer Fell admitted to "no literary aspirations," but editor Fell promised to include "as much practical information as possible on the methods and procedures for establishing nature reserves."[21] Publisher Fell hand printed each two-color, four- to eight-page, trifold issue. Scrupulously cost-conscious, frugal Fell had bought all of the conservancy's office equipment—including two offset printing presses, which he taught himself to operate and maintain in order to save on printing costs—at a steep discount at government surplus sales. Efficient Fell studied a book titled *The Technique of Getting Things Done* in order to teach his wife how to increase her speed at stuffing mailings into envelopes before she stamped them and walked them to the post office.[22]

Published four or five times per year, the newsletter made good on Fell's conviction that publicity was key for people who generally wanted to do the right thing for nature but did not know "exactly what needs to be done or what they can do" and "cannot [or were unlikely to] dig the facts out themselves."[23] Into each issue he poured regional, national, and international conservation news, addressing an impressive range of topics, including water policy, DDT, endangered species, exotic species, predator control programs, littering, vandalism, tourism, population control, and urban sprawl. He wrote short book reviews. He reported on relevant bills pending before Congress and various state governments, encouraging readers to take action. He provided updates about various individual conservation organizations and their direct preservation efforts, encouraging readers to send news of more such efforts.

In the first year alone, the Fells distributed twenty-seven thousand separate printed communications. The Wilderness Society contributed to the communications campaign by devoting an entire issue of its quarterly magazine to the conservancy's survey of nearly seven hundred nature sanctuaries in the United States and Canada. Several years in the making, the survey was a product of the Committee on the Study of Plant and Animal Communities, the body dissolved by the Ecological Society of America, resurrected by the Ecologists' Union, and carried over into The Nature Conservancy. Publication of the survey received widespread coverage, including a strongly supportive write-up by the *New York Times*: "Relatively little attention has been paid to a form of conservation activity that is at once more general in scope, more limited in appeal and yet of at least as great importance as anything else that is being done in the vital field of protecting America's renewable natural resources. This valuable survey will give the factual basis on which the need for new sanctuaries or nature reserves can be determined."[24]

As a result of such favorable press and the strategic distribution of conservancy outreach materials—based on Fell's detailed analyses of response rates to different kinds of solicitations—the conservancy increased its membership by 50 percent, to 552, within the first two years.[25] Admittedly, a membership base of some five hundred people was a far cry from "the thousands!" to which Fell aspired. Like Kendeigh, Fell knew "starting an organization without funds is a slow, difficult job."[26] But it was a promising start, not only for raising seed money but more so for laying the groundwork for what would become the conservancy's chapter system. From the outset, drawing on his Illinois experiences and as reflected in the "manifesto" he presented at the 1949 Ecologists' Union annual meeting, Fell believed that investing in a strong national organization would be the most effective means of organizing and encouraging preservation efforts at the state or regional level. Cultivating a larger, broader, grassroots membership base, he reasoned, would lead to the establishment of core constituencies within each state, which in turn could be organized under the umbrella of the national office.

With membership on the rise, in 1952 Fell urged the conservancy to appoint state representatives in thirty-four states. The representatives—generally conservancy members working in academia or government—were charged to "1) carry on promotional work, 2) organize committees to carry on projects, 3) work with and through other organizations by means of joint committees etc. and 4) initiate the establishment of a division of the Conservancy." One of the first divisions established—not surprisingly, building on Fell's earliest preservation efforts and headed by Charles Kendeigh—was in Illinois. Initially, the concept of a "division" was vague: "For the present, divisions shall be free to develop as they see fit," with the caveat that they generally had to subscribe to the bylaws of the conservancy. Announcing this initiative in the March 1952 issue of *Nature Conservation News*, Fell added a disclaimer: "This Policy is experimental. We urge you to help test it out and to send in your comments and ideas for improving it."[27]

Taking his own suggestion to heart, Fell spent the next eighteen months refining his ideas. This effort culminated in a detailed plan to formally charter conservancy chapters. He envisioned countless preservation efforts throughout the country but understood that it would be impractical, if not impossible, for any national organization to directly administer more than a small number of them. Local preservation projects, he argued, were best conducted by local groups that had the greatest knowledge of local natural areas, local issues, and local sources of financial support. But, harkening back to his proposed state-wide plan for Illinois, Fell was intent on moving away from the haphazard model of starting grassroots groups for each individual preservation effort. Such groups, he felt, were slow and difficult to establish and often waned or dissolved after the preservation objectives for which they were formed had been achieved. Rather, Fell envisioned a nationwide system of permanent, stable chapters that would serve as the local agents of a central governing body. The key for Fell in crafting this system was decentralizing authority among the chapters, yet maintaining strict standards of quality and accountability.

To inform his thinking, Fell carefully reviewed the chapter system arrange-ments of numerous nonprofit organizations, including the National Audubon Society. In 1905 independent state Audubon societies allied themselves under a new, central organization, originally named the National Association of Audu-bon Societies. By the early 1950s, the organization had changed its name to the National Audubon Society and had twelve thousand members, an annual bud-get of $750,000, an endowment of $3 million, and firm control over its thirty-six branches, some of which had fought hard to retain their autonomy.[28] In the course of their conversations, Audubon's executive director, John Baker, broached with Fell the idea of further expanding what was already far and away the country's largest, nonsportsman conservation organization at the time by incorporating the conservancy as the thirty-seventh branch of the National Audubon Society. Years later, Richard H. Goodwin, who became president of the conservancy in 1956, reported a related offer for the conservancy and Wild-life Preserves, a small, nonprofit organization founded in 1952 to protect natural land in and around New Jersey, to join with Audubon in establishing a Natural Areas Committee "that would carry out all the land acquisition functions for the entire country."[29] Both ideas were rejected, but Fell did lift a page out of the so-ciety's membership playbook, granting individuals membership in both the national organization and their respective local groups in return for a single membership fee. The society initially employed this device as a means to culti-vate allegiance to the national organization and thereby mitigate the autonomy of rogue chapters, which previously had retained 100 percent of the membership fees they generated.[30]

In addition to allegiance, Fell needed cash to support the conservancy's fledgling national office. Following the lead of the American Red Cross—then, as now, one of the largest public charities in the United States—he apportioned membership fees between local chapters and the national office. In the 1930s, the Red Cross allowed each of its chapters to retain all but fifty cents of each one-dollar, five-dollar, or twenty-five-dollar membership, with higher membership categories and bequests allocated entirely to the national office.[31] Fell, faced with limited revenue sources, allocated 70 percent of each membership fee and nonproject-specific dollar to the local chapter and 30 percent to the national office. Melding the American Red Cross and National Audubon Society models, Fell's membership fee arrangement "emphasizes the integral relation between chapters and the central organization. It induces the various components of the whole to work together cooperatively for the common good rather than to develop a selfish attitude of 'we'll go out after all we can get and let the others worry for themselves.'"[32]

The board of governors approved Fell's chapter plan in September 1953. In addition to providing the template for structuring a chapter's organization and its relationship to the national office, it stipulated that the national office would (1) provide chapters with technical and legal advice for preserving nature reserves; (2) establish criteria and standards for the identification, acceptance, and management of natural areas; and (3) require all chapters to abide by conservancy policies, including those related to the perpetual maintenance of nature reserves. The plan also outlined the need to provide chapters with financial assistance for acquisition and maintenance of nature reserves and to establish an emergency fund for "use in situations where quick action is necessary to save an area that is for sale or about to be destroyed."[33]

In January 1954 the Eastern New York division became the conservancy's first formally chartered chapter. In that same year, the number of conservancy members increased nearly fourfold to 1,800, with members in virtually every state in the nation. Yet, for all the organizational capacity building, the conservancy had yet to preserve a single acre anywhere. Fell was as impatient as anyone to achieve that first preservation success and thereafter many more. "We are living at the time of man's final conquest over the wilderness," he wrote in an early promotional piece for the conservancy, embellishing the battle cry he had used during his Illinois efforts. "What we have saved, and what we may save in the next few years, will be all the true wild nature that will remain to pass on from generation to generation in the years ahead. *There will never be another chance.*"[34] At the same time, he knew it would take time to set up the kind of structure that would provide for a strong national office and a nationwide network of local chapters. Most of his fellow members of the board of governors were understanding and supportive of the process and the accomplishments. Some, however, were not.

A Tale of Two Competing Leaders

Fell's fellow board member Richard Pough was equally impassioned and perhaps even more impatient to preserve that first acre. In fact, it was the impatience both he and Fell shared about the Ecologists' Union's lack of on-the-ground results that spurred them to morph it into a more activist organization. Pough first established himself as someone who got things done in the early 1930s, when, appalled by hunters' wholesale slaughter of migrating raptors at Hawk Mountain, in eastern Pennsylvania, he enlisted the support of the suffragist and New York society matron Rosalie Edge. Edge proved instrumental in acquiring the 1,655-acre mountain and ending all hunting at the site and then transferring title to the Hawk Mountain Sanctuary Association.[35] Soon thereafter, Pough hired on at the National Audubon Society and spent two months in Louisiana's Singer Tract monitoring a rare female ivory-billed woodpecker engaged in what turned out to be a futile effort to find a mate. He participated in an extensive eagle-banding project, the results of which led to him to be among the first to warn the public about the detrimental effects of DDT. Having found the feather of a golden eagle ornamenting his wife's new hat, he helped snuff out a resurgence in the illegal wild-bird plume trade. He authored three popular bird identification guides and in 1948 became chairman of the Department of Conservation and General Ecology of the American Museum of Natural History in New York City.[36]

Pough shared Fell's belief that the cultivation of local groups was critical to successful preservation efforts. Where they differed was that one held fast to a strictly methodical approach whereas the other preferred flexibility and opportunism. Fell labored to invest in the development of state chapters, which, with guidance and support from a national office, would be strong and enduring enough to engage in numerous local preservation efforts over the long term. Pough, on the other hand, favored throwing the conservancy's support behind whichever groups existed or were formed for each one-off conservation opportunity. In 1952, for instance, a year before Fell's chapter system was adopted by the board of governors, Pough pledged the conservancy's help to Rutgers University, which sought to preserve a sixty-five-acre hardwood forest near East Millstone, New Jersey. Mettler's Woods, as the tract was known, had not been logged since 1690, but a timber company had set its sights on harvesting the old-growth trees. The United Brotherhood of Carpenters and Joiners eventually acquired the site on behalf of the university, and Pough, at a time when the conservancy's entire annual operating budget was less than ten thousand dollars, personally helped raise fifty-six thousand dollars to establish a trust fund for ongoing maintenance. The successful preservation effort of the William L.

Hutcheson Memorial Forest, renamed in honor of a former president of the labor union, received national attention in an extensive 1954 *Life* magazine feature article titled "The Woods Near Home."

A "wheeler-dealer developer turned inside out," Pough thrived on such high-profile efforts, believing the positive press coverage would cultivate more opportunities and shake more dollars out of prospective donors.[37] Intent on moving the conservancy in this direction, yet personally finding its first two presidents, Stanley Cain and Catholic University of America's Herbert C. Hanson, to be ineffective leaders, Pough aspired to the presidency of the conservancy and was elected its third president in 1954.[38] In that same year, he signed on to another high-profile preservation effort, literally conducted amid the buzz of approaching chainsaws. A May 1954 issue of the *Saturday Evening Post* placed a national spotlight on the destruction of Corkscrew Swamp, which contained the nation's last stand of virgin, highly commercial bald cypress trees. Truly one of the most primeval-looking landscapes left in America, the roughly fifty-by-seventy-five-mile tract included towering cypress trees with girths measuring twenty-five feet. They rose up out of swampland that supported an astonishing diversity of plants and wildlife, including alligators and some of the largest breeding colonies of wood storks, egrets, and other showy plume birds. The National Audubon Society, which a half century earlier had posted seasonal wardens in the area to enforce game laws prohibiting the slaughter of birds for their plumage, had worked in concert with local leaders to establish the Corkscrew Cypress Rookery Association to acquire and manage the roughly five-thousand-acre tract. Pough committed the conservancy to raise a modest $5,000 through a general solicitation campaign and independently raised an additional $135,000 by persuading Theodore Edison, son of the famed inventor, who long had wintered in Fort Myers, Florida, to make a significant contribution. By December 1954, all parties, working together, had raised sufficient funds to save the rare, pristine habitat.[39]

Ironically, these early preservation successes also brought into the open the fundamental differences between Pough and Fell. In a lengthy report to the conservancy's board of governors in December 1954, Fell reiterated his perspective that piecemeal pursuit of a small handful of preservation projects, no matter how much positive press coverage they generated, ultimately undermined the goal of preserving a large number of strategically targeted natural areas nationwide. Rather than continue to invest in individual efforts, usually at a level several times the conservancy's entire annual operating budget, Fell argued, the conservancy should raise funds to bolster the capacity of the national office: "We must dispel the illusion that all we need to do the job is volunteers. It will never be done without professional help . . . to stimulate, direct, coordinate.

We have two paid employees when we should have at least 20. If only a fraction as much effort and money as goes into specific area preservation projects were invested in the organization and manpower [of the national office], we might not only hasten our present projects and lighten the load of those now supporting them, but we could increase the number of areas saved a hundred fold."[40]

Another bone of contention between Pough and Fell related to control and accountability. In 1951 developers and preservationists alike eyed one of the last remaining maritime forests on the eastern seaboard. Millennia in the making, Sunken Forest derived its name from being tucked behind two great sand dunes, which afforded protection for the American holly, sassafras, and shadblow trees that dominated the forty-acre site. Located on Fire Island, a long, thin sliver of a barrier island across the Great South Bay from densely populated Long Island, the forest offered the prospect of attractive second-home sites with ready access to beautiful white-sand beaches. A local preservation group wanted to keep the rare forest intact and unspoiled.

Before Fell completed his chapter plan, Pough encouraged the group to organize as an ad hoc committee of the conservancy, thereby allowing it to so-licit contributions in the conservancy's name and to use conservancy letterhead for all its correspondence. A second organizational partner, Wildlife Preserves, established in 1952 with an anonymous donation of twenty thousand dollars (funds that were, at the donor's request, held by the conservancy until Wildlife Preserves could secure its nonprofit status), became involved even though Sunken Forest was outside its mission-restricted geographic area of New Jersey's Passaic River Valley. Pough brokered an arrangement whereby the conservancy would raise and hold the majority of project funds while Wildlife Preserves agreed to negotiate agreements and hold title to the acquired lands.

In its early phases, the Sunken Forest project proceeded smoothly as funds were raised and individual tracts of land acquired, with Pough—"rhymes with dough"—serving as an active promoter and fund-raising agent.[41] Functioning as the conservancy's chief executive, Fell took seriously the organization's fidu-ciary role in administering the project's finances, and insisted on proper docu-mentation and reports before releasing project funds. In time, the local group rebelled against what it considered to be excessive oversight and publicly de-clared itself independent of and in no way accountable to the conservancy, even as the conservancy continued to operate as its fiscal agent. Furthermore, the group demanded that it retain exclusive right to issue any and all statements about the project and that the conservancy be barred from contacting any of the project's donors. Eventually, the group demanded that a separate bank account be established and the balance of project-related funds transferred to its exclusive control. The exclamation point to the group's dissolution of its relationship with both the conservancy and Wildlife Preserves was its demand to hold unrestricted title to the Sunken Forest site. Fell strenuously objected to the group's demands, especially regarding the lack of deed restrictions on the land, without which the prime acreage could be sold at any future time to a developer.

Pough may have had some informal assurances that the local group would preserve Sunken Forest as a natural area without a legal deed restriction. (A little more than a decade later, establishment of the Fire Island National Seashore, of which Sunken Forest was designated a key parcel, ensured that the National Park Service would preserve the site "in as nearly its present state as possible."[42]) In any event, he overrode Fell's objections, blamed him for the soured relationship with the local group, and acceded to the group's every demand.

What followed was a rash of competing appeals by Fell and Pough to the board of governors. "For a long time I have considered Dick Pough to be one of my closest friends," Fell wrote in one of many open letters, "and I hope that friendship will continue."[43] In another letter, to board member Joseph J. Hickey, he wrote, "All this correspondence about our differences . . . is in a way misleading. Whenever [Barbara and I] get together with Dick we get along fine. We look at some things with a mildly different view but just accept them that way."[44] On the heels of such preambles, however, Fell would enumerate the many reasons, ethically and legally, why he felt it was important to insist on strict accountability when dealing with chapters and outside groups. In doing so, he acknowledged that it was a challenge to strike the proper balance between local autonomy and accountability to the national office but held fast to his conviction that "our name must be kept synonymous with efforts in the public good, and to do this we must stick to certain specific standards."[45] Barbara, too, weighed in on the debate. In her own letter to Pough, she wrote, "I think we are agreed that the local groups must carry on the major part of the work, and they must be left to work out many of their problems. We can lighten the task here and there [and] we should have a standard procedure to point out their relationship to the Nature Conservancy as a whole."[46]

The sum of Pough's counterarguments ran along the line that Fell was misdirecting his efforts in not applying himself to on-the-ground preservation projects. "I think it is fair to say that we would not have been involved in any of the projects that we have been involved in to date if it had not been for my taking the initiative in going contrary to George Fell's frequently expressed opinion that all projects should be handled through chapters, and that, therefore, chapters should first be set up before we attempt to do anything. I practically had to battle every inch of the way on everything we have done except the setting up of chapters and the soliciting for more members."[47]

For all their efforts to convince each other which of them was right, Fell finally conceded, "It just all boils down to the fact that we all have our assets and our limitations. Dick's background, interests, and abilities are different from mine and as a result his attitude toward Nature Conservancy is different also."[48] Pough was more blunt. In August 1955 he wrote to Fell, "Let's face it. We simply have completely totally different ideas as to what the Nature Conservancy should be and how it should operate. No amount of talking by you is going to change my mind and apparently I have been unable to change yours. It seems to me the only possible way we can continue to work together is to place our points of disagreement before the Board and ask for definite instructions from them as to matters that can be reduced to statements of policy."[49]

In the midst of this welling controversy, the conservancy accomplished what it bills as its first land acquisition effort. Near the small town of Bedford, New York, the Mianus River shoots through a steep, granite-strewn gorge dense with 350-year-old hemlock trees. To save the wild and rugged site, the independently organized River Gorge Conservation Committee first successfully negotiated a compromise solution with the Greenwich Water Company to limit the size of a proposed dam that otherwise would have flooded a portion of the site. Fund-raising began in earnest in late 1954 when the owner of sixty acres, including a particularly scenic tract known as Hemlock Cathedral, notified the committee that she would accept an offer made on her property unless the committee could match the thirty-thousand-dollar bid. Three members of the committee pledged their life insurance policies to finance the down payment, and the deal went through. As the deadline approached to complete the acquisition, the committee had raised all but $7,500. Ernest Brooks, a new board member of the conservancy, urged the Old Dominion Foundation (today the Andrew W. Mellon Foundation) to grant the $7,500 to the conservancy with the understanding that it would be loaned to the River Gorge Conservation Committee to finalize the purchase of what later, in 1964, would be designated as the nation's first Natural History Landmark. The Old Dominion Foundation made the grant to the conservancy, which loaned the money to finalize the acquisition of the gorge property. When the $7,500 loan was repaid, the conservancy used the money as the nucleus of a revolving loan fund for future acquisitions.[50]

On the heels of the Mianus River Gorge success, Fell took up Pough's prescription for resolving their differences by formally making his case to the conservancy's board of governors. The sum of his white paper, titled "General Policies of Nature Conservancy," was embodied in this declaration: "because the organization exists to protect many areas, it shall be considered as being more important than any single area. A substantial organization capable of sustaining a widespread effort should therefore be developed."[51] Fell followed with a meticulous, point-by-point refutation of Pough's positions, including Pough's call to reconstitute the board of governors. Admittedly, the conservancy had been plagued since its inception with lackluster attendance at board of governors meetings because members had to travel to Washington or New York City from all over the country. The too-frequent lack of a quorum stymied the board's ability to move forward on important matters of business, especially related to urgent preservation opportunities. Pough's solution was to stack the board with East Coast representatives and to establish a new governance committee to be "selected solely on the basis of their ability to attend fairly regular meetings in New York."[52] Fell acknowledged the difficulties in achieving a consistent quorum at board meetings but stressed that a national organization required a "balanced representation of various interests and parts of the country." Fell also took Pough to task for raising large sums of money for individual preservation projects but failing to raise any money for the national office. Fell sought to check Pough in the future by advancing a policy that would require that "contributions . . . be solicited for the general purposes of the organization rather than for a specific purpose [and] to the extent possible projects . . . be financed with allocations from general funds."[53]

Pough responded four months later with his own written proposal for the "Reorganization of the Nature Conservancy." In contrast to Fell's vision for a broadly and equitably representative national board of governors, Pough called for the conservancy to "conform to the basic pattern of all corporate enterprises and the governments of most civilized nations." For Pough, this meant first reducing the number of board members from twenty-four to twelve, with the provision that each governor would have to commit to attend each quarterly board meeting. To assuage concerns that such an arrangement would concentrate the board of governor membership in and around New York and Washington, he recommended the establishment of an advisory committee made up of "men of mature judgment and high standing who are scattered about the country."[54]

Pough also insisted on making the presidency a full-time paid position and—stretching the bounds of what many might consider to be appropriate corporate and at least democratic government models—expanding the president's power to be "individual and absolute" over the executive staff. By "individual and absolute" he meant that he, as president, would have sole authority to hire and fire the executive director. He also suggested that the president be empowered to fire, with the board of governors' approval, the board-elected secretary and treasurer.

Pough's bid for a paid position was, in part, practical if not self-serving: he needed a job. As a senior staff member of the American Museum of Natural History, he had run afoul of his own board of directors for his vocal opposition to the Echo Park dam project, which would have flooded Dinosaur National Monument in northwest Colorado. The battle to oppose the dam was nearly as controversial and high profile as the unsuccessful antidam effort a half century earlier to spare Hetch Hetchy, the scenic and biologically rich valley located in Yosemite National Park, from becoming a reservoir to supply drinking water to San Francisco. Pough contended that he was dismissed from his position at the museum because "certain members of the board had interests that were to benefit from the dam at Echo Park and they were incensed that an organization of which they were trustees would be credited with playing a key role in its being defeated."[55]

Like Fell, Pough stood up for what he believed and was willing to accept the consequences. Unlike his counterpart, however, Pough was not willing to work full time for the conservancy for free. Neither would he back down from mandating in his reorganization plan that the conservancy "not have branches or chapters." To his way of thinking, Fell's chapter idea not only shackled his entrepreneurial style but also inappropriately decentralized the conservancy's decision-making authority. Pough preferred concentrating all decision-making power in a small, tightly controlled central governing body. From time to time, he acknowledged, it might be necessary to establish local groups where none existed to preserve particular natural areas and to provide them with "the technical skills, knowledge, and access to sources of funds that we possess. But," he hammered home, they "should not be . . . Nature Conservancy chapter[s]." Envisioning the conservancy as a lean, flexible facilitator of individual preservation efforts rather than any kind of permanent presence in each state, he further recommended that the conservancy confer title to preserved sites to unaffiliated local organizations in order to relieve the conservancy of "the legal problems and liabilities that go with the ownership of land."[56]

Largely divorced from the day-to-day conflicts between Fell and Pough, the board of governors could more dispassionately weigh the merits of the two competing visions for the future of the conservancy. Several members accurately perceived in Pough's proposal an excessive centralization of power. Herbert A. McCollough, of Howard College, went so far as to conjecture that Pough's plan "would certainly seem to produce a localized dynasty at best if not a permanent one man rule."[57] Other governors criticized Pough for his overstatement of the deficiencies of the conservancy. Robert W. Schery, of the O. F. Scott Company, wrote directly to Pough, "It is my feeling that the Conservancy has not been unsuccessful, as judged by its accomplishments. I would be hesitant to scuttle an existing workable system, developed carefully by George Fell, through the years, in favor of high pressure methods without the capacity to back them up."[58]

Not that Fell's way of operating was without its challenges. Several governors voiced concern about the state of relations between the conservancy's national office and its chapters and about divisions stemming from Fell's inflexibility in administering what many deemed to be a burdensome organizational structure. Charles Kendeigh, who had first urged his former student to join the Ecologists' Union and soon thereafter nominated him to the vice presidency, shared that the Illinois Nature Conservancy, formed as a division in 1952, "came within a narrow margin of withdrawing from the national organization entirely because of the rigid framework of organizational detail that has been set up, and the subordination of the local organization to the national officers remotely situated."[59]

Still other conservancy governors saw the dispute between Fell and Pough for what it was at its core. As board member Frank Engler wrote to Pough, "In the last analysis, I cannot help but wonder how much of this [conflict] is due primarily . . . to a fundamental personality-incompatibility between you and George Fell."[60] In a perfect world, their respective strengths would have complemented each other. In a perfect world, some compromise on both their parts would have resulted in a powerful management team. In the world that was, as Kendeigh observed in his unpublished memoirs, "Both Fell and Pough were dynamic personalities. Their ideas as to how the Conservancy should be run and the best way to promote the preservation movement in the country finally came into open conflict. The result was a proxy fight at an annual meeting in the late 1950s."[61]

The Proxy Fight

The proxy fight of which Kendeigh wrote was the climax of a calculated effort to displace Fell as the chief executive of the conservancy. Thwarted in his attempt to become the conservancy's first full-time paid president, in late 1955 Pough announced that he would remain on the board of governors but not seek re-election as an officer in order to devote sufficient time to his new job with Wildlife Preserves. In yet another open letter to the conservancy's board of governors, Fell expressed his hope that Wildlife Preserves would better suit Pough, as it had "a restricted membership and a small Board of Directors consisting entirely of New York and New Jersey people."[62]

In the same letter, Fell also expressed hope that the strife that had engulfed the conservancy during Pough's tenure would end with the election of a new president. That hope was ill founded. In spite of their differences, Pough genuinely liked Fell and consistently praised his role in transitioning the Ecologists' Union into The Nature Conservancy. But, after several years of struggle, he had determined that Fell was no longer "the man to run it." Unwilling to lower the boom on a friend, Pough recruited Richard H. Goodwin "to do the dirty job" of letting Fell go.[63]

Richard Goodwin was a professor of botany at Connecticut College and director of the Connecticut Arboretum. Before joining the conservancy in 1951, he had been active in several major preservation efforts in his home state, including the two-thousand-acre Bergen Swamp, the forty-acre Mamacoke Island in the Thames River, and a three-hundred-acre expansion of the land holdings of the Connecticut Arboretum.[64] In 1952 Goodwin was appointed conservancy representative for his home state, and in 1956, at Pough's urging, he was elected to the national board of governors as its fourth president.

In his autobiography, *A Botanist's Window on the Twentieth Century*, Goodwin confirmed that the "Fell issue" was one of his top priorities: "As soon as I became president in 1956, I realized that the organization was financially under-nourished and inadequately staffed . . . [and] someone other than the Fells had to be in charge of the national office." Goodwin cited several specific issues: "the staff consisted of one underpaid executive, the office his living room, and the annual budget was a mere $10,000." Added to this, Goodwin lamented that "no land had been acquired during the first four years of the Conservancy's existence, but after Richard H. Pough became president in 1953 the program began to take shape. By 1956, fifteen projects . . . had been undertaken."[65]

Goodwin's facts were a little off. Pough was elected in 1954, not 1953. Fell certainly was underpaid, as was Barbara, but by that time both of them were being paid honoraria for full-time work for the conservancy. Total annual revenues for the organization had peaked the year before at forty-five thousand dollars.[66] The conservancy's office was, indeed, in a dedicated space within the Fell home at 4200 Twenty-Second Street, but through 1956 the conservancy had played a direct role in no fewer than twenty-one land preservation efforts.[67] Goodwin did not mention membership, but by the end of 1956 Fell had increased the number of paid members to 2,500.[68]

These discrepancies aside, most troubling to Goodwin was what he referred to as the "public relations problem" with project committees. In drafting "A Review of Natural Area Projects" for the February 1957 *Nature Conservation News*, Goodwin learned firsthand just how disgruntled project leaders were with Fell and his inflexible attitude toward them. "[Fell] didn't play ball with these people and encourage them. He was interested in the national outfit and the result was that . . . some wanted to break off from the Conservancy."[69]

Given his impatience with those who disagreed with him, Fell was not blind to how others sometimes perceived him. In working with the Illinois division to negotiate a more favorable purchase price for Volo and Wauconda Bogs, he admitted, "I was strong minded and had certain things that I was aiming at and kind of going roughshod over the others." But in the end, he managed to knock ten thousand dollars off the purchase price by allowing continued hunting rights on the bogs for the duration of the owner's life.[70]

Whether or not Goodwin was aware of such attenuating circumstances, he remained convinced that the conservancy "required more competent staffing."[71] Many organizations, as they grow, must come to grips with "the difficulty, yet necessity, of leadership change . . . to move the organization to a higher level."[72] But Goodwin also was sensitive to the fact that several governors remained steadfastly loyal to the Fells. And so, taking a sabbatical from his teaching position, he embarked on a tour of what he called "persuasion and diplomacy," traveling the country to discuss the conservancy and its staffing issues with all thirty members of the board of governors, as well as with leaders from state chapters and divisions. Whereas his predecessor, Pough, had striven to affect change by attempting to wrest individual control of the organization, Goodwin carefully cultivated consensus among and more active participation by the entire board of governors.

In the five years prior to Goodwin's election to the presidency, the board of governors and the executive committee each had met a total of only six times. Although Fell communicated liberally with various governors, he had been left to administer the organization largely on his own. In the conservancy's infancy, this arrangement proved workable, even desirable, given the limited availability of the governors. However, as the conservancy grew, in no small part due to Fell's hard work, Goodwin sought to encourage board members to fulfill their responsibility to provide genuine oversight and governance. His first step was to establish a Committee on Management and Finance to provide for more accountability in the conservancy's administration. Another step was to reiterate Pough's call to establish the presidency as a full-time paid position, with the understanding that this change would be effective only after the next election of officers and that he would not stand for reelection.

Both of the Fells bitterly opposed Goodwin's proposed changes, which they viewed as a criticism of their abilities and ultimately a threat to their leadership role in the organization. Since moving to Washington with little more than the clothes on their backs, the Fells had committed more than their hearts and souls to the cause of the conservancy. Neither had received any salary for four and a half years until Fell cultivated a ten-thousand-dollar grant from the Old Dominion Foundation, which finally provided him what the board of governors termed an "honorarium" of four thousand dollars per year for his role as executive director. Shortly thereafter, Barbara demanded some level of compensation in return for her services as assistant to the executive director. The board— reflecting the concern of its Management and Finance Committee that "the wife of the Executive Director should not be a paid employee" — ultimately suggested that the same four-thousand-dollar salary be paid "to Mr. and Mrs. Fell together, to cover both his services as Executive Director and her services as assistant to the Executive Director, the amount paid to be divided in such proportion between them as they shall designate to the Conservancy in writing."[73]

Goodwin appreciated the Fells' hard work and sacrifice and understood why they felt threatened, but his vision for cultivating a strong, more effective national organization mandated a change in staffing.[74] At the July 1957 board of governors meeting, Goodwin raised the idea of hiring a new staff person. Seeing the handwriting on the wall and ever ready, Fell submitted for the board's consideration an alternative idea how to staff up the organization.[75]

In spite of the mounting tensions between Fell and Goodwin, not all was power play between them. Goodwin credits Fell with having brought to his attention a three-thousand-acre tract of old-growth redwood forest in the coast range of northern California. Goodwin flew to California and spent two days touring the property with its owner, Heath Angelo. Pledging a five-thousand-dollar grant from his own family foundation, Goodwin convinced the conservancy's board of governors to enter into a purchase agreement. It took twenty years to pay off the debt, but in 1977 Goodwin personally delivered the conservancy's final payment to the Angelos. Soon thereafter, the Heath and Marjorie Angelo Coast Range Reserve was designated a Global Biosphere Reserve by the United Nations Environmental Programme. The reserve is currently owned and managed by the University of California, as part of its Natural Reserves System.[76]

There were several other land conservation success stories, as well. On July 9, 1957, the conservancy signed purchase agreements to acquire Volo and Wauconda Bogs, located in Lake County, Illinois.[77] Fell had played an admittedly aggressive role in negotiating the agreements for the two rare, high-quality natural areas, which, in the 1970s, would be designated as National Natural Landmarks. In his own home state, Goodwin worked with local leaders to preserve Beckley Bog, which harbored one of the best remaining floating bog heaths in Connecticut. The conservancy entered into an agreement to work with a local committee to raise the purchase price of twenty-one thousand dollars by May 31, 1957.[78] In January 1957 the conservancy acquired title to yet another bog, named for the nearby town of Tannersville, Pennsylvania.[79] Beyond bogs, there were efforts under way to preserve a diversity of habitat types in Arizona, Florida, Georgia, Idaho, Maine, Missouri, Oklahoma, Virginia, and several other states.[80] A number of these efforts came about as a direct result of Fell's insistence — contrary to Pough's opportunistic instincts — on the need for additional surveys to identify natural areas of strategic conservation value and to be proactive in their preservation. On the basis of suggestions provided by Fell's Illinois colleague Julian A. Steyermark, an authority on the flora of Missouri, a survey in that state identified fifty-seven areas, mostly in the Ozarks region, which were prioritized in part based on the level of conservation threat. A conservancy survey of the Atlantic coast proved important enough in light of increasing development pressures that the National Park Service secured funding to continue the survey for several years.[81]

Fell and Goodwin wholeheartedly agreed that The Nature Conservancy should ramp up its land preservation efforts further still. Where they differed was on how to do so. At the December 1957 board of governors meeting, Fell brought the matter to a head. He presented a report that summarized the results achieved under his watch. "The only real test of management is in results," he proclaimed as he called attention to the logarithmic graph he had prepared, one that revealed the conservancy's steady upward trends in income, expenditures, salaries, members, publications, "man-months" of staff work, territorial units (chapters and divisions), and areas owned. "I believe the Board should consider all this," he asserted, "and come to a decision as to whether it wishes to have me continue managing the organization or prefers to turn the responsibility over to someone else." Fell did not compare the conservancy to other conservation organizations, which would have revealed that it still was one of the smallest in budget size and membership. However, he did make a viable case that with increased investment in the central office, he could promise even greater, more rapid growth in various metrics, primarily in the number of chapters established and acres owned.[82]

In the same memo, however, Fell seriously undermined his credibility with Goodwin and other board members. Earlier in the year, Fell had recommended moving the national office to the Midwest, specifically to his hometown of Rockford, Illinois. He all but tied himself in knots in an attempt to rationalize the proposed relocation, which but thinly masked an attempt to counter Pough's efforts at consolidating control of the conservancy among residents of the northeast. There may have been a personal reason, as well, something he would not have shared with anyone aside from his wife. During their time in Washington, Fell had had to return several times to Rockford to deal with a family issue. Fell's older brother Bill was a gifted inventor, but both he and his wife, Ella, suffered from severe alcoholism. They were in and out of various hospitals and treatment programs, and it was Fell who took on the responsibility for their care since their father—an expert in the treatment of those suffering from alcoholism—had grown too old to do so.[83] "We should like to know if he [Bill] is able to remain away from alcohol since his tolerance is so very low," a social worker had written to Fell, following his brother's discharge from the East Moline State Hospital.[84]

Fell replied directly to the attending physician: "I am happy to report that both William and his wife Ella are doing very well at this time. In fact, in spite of the relapses, he has shown steady improvement."[85]

Unaware of any personal reasons and unswayed by the rationales Fell had put forth, the board of governors voted to keep the national office in Washington. Rather than accept the decision, at the December 1957 board meeting Fell all but demanded that the decision be reconsidered, devoting a full page of his four-page "Memorandum on Nature Conservancy Management" to the subject. The board's decision not to relocate "was a severe blow to me," he stated. He then reiterated, "I cannot see the consistency of an organization dedicated to nature fearing to leave the heart of the metropolis. For my part, I do not believe I should spend my life in a city. I can continue on year by year as in the past but it will be without enthusiasm for I am convinced it is unnecessary."[86]

After Fell drew this line in the sand, the board of governors went into executive session and, upon the recommendation of the Management and Finance Committee, approved the search for a new executive director at a salary of between $9,000 and $12,500 per annum. Next, the governors passed a resolution that stated, "George and Barbara Fell are to be highly commended for their devoted efforts in managing the affairs of the Nature Conservancy so competently since its inception and the Board hopes they will continue this excellent service in the future." Then they voted to retain the Fells at their current salary levels—$6,500 for Fell and $3,500 for Barbara—but with new titles: executive secretary and assistant executive secretary, respectively. They were to report to an executive director—Fell's previous title—and their duties would be to manage the central office.[87]

On March 1, 1958, while the search for an executive director remained in progress, the Fells raised several issues that further eroded what confidence the board may have retained in them. Fell pressed the board of governors for specifics regarding the allocation of responsibilities between the executive director and the executive secretary. He stated that he "did not wish to be understood to have taken a position" on whether he would remain with the conservancy as executive secretary but that he "did not believe that over the long pull his function should be that of office manager." Fell also asked for confirmation that, since the board of governors had hired him directly as executive secretary, it would be the board's responsibility "to determine what action to take in case of differences that might arise between him and a new executive director." Barbara inquired whether the board had given any consideration to severance payments "in case the Fells elected to resign." One board member expressed his hope that the Fells would remain on the job, while another suggested that severance should be provided, "since it was normal in good corporate practice."[88]

Three months later, at the May 29, 1958, meeting of the board of governors, the Conservancy voted to hire Edward Munns. Munns, who had been chairman of the conservancy's Western Advisory Board and was recently retired from the US Forest Service, accepted. Goodwin championed the new executive director as "older, more experienced, especially dealing with people."[89] Not unsurprisingly, given the circumstances, the Fells found him difficult to work with. They complained of his coming from a large government bureaucracy and being unfamiliar with the mechanics of running a small nonprofit organization on a minuscule budget. Nonetheless, after a few months, relations had stabilized to the point where Goodwin felt he could step down as president and resume his full-time teaching duties, which he was eager to do. At the July 12, 1958, board of governors meeting, after congratulating Fell for receiving an American Motors Conservation Award of a bronze plaque and five hundred dollars, Goodwin announced a new slate of officers, headed by James B. Ross of Atlanta, Georgia, for president.

What stability Goodwin perceived was short-lived, if not an illusion. Not content to function as an office manager and against the advice of a number of colleagues, Fell conspired to wrest control of the conservancy's board of governors. In truth, Fell would have made a good manager; in many ways he *was* a good manager. "Looking back," he reflected years later, "I think that . . . a large part of my virtue was just systematically doing . . . things. Just figuring out what is needed."[90] His "Summary of Policies and Actions," compiled for the conservancy in August 1958, reveals that he was thorough, comprehensive, and adept in teaching himself about every operational facet of nonprofit organizations.

What skills Fell had as a manager, however, may have been trumped by the fact that—as a former Civilian Public Service commander observed—he was first and foremost an individualist. Because he believed that the current leadership of the conservancy was wrong in hiring someone to replace him as chief executive, Fell's self-professed "worst shortcoming" of becoming unreasonably irritated with those who disagreed with him bubbled to the surface and boiled over.[91] On conservancy letterhead—without the knowledge or approval of Munns or the board—he first queried select general members of the conservancy to determine whether they would be interested in serving a three-year term on the board of governors. Receiving a sufficient number of positive replies, he then filed an alternate slate of candidates with himself as president.

Many years later, Fell conceded that initiating the proxy war "was all a bunch of damn foolishness."[92] But, at the time, both he and the governors took the issue very seriously. The governors' reaction was swift and almost universally negative. Even more than senior staff of the Soil Conservation Service nearly a decade earlier, they found his actions inappropriate to the point of insubordination and proof positive that he was not the right man for the job. Several governors strongly urged Fell to reconsider. Particularly upset was William R. Huntington, who requested that his name be struck from the alternate slate when he learned that Fell had misled him into believing that he had been solicited to stand for election by the conservancy's official nominating committee.[93] Fell replied, "All I can say is that I am very, very sorry for my transgression against you. My efforts are clumsy and inept, I realize. I shall do what I can to mend the damage. I shall not withdraw from the contest because to do so would be to turn my back on what I believe is right."[94]

The election at the August 28, 1958, board of governors meeting began as a procedural chess match. Declaring his neutrality, eighty-one-year-old Victor Shelford, who many years earlier had cultivated his own share of controversy in breaking from the Ecological Society of America to establish the Ecologists' Union, made the first move by raising a point of order stipulating that all proxy votes should be discounted because of their doubtful legal validity. Ever since Fell had announced his alternative slate of candidates, both he and the board of governors had engaged in an aggressive campaign to secure proxy votes among new and existing conservancy members. In support of his point, Shelford introduced attorney Richard G. Davis, a professor of law at the University of Indiana School of Law, who pointed out that the use of proxies had not been properly provided for in the bylaws of the conservancy. Pressed on the point, Davis conceded that if the chair declared the proxies valid and his ruling was sustained by those members present, a court would probably uphold the decision.

Goodwin, presiding over the meeting as president, declared all proxies to be valid. His ruling went unchallenged, but immediately thereafter a motion was made to exclude the proxies of those members who were not members at the time the officer nominations were announced. The allegation fueling this motion was that certain governors had solicited new memberships expressly to obtain proxy votes to cast for the nominating committee's slate of officers. Some board members rose to refute this, but Goodwin had spent nearly five hundred dollars out of his own pocket to compete with Fell's proxy solicitation effort.[95] In his biography, Goodwin confessed that he felt compelled to counter Fell's proxy solicitations, in which Fell had accused Goodwin of "having been financially irresponsible," apparently for his "failure to approach financial donors while the Conservancy's administrative set-up was in turmoil."[96] By a vote of twenty-five to twenty-one, the motion failed, and all proxies remained valid. The vote for officers was taken by paper ballot. To review and count the proxy votes, Goodwin assigned a three-person committee, composed of one person from each faction and, because there was not an impartial third person in the room, a student intern who had been assigned to the meeting as a projectionist.

Fell lost the election by a vote of 762 to 667. With only minor variations in vote counts, each member of his alternate slate of candidates lost by similar margins. Of board members present, the vote swung decidedly against Fell, thirty-nine to five. Immediately following the meeting, Fell resigned his position, which eliminated the need for the board of governors to terminate his employment, as had been predetermined at an earlier meeting.[97] At the next board of governors meeting, Munns reported that the Fells had purchased about seven hundred dollars' worth of printing equipment that the conservancy no longer required (mostly because Fell was the only one who knew how to operate and repair the presses). The Fells left Washington on October 27, 1958—nearly seven years to the day after the conservancy was formally incorporated—and drove nonstop back home to Rockford, Illinois.

Fell was not the first "gifted, headstrong leader" whose singular vision eventually brought him into irreconcilable conflict with a governing board. William E. Dutcher of the National Audubon Society, Will H. Dilg of the Izaak Walton League, and Robert Sterling Yard of the National Parks Association all preceded Fell in building up their respective environmental organizations only to be summarily dismissed.[98] Nor was Fell the last, as David Brower would experience in 1969 with the Sierra Club.[99]

All things considered, a change in executive leadership at the conservancy was a necessary next step in its evolution. Nonetheless, it is important to keep in mind that when the Fells arrived in Washington on New Year's Day in 1950, the Ecologists' Union, with three hundred dollars in the bank, had not preserved a single acre and had no plan for how to do so. By the time the Fells departed, The Nature Conservancy existed. It had 2,900 members and peak annual revenues in excess of fifty thousand dollars.[100] There were three full-time staff in the national office in Washington, DC, with field staff in St. Louis, Missouri, and Berkeley, California.[101] There were eight chapters, with several divisions in the pipeline to become chapters.[102] The conservancy had had an active hand in sixty-eight land preservation projects, providing loans, helping to raise funds, and providing other kinds of support.[103] Fourteen of "the most important projects" completed or in process in 1957 alone protected more than eight thousand acres. Two loan funds had been established, which had helped preserve another sixteen natural areas with a combined acquisition cost in excess of $300,000.[104] The conservancy owned several natural areas outright, totaling a little more than 2,500 acres.[105] Most important of all, Fell left in place the fundamental structure that would underpin the conservancy's meteoric rise over the next half century.

Even more remarkable is that Fell did not allow his disappointment at being effectively squeezed out of the conservancy to diminish his passion and commitment. He remained unshakable in his conviction that natural areas needed to be preserved, that someone had to step up to do so, and that he remained the man for the job. Soon after returning to Rockford, he wrote to a colleague that he was considering launching a new nonprofit organization: "We have thought of 'Wild Land Institute,' 'Natural Land Institute,' and 'Nature Conservation Institute' as possible names. Do you have any comments on these?"[106]

George Fell and his mother, Olive Brady Fell, 1927. A gifted musician, Olive read Shakespeare aloud to her youngest son and instilled in him a deep appreciation for the arts. (Natural Land Institute)

Dr. Egbert Fell, 1912. Egbert was formal and reserved as a father, but his lifelong love of wildflowers and other native plants inspired his youngest son in his future career. (Natural Land Institute)

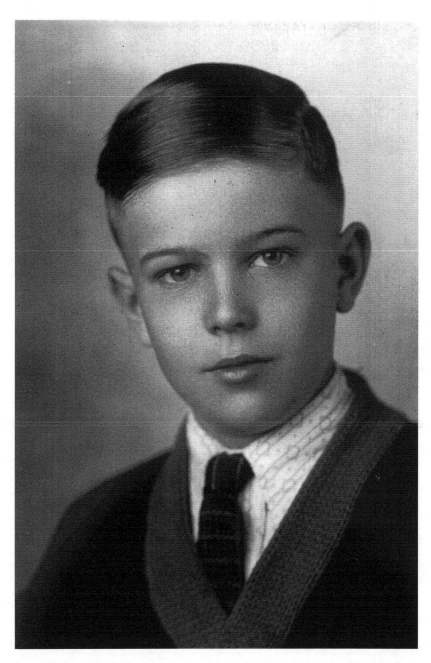

George Fell, Keith Country Day School, 1928. Even as a young boy, Fell perceived the development threats to the woods, wetlands, and gravel hill prairies he loved to explore along the Rock River. (Natural Land Institute)

George Fell, University of Illinois, 1938. As a botany student, Fell studied under some of the leading ecologists of the day, who would play important roles throughout his career. (Natural Land Institute)

George Fell, Civilian Public Service conscript, circa 1943. In spite of his father's impressive military record, Fell held to his own convictions and registered as a conscientious objector during World War II. (Natural Land Institute)

George Fell and Barbara Garst wedding day, May 1948. The couple sealed their "alliance" in a civil marriage ceremony and spent their honeymoon night camping on a remnant gravel hill prairie along the Rock River. (Natural Land Institute)

Top left: Civilian Public Service Camp, Germfask, Michigan, May 1945. Fell spent nearly five years in a succession of Civilian Public Service camps, frustrated not to be engaged in "work of national importance," as intended, and trying in vain to improve the operation of the camps. (Natural Land Institute)

Bottom left: George Fell working on his prewar Plymouth, 1948. An inveterate tinkerer with all things mechanical, Fell rigged the seats in his car to lie flat so that he and his wife could sleep in it during their many road trips scouting natural areas. (Natural Land Institute)

Top: George (*right*) and Barbara Fell in the Okefenokee Swamp with unidentified guide, 1952. The Fells traveled far and wide together in search of natural lands to protect. (Natural Land Institute)

Bottom: Barbara Fell in The Nature Conservancy office, circa 1955. Like her husband, Barbara worked for little or no pay during the critical start-up years of the conservancy. (Natural Land Institute)

Top right: Dr. Egbert Fell tending his wildflower garden at his Rockford home, circa 1958. During his retirement years, Dr. Fell compiled *The Flora of Winnebago County*, which his son published while serving as the executive secretary of The Nature Conservancy. (Natural Land Institute)

Bottom right: Governor Otto Kerner signing the articles of dedication for the Illinois Beach Nature Preserve, 1964. Flanked by George Fell (right) and William T. Lodge, director of the Illinois Department of Conservation (*left*), Kerner signed the articles establishing the first dedicated nature preserve in Illinois. (Natural Land Institute)

George Fell at the dedication of the two-hundredth nature preserve, 1991. Joining Fell at the dedication were Barbara Fell (*third from left*) and Frank Bellrose (*far left*), with whom Fell had shared a youthful dream of protecting natural areas. (Kenneth R. Robertson, Illinois Natural History Survey)

Barbara Fell at the dedication of the three-hundredth nature preserve, 2001. Barbara (*far right*) attended the ceremony at which a portion of White Pines Forest State Park—where she and her husband had spent a part of their honeymoon—was designated as an Illinois nature preserve. (Kenneth R. Robertson, Illinois Natural History Survey)

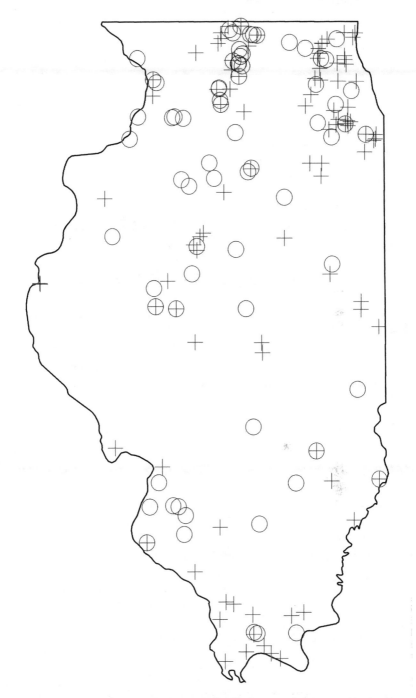

Map of Illinois natural lands protected by George Fell. Fell protected more natural land in Illinois than any other individual. The circles represent natural lands in which Fell played a direct role protecting by acquisition or easement. The crosshatches represent lands designated as Illinois Nature Preserves during his tenure with the Illinois Nature Preserves Commission, 1964–82. (Natural Land Institute; map by Susan B. Clark)

4

The Illinois Natural Areas Preservation Act

If at First You Don't Succeed . . .

In his landmark essay "The Land Ethic," published posthumously in 1949 in *A Sand County Almanac*, Aldo Leopold observed that small, scattered natural areas and the significant biotic communities they represented had been effectively "relegated . . . to ultimate extinction." Leopold reasoned that it was impractical if not impossible for government to own or control such parcels. One solution, which he acknowledged could take countless generations to achieve, was to cultivate "a land ethic, or some other force which assigns more obligation to the private landowner."[1] In theory, George Fell agreed with his former mentor. In practice, he feared that remnant natural areas would be long gone by the time any such ethic might take hold.

Deprived of the opportunity to follow through on the national preservation organization he had launched in Washington, DC, Fell returned to Rockford, Illinois, and his original idea of a statewide system for preserving natural areas. With a heightened sense of urgency, he studiously applied the lessons learned during his years of on-the-job training with The Nature Conservancy to inform both the structure and the content of an entirely new kind of state preservation effort. Failing in his first attempt to pass the enabling legislation required, he took up a second legislative campaign, which led to the passage of the Illinois Natural Areas Preservation Act, making Illinois the first state in the nation to establish a statewide system for preserving natural areas. Although the act ultimately passed was a competing version of the one Fell had championed, he embraced it as his own and shaped it to conform to his original vision.

The Natural Land Institute

Upon their arrival back in Rockford in late October 1958, the Fells wasted no time. They rented an apartment from Barbara's mother and within the first week began drafting articles of incorporation for a new nonprofit organization. A little more than a month later, the articles were signed by Fell, his brother-in-law and local businessman Edward (Ned) Garst, and Milton W. Mahlburg, head of Rockford's Burpee Museum of Natural History. On December 24, nine years to the day after the Fells left for New York and eventually Washington to launch what would become The Nature Conservancy, they celebrated Christmas Eve by holding the first meeting of the Natural Land Institute.

Starting up a new organization so soon on the heels of The Nature Conservancy experience was not easy. Years later, Fell would reflect, "You've got to remember that . . . there was quite a pall hanging over our efforts when we left Washington and started doing things here [in Rockford]. I mean, we created a huge mess in having a proxy war. People knew about it. So . . . they'd automatically think 'what's he trying to do?'" However, Fell was adamant that "we didn't want to set up a competitor to The Nature Conservancy. We had no intention of doing that."[2] Nonetheless, as outlined in the bylaws of the Institute, its conservation goals were indistinguishable from those of the conservancy. Essentially, both organizations were founded to establish and maintain nature preserves to be used for scientific, educational, and aesthetic purposes. Where they differed—aside from geographic emphases, with the conservancy targeting natural areas throughout the country and the institute focused on preserving those within Illinois—was in how they were structured. With the experience of an independently minded conservancy board and a proxy war fresh in his mind, Fell forwent a large, broadly representative board in favor of a small handful of close friends and family. He handpicked Garst and Mahlburg to join him in making up the institute's entire board of trustees, three being the minimum number of directors required to incorporate as an Illinois nonprofit organization. Fell likewise opted not to cultivate a large general membership base. Instead, the institute's bylaws stipulated that members were to be selected by the trustees. At the institute's first meeting, the three trustees selected themselves and Barbara as members. The four inaugural members then elected the following officers: Fell as chairman, Mahlburg as vice chairman, and Garst as secretary.

Over the next couple of decades, the number of institute members increased negligibly, and the number of trustees—although the bylaws allowed for up to nine—never totaled more than five. With a purposefully limited membership, there was never the least hint of challenge to each year's slate of trustees and officers. Then again, there was seldom any change. For many years, the board remained not only intentionally small but exceptionally stable in composition. Garst and Mahlburg served as board members for thirty-two uninterrupted years (perhaps the only instance in which Fell did not strictly abide by his own bylaws, a provision of which limited institute trustees to six consecutive one-year terms). As chairman and executive director for thirty-six years, Fell kept a firm grip on all facets of the organization, taking the lead on everything from finances, to administration, to policy, to on-the-ground preservation efforts. When board action was required, generally it was Fell who asked that a motion be made. A trustee obliged. The motion was seconded and approved, often unanimously and without much debate. Even in later years, one board member would recall, "George didn't want oversight, he wanted endorsement."[3]

As much as Fell cultivated tight control of the institute, he did not surround himself with rubber stamps. Without exception, each trustee was an accomplished professional with deep convictions about natural areas preservation. Lee Johnson, for example, a trustee for twenty-two consecutive years beginning in 1969, succeeded Mahlburg as head of the Burpee Museum of Natural History and founded the Sand Bluff Bird Observatory and Banding Station, one of the largest volunteer banding stations in the country. Fell relied heavily on his trustees, calling them virtually any time of the day or night to solicit their opinions on a wide range of preservation issues or to ask them to accompany him scouting out natural areas in need of protection. Often by the time the trustees met, most of them were well informed and in agreement on the various agenda items. From time to time, a trustee would raise a dissenting voice. Ned Garst, for instance, recalled his recurring frustration over his brother-in-law's lack of interest in raising money to sustain and expand the core operations of the institute. "When the board wanted something different than George did," Garst explained, "he'd go along with it, but six months later, by God, we'd find that he ended up doing it his way."[4]

That Fell exhibited so little interest in raising funds to support and expand his new organization underscores that he did not want to create another Nature Conservancy. He had no interest in spending several more years struggling to build an organization that might on its own preserve only a scattered handful of natural areas or that could—perhaps more important—oust him from his leadership position. Rather, he purposefully set up the institute as a "shell corporation," as he put it, a small, insular group of trusted individuals that would provide him both the control and the flexibility he required to pursue what he deemed necessary to achieve his vision for a statewide system of natural areas preservation.[5] Ironically, this was not so different from the control and flexibility Richard Pough had sought in structuring The Nature Conservancy to achieve his vision of natural areas preservation nationwide.

Although Fell felt an oft-described urgency to launch a statewide system as soon as possible, he initially involved himself and, by extension, the institute in an eclectic mix of efforts. "I've always been kind of susceptible to my energy being diverted in various ways," he confessed.[6] During his years with The Nature Conservancy, he had aided the ailing Percy Ricker of the Wild Flower Preservation Society by offering administrative assistance through the conservancy. The society, which sought to preserve rare native plants and to establish wildflower preserves, maintained an extensive collection of photographs of wildflowers, trees, and shrubs from all across the country.[7] After Fell's departure, the conservancy had no interest in maintaining its relationship with the society. Fell, named the society's vice president, filled the void by offering continued administrative support through the Natural Land Institute.

In 1959 Fell was among the founding members of the Prairie Chicken Foundation of Illinois. The only grouse native to Illinois, the greater prairie chicken is notable for its extraordinary spring mating rituals. The males compete for mates by inflating bright orange air sacs on their breasts, raising their neck feathers like spiked collars, stomping their feet, and emitting a tympanic "who-OOM-oom" that can be heard up to a mile away. In pre-settlement times, the population of these shy birds was estimated at between ten and fourteen million. Beginning in the mid-nineteenth century, however, sportsmen and market hunters engaged in a wholesale slaughter of prairie chickens. In 1869, to cite but one example, Captain A. H. Borgardus wrote a letter to the editor of the *Chicago Tribune* offering a challenge to "any man in America to shoot prairie-chickens against me . . . for a stake of $100 to $500 a side. The man who kills the most during the time specified to take all the game and the stakes." Over the course of ten days, Borgardus and a partner won the bet, bagging six hundred birds.[8] According to a survey by Aldo Leopold conducted between 1928 and 1930, the conversion of prairie to farmland initially helped populations of prairie chickens to recover somewhat. As late as 1940, there were estimated to be thirty thousand prairie chickens scattered across nearly three thousand square miles of Illinois. But, with the intensification of agricultural practices during World War II, prairie chicken habitat decreased significantly. By the time the Prairie Chicken Foundation of Illinois was established, there remained "between 1,000 and 2,000 birds, scattered in a few pityful [*sic*] remnant flocks in southern and north central Illinois."[9]

Although Fell modeled the Prairie Chicken Foundation of Illinois in part on the Society of Tympanuchus Cupido Pinnatus (Latin for "greater prairie chicken"), which had been successful in acquiring prime prairie chicken habitat in central Wisconsin, there is no indication that he had any direct contact with the society's guiding lights, Frederick and Frances Hamerstrom. Had there been, he would have discovered that he and Barbara were kindred spirits of the couple. Like the Fells, the Hamerstroms were a husband-and-wife team who shunned convention in their total devotion to their particular conservation cause. However, Fell did manage to recruit his old University of Illinois friend Frank Bellrose to join the Prairie Chicken Foundation of Illinois effort. At long last, some thirty years after the two of them shared a youthful dream of "sav[ing] natural areas from disappearing," they were able to work together to accomplish precisely that; the primary objective of the foundation was to acquire a total of two thousand acres for the establishment of two downstate management areas—one in Jasper County and one in Marion County. With Bellrose's encouragement, Fell had earned a master's degree in wildlife management, which may have qualified him to assist in the development of on-the-ground recovery plans for the greater prairie chicken. But that was neither Fell's interest nor his strength. Elected the foundation's first treasurer, he drafted its bylaws and provided bookkeeping and mailing list services through the Natural Land Institute.

Fell likewise offered the cooperation of the institute to the Hugh Moore Fund. Established in 1944 by the founder of the Dixie Cup Corporation, the fund focused on world peace. Believing that an exploding world population meant more and often violent competition for basic resources, Moore placed a strong emphasis on population control.[10] Sparked by his own experience of the negative consequences of the postwar population boom on natural areas, Fell also had developed a firm belief in the need for population control, so much so that he had included it in the original mission statements of both The Nature Conservancy and the Natural Land Institute. At the conservancy, whose first board of governors included William Vogt of Planned Parenthood Federation of America, population control never gained much traction beyond a small research scholarship program funded entirely by one board member, Conrad Chapman of Boston.[11]

The Fells had no children of their own. During their time at the conservancy, Barbara had become pregnant, but it was a difficult pregnancy that ended in a late-term miscarriage. Because of the complications she experienced, they decided against trying again, a decision perhaps eased by their strong, shared convictions regarding population growth. In fact, upon their return to Rockford, they considered starting a local chapter of Planned Parenthood. Ultimately, they decided that doing so would take too much time away from their natural areas preservation efforts, to which they were as devoted as were the best of parents to their children. Years later, in planning the disposition of their estate, they remained just as passionate about population issues. "I'm very much interested in Planned Parenthood," Barbara noted in an interview. "That's where our money's going."[12]

Ironically, providing administrative support for the Illinois Prairie Chicken Foundation, the Hugh Moore Fund, and other organizations played into Fell's strengths as a manager, a role he had fulfilled admirably, if controversially, at the conservancy and by which he refused to be limited in the end. A related set of skills in which he excelled at the conservancy was writer, editor, and publisher, services he offered through the Natural Land Institute as well. Using the massive, antiquated presses he had brought with him from Washington and on which he lavished untold hours for maintenance and operation, Fell printed sheaves of brochures, newsletters, and informational pieces, including the fund-raising appeal he authored to help the Prairie Chicken Foundation of Illinois acquire its first seventy-seven acres of protected habitat in Jasper County: "The open grasslands of the Midwest belonged to the prairie chicken. The Indians knew and loved this little brother of the plains. They copied his strutting and stomping in their dances. We have a chance of saving the prairie chicken. Failure will spell the doom of this population. Surely we can do this much for a wild creature our prosperous civilization has deprived of a home. If you agree, we welcome your help with a warm heart."[13]

Perhaps most gratifying for Fell were the print runs he made of conservation articles authored by his father. While at the conservancy, Fell had had the privilege of publishing his father's *Flora of Winnebago County, Illinois*; *The Gravel-Hill Prairies of Rock River Valley in Illinois*; and *The Ravine Flora of Winnebago County*. Through the Natural Land Institute, he printed his father's *Plants of a Northern Illinois Sand Deposit* (reprinted from the *American Midland Naturalist*); *The Genus Carex in Rock River Valley in Northern Illinois*; *Notes on a New Hybrid Carex*; and *Bell Bowl Prairie*, the latter coauthored with Fell's mother, Olive, who sometimes participated in her husband's botanizing by driving him to natural areas and typing up his field notes. These articles were among Dr. Fell's last, for on July 16, 1960, at the age of eighty-two, he died.

Neither Fell nor his father was demonstrative. Fell made no mention of his father's death in the journal he and Barbara faithfully kept. In fact, Fell's only known mention of the subject occurs in the institute minutes for December 30, 1960. In them, he recorded that he began negotiations to acquire a portion of Easton (now Harlem Hills) Prairie in memory of his father. Located within walking distance of the Wilgus Sanitarium, where Fell grew up, it was among his father's favorite sites for collecting plant specimens and one of the places where the reserved doctor first awakened his solitary son to the wonder of native wildflowers.[14]

In addition to Harlem Hills Prairie, Fell initiated efforts to preserve other individual sites that were threatened with imminent destruction. Among these was Bell Bowl Prairie, a twenty-five-acre prairie remnant on the grounds of the former Camp Grant that Fell's father had discovered while treating psychiatric casualties during World War I. Once Dr. Fell took to botanizing as a full-time avocation during his retirement, he returned to the site many times. In the article he coauthored with his wife in 1958, he described Bell Bowl as "a natural amphitheater formed by a bend in the terrace bluff . . . one-half mile [long by] about 150 yards wide. The bluff was used for the training of troops in trench warfare maneuvers but it has since been untouched except by an occasional burning. The prairie is one of the best preserved in northern Illinois [and] now a part of the Greater Rockford Airport."[15]

For one who typically shied away from direct preservation efforts, Dr. Fell was credited by several local newspaper writers with undertaking the first effort to save Bell Bowl Prairie from destruction. In the preface to his landmark *Flora of Winnebago County*, he related, "We are mindful of the rapid changes which must accompany the passing of time and we believe that those who will come tomorrow will be interested in the conditions of today, so we will try to picture the plant life of our county as it is now—we will attempt nothing more."[16] But in 1957, he did something more: he extracted a promise from the airport authority not to disturb the prairie tract "if at all possible." The "chairman of the board which operates the Airport," Dr. Fell wrote in his Bell Bowl Prairie article, "has agreed that, because of its educational value, the bluff will be used by the Airport only for essential operation. The steepness of the terrain makes such use unlikely."

Unlike his father, Fell had little confidence in a vague promise by a chairman who might give way to another chairman with an entirely different perspective on the matter. A year after publishing his father's article about Bell Bowl Prairie, Fell sought to negotiate a lease or sales contract between the Greater Rockford Airport Authority and the Natural Land Institute to ensure the site's permanent protection and stewardship. The airport authority rebuffed each offer. Within a decade of the handshake deal to preserve the prairie, Fell's suspicions proved justified: the airport authority secured permission from the Federal Aviation Authority to excavate the site's virgin soils for use as substrate for a runway expansion. Word of the prairie's impending destruction caused Fell to redouble his preservation efforts. He raised money, wrote letters, made speeches, provided expert testimony, and led field tours for politicians, press, business leaders, the general public, anyone whom he thought might be an ally. Once again, his trademark persistence—this time backed by strong editorial support from the local papers and an eleventh-hour intervention by Governor Samuel H. Shapiro of Illinois—eventually paid off. The airport authority relented. The remnant prairie was spared and remains stewarded by the Natural Land Institute to this day.

The Illinois Natural Areas Preservation Bill: The First Campaign

Preserving the likes of Harlem Hills Prairie and Bell Bowl Prairie were heroic efforts. Each campaign or "grass-fire war," as a local Rockford paper reported it, took an enormous amount of time and energy. Yet, as important as such efforts were, in the end they were one-offs, leaving in place no infrastructure for the next inevitable rescue operation. Neither did they advance Fell's goal of a systemic solution to stem the tide of natural areas destruction throughout the state.

In the decade after Fell first introduced and pursued the idea of a statewide system of nature preserves, no agencies or organizations emerged as willing or able to take up the cause. Without Fell, the Illinois State Academy of Science all but abandoned its natural areas preservation pursuits. The Illinois chapter of The Nature Conservancy, initiated in 1951 as part of Fell's strategy to establish a conservancy presence in every state, enjoyed early success in acquiring title to the two bog areas in Lake County. By the time Fell returned to Rockford in late 1958, however, the Illinois chapter had reverted to being a small, struggling entity with limited capacity and prospects for success, quite the opposite of what he had hoped in setting up the conservancy's chapter system.

On the other hand, in the years that had passed, an increasing number of preservation efforts were gaining traction through government. The Wilderness Act pending before Congress in 1959 was still five years and numerous drafts away from becoming law, but Fell had been intimately familiar with the effort to establish a national system of wilderness areas through his close association with Howard Zahniser during the 1950s. Zahniser first envisioned such a system in the late 1940s, but the stage was set for the introduction of a wilderness bill after the successful, high-profile effort to defeat a proposal to build a dam at Echo Park, which spared Colorado's famed Dinosaur National Monument from being flooded to create a reservoir. A leader of the antidam effort and head of the Wilderness Society, Zahniser embarked upon an eight-year ordeal to establish a nationwide system of preserved wilderness areas under federal jurisdiction. Several aspects of the bill greatly appealed to Fell. It provided for an unprecedented degree of protection by making it illegal to alter any wilderness area within the system. Even more important, it established a proactive system of preservation. Up to that time, national-scale preservation efforts had been largely crisis driven, a reaction to a never-ending succession of development proposals. For the first time in the history of American conservation, the bill put wilderness preservation on the offensive.[17]

For state-level models, Fell turned to the Scientific Areas Preservation Council, established in 1951 within the Wisconsin Department of Natural Resources. Limited then, as it is now, to an advisory role and initially afforded no funding for staff or acquisition of land, its primary responsibility was to recommend sites for federal designations or acquisition by the state as scientific research areas.[18] A year earlier, the Michigan Natural Areas Council, a nonprofit, membership-based advocacy organization founded in 1946 by The Nature Conservancy's first president, Stanley A. Cain, was formally incorporated to "*permanently* preserve typical examples of all kinds of plant and animal communities that exist within the State [of Michigan]." The council proposed that suitable lands be preserved by designating them as "Natural Area Preserves."[19] However, as a nongovernmental body, the council had no statutory authority to implement or enforce its plan.

Fell envisioned something decidedly more than an advisory or advocacy body with few resources and limited power. In November 1960 he crafted a rudimentary bill that called for the establishment of a state commission empowered to locate, acquire, and dedicate sites as state nature preserves. Following in the footsteps of Zahniser, Aldo Leopold, and John Muir, each of whom championed the establishment of wilderness areas for nonutilitarian purposes, Fell proposed that dedicated nature preserves be "declared to be assigned to their highest use for public benefit," which precluded their use for recreational or resource purposes. To safeguard nature preserves from recreation, extractive, and hunting interests within the Illinois Department of Conservation or other environment-related state agencies, Fell slyly called for the commission to be placed under the umbrella of the Illinois Department of Registration and Education.[20]

Underscoring his foresight and his scrupulous attention to detail, Fell took steps to protect the nonprofit status of the Natural Land Institute before he circulated copies of his draft bill. Then, as now, federal tax code limits the ability of nonprofit organizations to engage in lobbying activities. To avoid the risk of an excessive amount of lobbying by the institute, Fell informally set up the Citizens Committee for Nature Conservation, through which he channeled all lobbying efforts on behalf of the natural areas bill. Some of Fell's colleagues perceived the establishment of yet another "shell" organization as overly cautious, but the extra step was appropriate; a few years later, the Sierra Club would have its nonprofit status revoked by the Internal Revenue Service for its active role in lobbying against a legislative bill to dam the Colorado River.[21]

Through the Citizens Committee for Nature Conservation, Fell undertook an extensive lobbying campaign. Over the course of several months, he mailed copies of his draft bill and related promotional materials to every garden club, conservation organization, and civic group he identified within the state. Then, calling on the skills he had developed while promoting his federal Nature Conservancy bill a decade earlier, he approached several potential sponsors of the bill. On January 18, 1961, Fell presented his idea to State Senator Robert Canfield (R-Rockford), who responded dryly, "It's simple to set up a commission, but not so easy to get funds."[22] Nonetheless, Senator Canfield was sufficiently impressed with Fell's passion and persistence that he agreed to help and referred Fell to the Illinois Legislative Reference Bureau to polish the bill.

In 1961 the Illinois Legislative Reference Bureau had only three or four full-time draftsmen and a similar number of part-timers hired for the duration of the legislative session. Most of the temporary staff received minor bill drafting assignments, such as congratulatory resolutions or amendment corrections. Perhaps indicative of the priority Senator Canfield placed on the nature preserves idea, he tapped one of the temporary staff, Edward M. Levin, to work with Fell. A recent law school graduate, just two years out of the army, Levin was thrilled to work on an unexpectedly substantive assignment. At their first meeting, Levin recalled that Fell had modified his thinking and was adamant about establishing a commission independent of any existing state department or agency. In revisiting his earlier investigations of a prospective state government system of natural areas preservation, Fell had determined that the competing interests among existing agencies, at both an inter- and an intra-agency level, were too entrenched and therefore would be difficult if not impossible to overcome.

Working closely with Fell, Levin crafted a bill that outlined a substantial measure of independence for a new nature preserves commission. Operating as an entirely free-standing entity, the commission was to be composed of nine members appointed by the governor and serving without compensation, a fact intended to restrict the appeal of the appointment to those who were inspired purely by a wish to preserve natural areas. Commissioners would serve in staggered three-year terms to insulate the commission from any wholesale, politically motivated takeover. On equal footing with the Illinois Department of Conservation, the commission would be empowered to enter into agreements with any agency, organization, or individual and to establish policies related to the management of lands within its jurisdiction and to enforce its rules by use of police power. Reaching beyond the powers of the Department of Conservation, it would be empowered to designate natural areas on both public and private lands. Refining the phraseology Fell had employed in his early draft of the bill, Levin stipulated that dedicated areas would be put to their "highest, best, and most important use" for the public interest. These were "magic words," according to Levin, "that would keep the area from being condemned for any other purpose under state law."[23] So magic were they that this exact phrase would later find its way into legislation establishing similar commissions in other states. Finally, in acknowledgment of the reality that independence without funding is not much independence at all, the bill included an appropriation of seventy-five thousand dollars.

Senator Canfield introduced Senate Bill 465 on April 12, 1961: "The purpose of [the Natural Areas Preservation Act] is to promote the public welfare by securing for the people of Illinois of present and future generations the benefits of an enduring resource of natural land."[24] While the bill made its way through various committees, Senator Canfield arranged a meeting with Governor Otto Kerner, a Democrat. Fell, accompanied by his former professor and Nature Conservancy trustee S. Charles Kendeigh and by Willard D. Klimstra, founder of the Cooperative Wildlife Research Laboratory at Southern Illinois University at Carbondale, made his appeal to the governor. The governor was "very tough at first," Fell recorded in his journal, questioning the cost and whether there was sufficient public support. The governor raised his strongest concerns about the one element that Fell deemed the most important: the independence of the proposed new government body.[25] Fell defended his bill well enough that Governor Kerner agreed to lend his support provided Fell eliminated the seventy-five-thousand-dollar appropriation.

The loss of start-up funding was difficult for Fell to swallow but not a deal breaker. He had launched The Nature Conservancy with only three hundred dollars in the bank. Nonetheless, in exchange for striking the seventy-five-thousand-dollar appropriation from the bill, Fell convinced Senator Canfield to introduce four companion bills. Senate Bills 694 and 695 had nothing to do with funding but authorized the Department of Conservation and park districts throughout the state "to designate areas as nature preserves." Together, these bills effectively would have provided for the establishment of state wilderness areas within certain public lands. Senate Bill 692 addressed the money issue and raised some eyebrows in calling for the establishment of a separate Nature Preserves Fund to ensure that any monies raised independently by the commission would not go into the general treasury, thereby avoiding the risk that the funds would be siphoned off for other purposes. The fourth Senate bill was more controversial still: it would have exempted all employees of the Illinois Nature Preserves Commission from the state's personnel codes. Because of his own experiences in government, Fell was unshakable in his low opinion of government workers, an opinion that would be validated a few years later when a task force found rampant patronage at the expense of hiring qualified professionals within several Illinois state departments, including the Department of Conservation.[26]

Several editorials came out in strong support of the natural areas bill. In their endorsement of the natural areas bill, along with the federal wilderness bill then pending before Congress, the editors of the *Chicago Daily Tribune* insightfully pointed out that "at present, there is no effective way to protect existing nature preserves from the decisions of subsequent owners or administrators. A single heavy handed bureaucrat or board can often by a single decision demolish an irreplaceable natural area that had been a delight for generations. We commend . . . nature conservancy legislation of the sort proposed . . . to the Illinois legislature and the national Congress."[27]

Response among state agencies was mixed. The Illinois Natural History Survey's Lewis J. Stannard Jr. and Harlow B. Mills—the latter of whom supported Fell's earliest ideas for preserving natural areas and appointed him to the Illinois State Academy of Science's Conservation Committee—applauded the idea of a nature preserves commission but viewed it as a natural fit within their agency.[28] William T. Lodge, director of the Illinois Department of Conservation, argued that the commission should fall under the authority of his department to avoid overlapping powers and responsibilities.[29] Less than a month after introducing what came to be known unflatteringly as "Canfield's Bog Bill," Senator Canfield himself called Fell into his office and asked point blank why the commission should not be placed under the Department of Conservation. At the House debate on the bill, legislators posed the same question.

Time and again, Fell answered his critics convincingly enough to keep the bill intact and on track. At the end of June 1961, the natural areas bill and its four attendant bills passed the state legislature. Thirty days later, Governor Kerner vetoed all of them. Acknowledging in his veto message that he was "wholly in sympathy" with the purpose of the bill, he stated plainly that he did not "look with favor upon" a bill that "creates an entirely new operating department in a field of government operations where other departments and agencies are now available to carry on administrative functions. The purposes of this Bill can and should be served without the creation of this superstructure."[30]

In the conclusion to his veto statement, the governor noted that he had signed into law an alternative bill to extend the Department of Conservation's jurisdiction "to cover flora and fauna generally."[31] At first blush, this may appear to have afforded Fell some small measure of victory, but in truth it underscored what would become an ongoing struggle for control between Fell and the

Department of Conservation. At the time of Fell's first failed attempt to establish an independent nature preserves commission, the Department of Conservation was headed up by William T. Lodge. A native of Monticello, a small agricultural community in central Illinois, Lodge had graduated from the University of Illinois about a decade before Fell, with a degree not in botany but in political science and economics. He spent his early career as a general contractor, an engineer for Roosevelt's Works Progress Administration, and a farmer before becoming vice president of a pharmaceutical firm in his hometown. An avid hunter and fisherman, he had served as president of the Illinois division of the Izaak Walton League of America and for several years as the central zone director and then executive secretary of the Illinois Federation of Sportsmen's Clubs. He was equally active in state politics, serving as chairman of the Piatt County Democratic Central Committee for nine years.[32] Two different governors appointed him to conservation-related advisory boards and legislative committees before a third governor, Kerner, tapped him to become director of the Department of Conservation.

Given Lodge's political clout, Charles Kendeigh counseled his former student "to work out some arrangement with . . . Lodge . . . for the Nature Preserves Commission to be a semi-independent unit in the Department of Conservation."[33] Fell ignored the advice and refused to compromise, believing he was right in seeking a wholly independent commission—so right, in fact, that following the governor's veto he immediately sought to have his bill, unaltered, reintroduced during a special session of the General Assembly in an effort to have the veto overridden. In this, he displayed the kind of stubborn single-mindedness that had fueled the proxy war at The Nature Conservancy. Once again, his resistance was in vain; the bill was not reintroduced, which meant that he would have to wait two years to try again, since the General Assembly met only biannually at the time. Never content to idle away the time while natural areas continued to disappear from the Illinois landscape, Fell placed his nature preserves idea temporarily on a back burner and tended to one of several other irons in his perpetual fire.

The Illinois Chapter of The Nature Conservancy

In the midst of his legislative effort to establish a nature preserves commission, Fell received a letter from Lewis Stannard in his capacity as secretary of the Illinois chapter of The Nature Conservancy. In its ten years of existence, the chapter had managed to preserve two Lake County bogs, but the effort had left the organization all but spent. In 1960 it had about four hundred dollars in its bank account, officers were resigning for various reasons, and—although no one seemed able to provide an accurate count—the total number of members probably numbered somewhere around fifty. Stannard asked Fell if he would allow his name to be put forth as secretary of the chapter, confessing, "We suffer from lack of leadership, lack of causes to work for, and general indifference. Because of your abilities and interest it is only logical that we turn to you. I'd be happy to continue as secretary if someone like you were chairman, that is, if we had a chairman who acted like an executive director."[34]

Given how his employment had ended with the national Nature Conservancy, it would have been understandable if Fell had turned away from the organization and never looked back. But when he returned to Rockford, he could not resist attending meetings of his home state chapter. The Illinois chapter had gotten off to a particularly slow start, its handful of members initially meeting only once a year and spending much of their time discussing various organizational matters rather than accomplishing much in the way of on-the-ground preservation. Part of the challenge was that, unlike most other grass-roots preservation groups, the Illinois chapter was not organized around the preservation of any particular site threatened with imminent destruction, which made it difficult to generate enthusiasm, support, and momentum. As early as 1951, the idea of preserving Volo Bog was raised, but only in 1956, as the prospect of actually acquiring it, along with nearby Wauconda Bog, became a reality did the chapter gain focus and spring to life.

Located about seven miles apart, Volo and Wauconda Bogs—named for their proximity to a pair of Lake County towns—were well known to naturalists, being among a very small number of tamarack bog communities in the entire state. Volo Bog began as a fifty-acre kettle lake some six thousand years ago, a relict of the region's glacier age. As the early plant community of sphagnum moss and sedges encroached on the water's surface, dead plants did not decompose but formed a floating substrate of peat, which eventually supported cranberry, leatherleaf, sumac, and deciduous tamarack pine trees. Evolutionarily younger than Wauconda Bog, the surface of which was entirely covered with a floating mat of vegetation, Volo Bog still retained open water on its surface.[35] In 1956 the Illinois chapter had $1.50 in its bank account. A little more than a year later, with Fell making a couple of trips from Washington to help negotiate deals, the Illinois chapter had signed purchase agreements to acquire the two bog sites for a combined price of forty thousand dollars. By November 1958, 1,200 persons had contributed a total of twenty-two thousand dollars toward the purchase-price goal.[36]

Acquisition of the bog areas, completed in 1959, was an extraordinary accomplishment. In Fell's vision, Nature Conservancy chapters would build on the momentum of such preservation successes, but once the Illinois chapter's first multiyear acquisition effort came to an end, so did much of the energy of its all-volunteer board. At the time Stannard made his offer for Fell to join the board, Fell was still embroiled in his Nature Preserves campaign. Nonetheless, sensing an opportunity to breathe life back into the chapter, Fell ultimately accepted Stannard's offer.[37]

Fell was elected secretary of the Illinois chapter in April 1960 but did not become active beyond his basic responsibilities until after Governor Kerner vetoed the natural areas bill, in July 1961. At that point, he effectively assumed the role of unpaid executive director, much as he had in the early years of the national Nature Conservancy. At the chapter's December 1961 board meeting, Fell proposed publishing a regular newsletter pertaining to nature preservation in Illinois. It would be copublished by the chapter, the Natural Land Institute, and the Citizens Committee for Nature Conservation, which would supply its extensive mailing list, amassed during its lobbying campaign in support of the natural areas bill. At the same meeting, Stannard reported that his virtual one-man effort to protect a pristine ravine area known as Rocky Branch in Clark County, in central Illinois, had gained traction with a six-thousand-dollar loan from the national Nature Conservancy. For the first time in many years, however, it was not the only prospective site to be discussed. Fell made reports on seven different potential preservation areas. They included an old-growth bottomland forest on the Wabash River in the county of the same name, a sixty-nine-acre tract of prairie near the Illinois–Wisconsin state line in Winnebago County, Baker Lake in Lake County, Danville Orchid area in Vermillion County, and three parcels around and inclusive of Castle Rock, the namesake sandstone feature of the Rock River's Castle Rock area.[38] Fell and his wife had visited each of the sites, met with their landowners, and initiated negotiations to buy them, either through the chapter or the Natural Land Institute.

By far the most astonishing thing Fell did at the December 1961 meeting was to recommend suspending the operations of the Illinois chapter for a one-year trial period in favor of incorporating as an independent Illinois Nature Conservancy. The impetus for the recommendation was actions taken by the national Nature Conservancy following Fell's departure. While still with the national organization, Fell had crafted a chapter system that allocated 30 percent of locally generated membership and nonproject-specific revenues to the national office, with 70 percent remaining with the local chapters. His purpose in devising this allocation was as much to cultivate a cooperative spirit among chapters and the national office as it was to provide operating revenue for all parties. However, at the same August 1958 board meeting at which Fell lost his bid to be elected president of The Nature Conservancy, the governors, against Fell's strident objections, voted to allocate 100 percent of all general-purpose contributions in excess of fifty dollars to the national office, which significantly reduced the amount of money available to individual chapters. Fell had argued that this reallocation would discourage chapters from raising sufficient funds to support their own operations, thereby weakening their capacity to preserve natural areas.[39] In proposing that the Illinois chapter incorporate independently, Fell did not advocate severing ties with the national office. In fact, he suggested few changes in the relationship other than to allow the local group to acquire and hold land without the approval of the national office and to reinstate the 30–70 apportionment formula in order to provide an incentive for the Illinois chapter to raise sufficient operating dollars to allow it to hire staff and build organizational capacity.[40]

The board of the Illinois chapter tabled and never formally acted on Fell's recommendation to incorporate independently. In effect, then, the members voted in favor of Fell's chapter system, as imperfectly as the national board of governors may have altered it. They supported only a single issue of Fell's newsletter, *Illinois Wildland*, because it consumed more than half of their available cash reserves. In spite of all this, they embraced Fell's proactive identification of preservation projects, which, as board member Charles Kendeigh recalled, breathed "new life" into the chapter.[41]

With Barbara as his constant traveling companion, Fell barnstormed the state in search of additional natural land remnants in need of protection, which he compiled in an Illinois chapter white paper, "Wilderness Remnants for Illinois." Fell's list of twenty-five "proposed living museums" ranged from general areas such as the "Pasque Flower Prairie Hills" along the Illinois–Wisconsin border and the bogs and sand prairies along the Illinois River to specific sites, including the Elgin Botanical garden and the Grand Canyon of Jackson County, down near the southern tip of the state. This list also included two sites first identified in *Proposed Park Areas in the State of Illinois*, published in 1921 by the Friends of Our Native Landscape. In the chapter devoted to "The State Park Possibilities of Southern Illinois," Henry C. Cowles, the pioneering ecologist of the Indiana Dunes fame, described Fountain Bluff, another site located in Jackson County, as

> an isolated area of great ruggedness and beauty, separated by many miles of flood plain from the main body of the Ozarks, with which it was once connected. This rock island stands up like a mountain from the flood plain extending on every side, reaching a height of three or four hundred feet at its highest point. At the south-west portion of the bluff the Mississippi washes its banks, and from the top of the bluff, the Father of Waters forms an impressive feature of the landscape. Within [its] four thousand acres are

many beautiful ravines, grottos, and springs. The whole tract is beautifully wooded. There is a fine display of hickory, oak, and beech. The spring flowering display of the service berry and later of the dogwood beggar description.[42]

As he did with many of his promotional pieces, Fell concluded his "Wilderness Remnants for Illinois" with the exhortation that "we in this generation have a great moral obligation. We have the last chance to set aside natural land. We are witnessing the final conquest of the wild, the domestication of the earth. What we have saved, and what we save in the next few years, will be all the natural land that will remain to pass on from generation to generation. There will never be another chance."[43]

The Illinois Natural Areas Preservation Bill: The Second Campaign

Fell's active involvement in the Illinois chapter of The Nature Conservancy was short lived. Although he would remain on the board through 1968, in 1962 he announced that he would not stand for reelection as secretary in order to prepare for the upcoming legislative session. In early 1963, while traveling by train between Chicago and Springfield, Fell met Ed Levin, the former part-time legislative bill writer with whom Fell had crafted the first natural areas bill. Levin had gone into private practice as an attorney but was eager for a second chance at the natural areas bill. He readily accepted Fell's offer to re-draft it for the 1963 legislative session. In revising the bill, he stripped it of "anything . . . that the veto message had hinted was a problem"—anything, as it turned out, except the independence of the commission, which, for Fell, was nonnegotiable.[44] Senator Canfield supported the new bill by tagging on a twenty-five-thousand-dollar appropriation and introducing it, along with the four earlier companion bills, as Senate Bill 579.

Immediately, the bill ran into opposition from William T. Lodge, director of the Illinois Department of Conservation. Senator Canfield postponed a scheduled committee hearing on the bill in order to broker a compromise between Fell and Lodge. In an echo of the struggle for control that Fell had experienced earlier between himself and Richard Pough of The Nature Conservancy, Fell and Lodge were two strong-willed men who shared a similar goal but differed mightily as to the means by which to achieve that goal. After weeks of failed negotiations, in early May 1963 Lodge appeared to capitulate, stating that his agency would give Fell no more trouble on the bill.[45] Within a month, Levin tipped off Fell that the Department of Conservation had drafted its own pair of natural areas bills, which were introduced into the House by seven state representatives. Clearly patterned after Fell's Senate Bill 579, House Bills 1538 and 1539 contained many of the provisions of their Senate counterpart, the principal difference being that a new nature preserves commission would operate under the umbrella of the Department of Conservation, which alone would possess the power to acquire land and manage nature preserves.[46]

In response to the House bills, Fell did adopt some minor changes to his Senate bill, but he held fast to his call for an independent commission. Staking out an essentially all-or-nothing position was particularly risky given the political insider credentials of Lodge, who, in advancing his own version of the bill, was confident enough to let the governor who appointed him choose which bill to sign into law.[47]

Elevating the stakes even higher, Fell crafted an additional bill for introduction during the same 1963 legislative session. In 1961 he had conducted an investigation to determine why only eight of Illinois's 102 counties had established forest preserve districts under a 1913 state law that enabled them to do so. Fell certainly had his issues with the way forest preserves were managed first and foremost for recreation, but more county forest preserves, he reasoned, would complement his vision for a statewide system of nature preserves. Fell sent out his survey, and thanks to its astonishing 95 percent response rate he learned that, with the exception of central Illinois's Sangamon County, where a ninth forest preserve district had been proposed (but would not come to pass), most of the remaining counties had little knowledge of or interest in the forest preserve law.

Fell's survey failed to determine why there was so little interest in the law. Perhaps part of the reason was the incongruity of Illinois providing for the establishment of forest preserve districts in a state that historically had been mostly prairie. At the turn of the twentieth century, even as some voices began to urge the protection of the remaining natural lands in Illinois, there was considerable resistance—mostly from developers and pro-development elected leaders—to doing so. The first attempt at passing a forest preserve act was struck down by the courts for being overly broad in allowing for the protection of prairie and other kinds of land, land that was eminently developable. The third and final iteration of the act, passed in 1913, restricted the kinds of lands that could be acquired to "natural forests," which proved a winning "legal strategy [for Chicago interests] to achieve the greater goal of providing Chicago's public with more open space." As it turned out, the administrators of the newly formed Forest Preserve District of Cook County quickly realized just how little forested land there was in Cook County. This led the county to acquire a range of different kinds of land, including prairie and old farm fields that used to be prairie. Rather than restoring the prairie lands, however, managers were compelled to plant trees in order to comply with the enabling legislation.[48]

Because of the limitations and land management ironies inherent in Illinois's forest preserve act, Fell turned to Iowa for a better, more widely applicable model. In 1955 the state of Iowa had passed the County Conservation Law, which enabled Iowa counties "to acquire, develop, maintain, and make available museums, parks, preserves, recreational centers, forests, wildlife and other conservation areas, to promote the health and general welfare of the people, to encourage the conservation of natural resources, and to cultivate good citizenship by providing programs of public recreation."[49] In time, each of Iowa's ninety-nine counties would establish a conservation board, overseeing a combined 160,000 acres of park and conservation areas.[50] Aspiring to match the 100 percent participation rate of his neighboring state, Fell used the Iowa statute as a template and drafted a bill that would enable the establishment of county conservation districts in Illinois. It underwent relatively few changes as it sailed through the General Assembly.

Unlike the natural areas bill, the conservation district bill ran into few difficulties with the Department of Conservation. From the very first draft, the bill stated that "districts shall obtain approval of the State Conservation Department on all proposals for land acquisition and plans for development," which provided the Department of Conservation with its accustomed degree of oversight and approval.[51] The bill also encountered little resistance from legislators because, like the Iowa law, it allowed for the conservation of land for recreational purposes. Fell seized upon this aspect of the bill in his promotional efforts: "The demand for outdoor recreation areas is increasing at a tremendous rate. Far from keeping pace with the need, Illinois has been rapidly losing ground." Fell took the argument for recreation a step further by tenuously tying it to the state's economic future: "The shortage of attractive recreation areas in Illinois also means a serious loss to our economy as recreation dollars are spent elsewhere. Perhaps even more important in the long run, our economic base suffers from the loss of industries which locate in regions that provide the most attractive living conditions for their employees. Availability of recreational resources ranks high in the factors which an industry considers when seeking a new plant location."[52]

Fell had not suddenly changed his stripes. What he left unmentioned in his promotional efforts was a significant difference from the Iowa statute. In Section 11 of his Illinois conservation district bill, buried more than halfway through the text, he revealed his true colors: "Every district shall consider the preservation of natural conditions and protection of flora and fauna as a *primary objective* and to that end shall set aside an ample portion of its land to remain in an essentially undisturbed condition."[53] By trumpeting the conservation district bill's recreational benefits while soft-pedaling its natural areas preservation emphasis, Fell betrayed a political savvy that might have served him well in his standoff with director Lodge over the natural areas bill.

By mid-July 1963, the conservation district bill and the two competing natural areas bills had passed the General Assembly, leaving the final decision up to Governor Kerner. The governor's office advised Fell that no decision would be made for a couple of weeks, so Fell and Barbara left for a two-week working vacation, which included attending the annual meeting of the national Nature Conservancy and staying overnight at the New London, Connecticut, farm of Richard Goodwin, the former Nature Conservancy president. Only five years had passed since Fell's difficult departure from the conservancy. In the intervening years, whatever personal animosity there was between Fell and Goodwin had disappeared. Fell remained a member in good standing of the conservancy and kept up a friendly and semiregular correspondence with its succession of executive directors. In spite of a high rate of staff turnover, the conservancy had increased its annual operating budget more than threefold to $180,000, increased the number of projects from 15 to 125, acquired $100,000 worth of land, and possessed an additional $1.3 million in net assets.[54] Reflecting back, Goodwin echoed Richard Pough's assertion that none of this ever might have come to pass without the selfless early efforts of the Fells.[55]

While at The Nature Conservancy annual meeting, Fell received word that the governor had signed into law his conservation district bill. However, the good news was offset by the news that the governor had also vetoed his natural areas bill in favor of the one advanced by the Department of Conservation. In his veto message, Governor Kerner stated, "Two years ago I vetoed a series of bills designed to establish a nature preserves system. At that time I expressed sympathy with their purpose but found the substance of the bills deficient. I am afraid that a basic objection is still inherent. . . . It entrusts all of the powers of negotiation, acquisition and promotion of the use of the property to the independent Commission." Then, as if addressing Fell directly, he continued, "An unfortunate distrust of government has been the cause of too many misguided legislative efforts to divorce a program or an officer from 'politics' or even from government itself. Rarely does it achieve anything other than the proliferation of independent agencies or of independent officers."[56]

In his journal entry for August 27, 1963, Fell recorded only the bare facts of which bills the governor had signed and which he had vetoed. Fell had lost the battle a second time but decidedly won the war on behalf of the state's remaining natural areas, a victory that would not have come to pass had Fell not instigated the fight. As enshrined in law, the Illinois Natural Areas Preservation Act—the first of its kind in the nation—established a new Illinois Nature Preserves Commission that was empowered to dedicate natural areas throughout Illinois, on public and private lands alike, affording them the highest level of legal protection. In concert with the Conservation District Act, authored by Fell; the Illinois Forest Preserve District Act of 1913; and efforts of the Illinois chapter of The Nature Conservancy and other conservation organizations encouraged by Fell, the law set the stage for a robust, multifaceted, statewide approach to natural areas preservation. The fact that the Nature Preserves Commission operated under the aegis of the Department of Conservation and was allocated no budget would not prove a setback for Fell. As with nearly every obstacle he faced, he would parlay the challenge into an opportunity.

5

The Illinois Nature Preserves Commission

Where Once We Were Opportunists

In his career-long quest to preserve natural areas, George Fell suffered several notable setbacks. As relentless as rainwater in search of the sea, however, he let no obstacle impede the ultimate achievement of his goals. When his earliest efforts to cultivate a statewide system of natural areas preservation stalled, he went on to transition the Ecologists' Union into The Nature Conservancy. After he unsuccessfully challenged the leadership of that organization, he immediately started up the Natural Land Institute. His first attempt at securing passage of a natural areas bill having failed, he threw himself into the secretariat of the Illinois chapter of The Nature Conservancy before taking up a second legislative campaign to establish the Illinois Nature Preserves Commission. And when a competing natural areas bill, not the one he championed, was signed into law, he embraced the alternative commission as if it were his very own.

With the passage of the Illinois Natural Areas Preservation Act, in 1963, Fell finally achieved the statutory means to shift preservation efforts away from a chronically haphazard, opportunistic course toward one that was purposeful and strategic and that had the force of law behind it. "Where once we were opportunists, preserving what we could when we could," he would relate in a summary overview of the natural areas preservation movement, "we now plan and direct our efforts deliberately."[1] But all the planning and direction would have amounted to very little without the money needed to manage a program and, most important, to buy and steward land. For financial support, Fell turned to the shell organization he had set up for just such a purpose. The creative public-private partnership Fell fostered between the Illinois Nature

113

Preserves Commission and the Natural Land Institute, coupled with his willingness—once again—to work full time for little or no compensation, allowed the commission to flourish from the outset and to function for many years thereafter, nearly as independently as he originally envisioned.

Protection by Dedication

The Illinois Natural Areas Preservation Act broadly outlined a threefold system for protecting natural areas: (1) dedicating existing natural areas, either in private or public ownership, as nature preserves; (2) acquiring new natural areas by the state for the purpose of dedicating them as nature preserves; and (3) managing all dedicated nature preserves to ensure that their ecological features were passed on to future generations unimpaired or improved. As with any new system, there were innumerable details to work out, including the operational mechanics of an entirely new entity. This was familiar territory for Fell. Yet, before he could flesh out the bare bones of the statute language, he would suffer yet another unexpected setback.

The first order of business at the Illinois Nature Preserves Commission's inaugural meeting, held in Chicago on January 30, 1964, was the election of officers. Governor Kerner, in accordance with the statute, had consulted with the chief of the Illinois Natural History Survey and the director of the Illinois State Museum to appoint a well-qualified and well-balanced group of commissioners. Among the ecologists named, in addition to Fell, were Margery C. Carlson, retired professor of botany at Northwestern University; S. Charles Kendeigh, Fell's former University of Illinois professor and colleague from both The Nature Conservancy and its Illinois chapter; and Willard D. Klimstra, professor of zoology at Southern Illinois University. Conservation organization and agency representatives included Elton Fawks, of the Izaak Walton League in Illinois, and Charles G. "Cap" Sauers, general superintendent of the Forest Preserve District of Cook County. Representing those with general interests in natural areas preservation were James Brown IV, executive director of the Chicago Community Trust; Edward M. Levin Jr., an attorney and the author of Fell's alternative nature preserve bills; and Mary Ann Leslie Walgreen, a noted nature photographer and the wife of the chairman of the Walgreen's pharmacy chain, whom Fell had approached as a prospective donor for the start-up of a statewide nonprofit preservation organization fifteen years earlier.

Prior to the first meeting, Kendeigh had suggested that Fell deserved the chairmanship of the commission as the unquestioned leader for natural areas preservation in Illinois. Fell agreed.[2] Aside from the Natural Land Institute, he had never been elected the head of anything, dating all the way back to his high school botany club, where he served as vice president. Even though his version of the Illinois Natural Areas Preservation Act was not signed into law by the governor, it was commonly understood that had it not been for Fell, no act would have been passed at all. He fully expected to be elected chairman. What Fell failed to appreciate, however, was that his uncompromising pursuit of an independent body had created an irreparable rift between him and the director of the Illinois Department of Conservation, William Lodge. Lodge was not a commissioner but had agreed to serve as the commission's temporary chair pending the election of officers. Levin recalled that as the commissioners entered the room for the first meeting, Lodge cornered several of them, "undoubtedly related to the election of officers."[3] Gaveling the meeting to order, Lodge accepted nominations for chairman. Both Fell and Kendeigh were nominated. By a 4 to 3 margin, with one abstention and one vote not cast because of the member's absence, the election swung to Kendeigh, who later echoed Levin's suspicion: "I suspected that Lodge had reservations about Fell and had previously connived for my election."[4]

Following the uncontested election of Fawks as vice chairman, Fell was put forward as the sole nominee for secretary—his accustomed role—and unanimously elected. In the end, it mattered not at all to which, if any, office Fell was elected. Unlike his fellow commissioners, each of whom was busy with a demanding job or other responsibilities, Fell intended to devote himself full time to ensure that the commission realized its full potential. In other words, he was prepared to perform essentially the same chief executive role, for no compensation, that he had during the start-up years of The Nature Conservancy. He was able to do this with the support of his wife, who, just as she had during their time with the conservancy, earned enough as a lab technician to meet their modest personal needs.

Following the election of officers, the new commission took up its second order of business: a proposal to dedicate a considerable portion of Illinois Beach State Park—nearly 20 percent of its 4,160 total acres—as the first Illinois Nature Preserve. As early as 1888, the noted landscape architect Jens Jensen, along with a Waukegan, Illinois, nurseryman, Robert Douglas, had petitioned lawmakers to establish a regional park along a swath of the Lake Michigan shoreline, immediately south of the Wisconsin–Illinois border, to protect its ecological and aesthetic values.[5] Similar petitions continued through the early part of the twentieth century, but not until 1948 did the state acquire the first acres, which eventually led to the establishment of Illinois Beach State Park.[6]

With its 6.5 miles of prime swimming beaches located fewer than twenty-five miles from both Chicago to the south and Milwaukee to the north, Illinois Beach State Park quickly became the most visited state park in Illinois. To capitalize on its popularity, in the 1950s the mayor of Waukegan petitioned the state to cede 160 acres at the south end of the park for a golf course, marina, and swimming pool. To some, the south end of the park seemed nothing more than sandy scrubland, all but begging for development as an active recreation area. However, the Illinois Dunesland Preservation Society, formed to protect the park's ecological features, knew the south end of the park constituted one of the largest remaining examples of a rare and interdependent network of lake-shore, foredune, sand prairie, sand savanna, fen, panne, sedge meadow, marsh, and pond communities in all of Illinois.[7]

With the backing of the Illinois Department of Conservation's advisory board, the society successfully petitioned Governor Kerner to reject the transfer of any portion of Illinois Beach State Park to the city of Waukegan. However, as Fell well knew, there was nothing in state law to prohibit a future governor from making a different decision. The establishment of state parks and forests, along with their county and municipal counterparts, afforded a modicum of protection to natural areas by placing them under public ownership, but that did not preclude their being developed or destroyed for public use as recreational areas. Providing ironclad protection for ecological gems such as the south end of Illinois Beach State Park was one of Fell's main objectives in championing passage of the Illinois Natural Areas Preservation Act.

Dedication of areas as nature preserves does not guarantee inviolable permanent protection, but it comes close. By virtue of Article VI of the US Constitution, which states that laws of the United States "shall be the supreme law of the land . . . anything in the . . . laws of any state to the contrary notwith-standing,"[8] the federal government could exercise its right to "take" even those lands dedicated as nature preserves if there was some compelling reason for doing so. However, there are certain federal laws and legal precedents that recognize the importance of parklands, rendering the likelihood of federal action extremely unlikely. The state of Illinois is even more restricted than the federal government in its authority. Declared by state law as lands "put to their highest, best and most important use for public benefit," dedicated nature preserves are held in trust and may not be used for any public use without a finding of "im-perative and unavoidable public necessity" by the Illinois Department of Conservation and with the subsequent approval of the Illinois Nature Preserves Commission and the governor. Before a finding of imperative public necessity can be rendered, the Department of Conservation must provide a reasonable opportunity for public comment.[9] This system of checks and balances was purposefully constructed to make it practically impossible for "future public officials to casually cause or allow" the destruction of natural areas.[10]

The underlying strength of the Illinois Nature Preserves system lies in its being anchored in two powerful common law doctrines: dedication and public trust. According to common law, "a dedication is the deliberate commitment of land to a public use by the owner, with the clear intention that it be accepted and used for some public purpose."[11] In the case of the Illinois nature preserves system, an area of land may be dedicated by its owner as a "means to set [it] aside . . . in perpetuity as a nature preserve or as a buffer area . . . for the benefit of the public."[12] Articles drafted for each area accepted into the nature preserves system specify the terms of the dedication, including provisions related to use, management, and sale or transfer of the land, and are permanently attached to the deed. Permanently attaching the articles to the deed means that future owners of the land are bound by the terms of the dedication, thereby providing protection for the nature preserve in perpetuity.

The doctrine of public trust dates back even further, to Roman law, and underpinned the tradition of the public commons in medieval European towns and the earliest towns in America. The doctrine, the essence of which is that the public has a legal right to certain lands and waters, is in evidence today in our nation's innumerable parks, preserves, and public rights of way. Historically well established, the doctrine stipulates that "a public agency must act as trustee for the trust, guarding the public's interest [and that] the trustee may not create or allow uses on dedicated land which violate the original purposes of the dedication."[13] The Illinois Department of Conservation, as the principal administrative agency of the Illinois nature preserves system, must enforce the articles of dedication for each nature preserve. Although the issue of legal standing is a complex one (the term refers to a party's right to bring a lawsuit), "the legal standing of citizens to enforce a trust held on their behalf where their rights are likely to be injured by misuse or diversion of dedicated property is also established in common law tradition."[14] In other words, were the Department of Conservation to fail to enforce the terms of a nature preserves' articles of dedication, citizens could take legal action to compel agency officials to perform their nondiscretionary duties.

Ironically, perhaps the only person conflicted about the prospect of dedicating the south end of Illinois Beach State Park as a nature preserve may have been William Lodge, the director of the state Department of Conservation. In his biennial report for 1963–64, he trumpeted his agency's investments in recreational infrastructure, including boat access areas and marinas, and $9 million for the establishment of additional revenue-generating enhancements to state park lands.[15] A new marina at the state's most popular state park would have generated yet more revenue for the state. But with the governor and his own advisory board in support of retaining the park's southern portion in its undisturbed natural condition, Lodge recommended its dedication as a nature preserve. The commissioners readily concurred. Over the next several months,

boundaries were surveyed and commissioner Levin drafted articles of dedication, which served as a template for subsequent dedications. Although the governor did not sign the articles until October 16, 1964, about a month prior to that
date the commission held its fourth meeting at Illinois Beach State Park; immediately following the meeting, members of the Illinois Dunesland Preservation
Society joined the commissioners for a luncheon and ceremony celebrating the
dedication of the state's first nature preserve, the 829-acre Illinois Beach Nature
Preserve.

Hardly expecting all nature preserves to be similarly handed to the commission on a silver platter, Fell pressed his fellow commissioners to canvass the
state for additional dedication possibilities. He compiled a list of likely sites at
state universities and private colleges, along railroad rights of way, in private
ownership, even on federal lands, and assigned commissioners to investigate
them. Fell reserved for himself several state parks and the area around his
hometown of Rockford. He sent his fellow commissioners into the field with
exceptionally broad criteria for assessing candidate sites. Beyond placing the
highest priority on prairie and wetland communities, undisturbed examples of
which were "extremely rare in Illinois [with] remaining areas . . . being destroyed
at an alarming rate," his basic idea was to preserve adequate samples of all
natural community types throughout the state, with special consideration given
to unique and outstanding areas and those that afforded habitat for endangered
species of plants and animals.[16]

Among the potential sites identified by commissioners were several exceptionally high-quality natural areas within Shawnee National Forest. Pushing
the limits on how far the commission might be able to extend its reach, Fell
broached the subject of dedicating federal lands as state nature preserves with
the US Forest Service. Staff of the Forest Service reacted favorably to the idea
as an additional means to safeguard the flora and fauna of high-quality areas.
The LaRue-Pine Hills Area, for instance, whose dramatic, Devonian-age limestone bluffs support a complex of plants and animals unique in the country,
suffered from excessive collecting of its rare fish, salamanders, copperhead
snakes, and cottonmouth snakes. "At present there is no way in which nongame animals can be protected," the Forest Service acknowledged in its early
correspondence with the commission.[17] Designation of federal areas as nature
preserves would have provided a missing legal protection, but there arose the
issue of whether federal lands could be subject to state authority.

In time, commissioner Levin and attorneys for the federal government
determined that Article VI of the US Constitution prohibited the federal government from entering into agreements that would bind federal lands to restrictions
imposed by state programs without explicit authorization to do so. Nonetheless,

in the course of this exploration, the Forest Service identified nine candidate sites of exceptional ecological significance and the US Fish and Wildlife Service identified three. The commission inquired of the administering agencies whether there were any federal programs in which the sites could be enrolled to afford them protections similar to those afforded by the state nature preserves system. There were no precise parallels, but the Forest Service did respond by designating, by administrative action, its nine sites as Botanical, Ecological, or Scenic Areas. The Fish and Wildlife Service designated its three sites as Research Natural Areas. Although the dozen federal sites did not become part of the Illinois Nature Preserves System, the efforts of the commission led to their combined 4,712 acres of high-quality natural areas—including the two-thousand-acre LaRue-Pine Hills Swamp Ecological Area—receiving a greater degree of federal management and protection.

After designating a portion of Illinois Beach State Park as a nature preserve and initiating efforts to achieve heightened protection for a dozen high-quality natural areas on federal lands, the commission celebrated the conclusion of its first year by adding eleven sites within the Forest Preserve District of Cook County. A year after the passage of the Forest Preserve Act of 1913, the voters of Cook County had voted to establish the nation's first county forest preserve district. The district acquired its first land in 1916 and today holds sixty-nine thousand acres, which represents about 11 percent of the entire land mass of Cook County. The move to protect so much land within the second-most populous county in the United States was fueled by the idea that natural areas "should be preserved for the benefit of the public in both the city and its suburbs, and for their own sake and scientific value, which, if ever lost, cannot be restored for generations."[18] Taking this charge to heart, Cap Sauers, the Nature Preserves commissioner and district general superintendent, recommended the dedication of eleven district sites of exceptional value, covering a total of 4,025 acres, as nature preserves. Although there were no imminent development threats to these sites, they were recommended for dedication essentially for the same reason the commission dedicated the southern portion of Illinois Beach State Park: there was nothing in the Forest Preserve District of Cook County law that explicitly prohibited their development or destruction for active recreational use.

The Forest Preserve District sites dedicated as nature preserves reveal the unexpectedly rich biological diversity that remains within the nation's third-largest metropolitan region. Among the sites dedicated was Cap Sauers Holdings, named in honor of the man who faithfully served as the district's general superintendent for fifteen years. The 1,520-acre site, still the largest dedicated nature preserve in northeastern Illinois, contains rare, undisturbed prairie and oak savanna communities, along with one of the state's best remaining examples of an esker, a ridge formed by rivers that cut under or through the region's last glaciers. Remnant glacial features figured prominently in the dedication of other district sites, as well. Within its 560-acre boundary, Spring Lake Nature Preserve has two glacial lakes, surrounded by a peat-filled depression that underlies small fen, sedge meadow, and wet prairie communities. Cranberry Slough Nature Preserve, encompassing 372 acres within the 14,000-acre Palos Preserve unit, historically supported a mosaic of prairie and oak savanna along with sedge meadow and marsh communities in its two glacial-era depressions, called kettle holes. The 245 acres of Salt Creek Woods Nature Preserve comprise a diversity of community types ranging from oak-dominated upland woodlands to communities of elm, cottonwood, and silver maple around a scattering of small glacial ponds in the creek's floodplain area. Measuring only nine acres, Shoe Factory Road Prairie Nature Preserve supports more than one hundred dry to semi-dry native prairie plant species perched atop a glacial kame, a cone-shaped hill of gravel formed as a retreating glacier melted. Two sites were designated for their features shaped by Lake Chicago, the ancient and larger forebear of Lake Michigan: Sand Ridge Nature Preserve, which contains one of the finest remaining inland dune and swale topographies from the retreating Lake Chicago; and Thornton-Lansing Road Nature Preserve, whose sandy, poorly drained soils support rare marsh and bog-like communities that represent some of the last remnants of the natural vegetation of the southern part of Lake Chicago's lake plain.

Following through on his first-year self-assignments to investigate prospective areas around the Rockford area and within several state parks, Fell made the most of his broad assessment criteria by recommending the dedication of nearly every one of the many sites he visited, including large swaths of state parks. Director Lodge, who had no vote in commission matters but whose opinion carried considerable weight because of his budgetary authority over the commission, cautioned against Fell's aggressiveness: "The Commission should endeavor to secure dedication of areas of exceptional quality rather than aiming at maximum quantity."[19] Standing his ground, Fell shot back that if "exceptional" was the qualitative benchmark by which natural areas would be assessed for potential dedication, few sites would be eligible: "all [Illinois natural area community types] are in jeopardy and in most cases the samples available are pitiful, partly mutilated remnants that have escaped complete destruction only by accident. Probably there is not an acre of ground in the State of Illinois that can be considered as virgin land, unchanged by the influence of civilized man."[20]

Fell's substantively true but hyperbolic statement regarding the condition of the state's remaining natural areas was a deliberate rebuff to Lodge, whose preference was to keep state lands unencumbered for potential recreational development.[21] As director of an agency whose mission included managing lands for hunting, camping, and other active recreational activities, Lodge had a legitimate obligation to evaluate recommended nature preserve designations from a broader perspective. Fell understood this too well, and it underscored for him the fatal flaw in placing the commission under the Department of Conservation. From his perspective, the goals of the two entities were at cross purposes, with the commission seeking to preserve what little was left of the state's native plant and animal communities and the Department of Conservation, in Lodge's words, paying "ever increasing attention to secure the utmost multiple use of all . . . areas and facilities for all types of outdoor recreation."[22]

The schism between Fell and Lodge was the same one that has run through the American conservation movement since its very inception. On the one side, beginning with John Muir, have been those who seek to preserve the environment for its aesthetic, spiritual, and ecological values. On the other side, beginning with Muir's protégé-turned-protagonist Gifford Pinchot, have been those who extol a utilitarian view of the nation's natural resources.[23] "The greatest good of the greatest number in the long run" was the standard Pinchot applied in his administration of the nation's forest lands in his role as the first chief of the Division of Forestry (later the US Forest Service) within the US Department of Agriculture.[24] From the perspective of such "wise use" advocates, forest preserves, for example, are to be managed to ensure a steady supply of lumber and other forest products to meet the nation's needs. For preservationists, forest preserves serve as refuges for their unique assemblages of native plants and animals and provide the human community with the opportunity for passive recreational opportunities and a spiritual and physical escape from the built world.

In spite of the philosophical differences between Fell and Lodge, within the commission's first year it had dedicated a dozen nature preserves, thereby ensuring the permanent protection of 4,854 acres of high-quality natural areas. Yet, as Fell well knew, these first dedications were low-hanging fruit; eleven were volunteered by a single agency and one was actively supported by the governor. Because the commission had no staff and no budgetary appropriation, its first-year dedications might well have proved its high-water mark. But the energy Fell poured into his legislative effort to establish the commission paled in comparison to the devotion he exhibited in making sure that the commission, underpinned by the Natural Land Institute, lived up to his personal expectations.

Protection by Acquisition

Back in 1950, when Fell filed the incorporation papers to establish The Nature Conservancy, the organization had a few hundred bucks in the bank. The Nature Preserves Commission began in 1964 with zero dollars. Part of the reason for the lack of a direct appropriation was that passage of the natural areas bill was far more likely to occur if it came at no additional cost to the state. Furthermore, the lack of an appropriation, intentional or not after Fell's unsuccessful bid for the establishment of an independent commission, also reinforced the commission's subordination to the Department of Conservation, its primary potential source for state funding. The law establishing the commission did not provide for any mechanism or authority by which the commission could raise or hold funds independently, as Fell had proposed in his unsuccessful version of the natural areas bill. However, neither did it preclude an independent organization from raising money and incurring expenses on the commission's behalf. Intent on an aggressively proactive role for the commission, which would require considerably more financial support than the travel reimbursements Lodge offered out of his agency's general budget during the commission's first year, Fell turned to the Natural Land Institute. He asked his trustees to fund a number of the commission's expenses, namely secretarial support and seasonal staff to conduct the ever more detailed field studies needed to identify prospective nature preserves before they were destroyed. The trustees voted unanimously in favor of Fell's requests.[25]

Thus began, with no formal agreement, a public–private partnership between the commission and the institute, one that would continue and expand significantly over the course of nearly twenty years. At first, the financial support the institute offered was modest because its own resources were meager. With no membership base to provide contributed income to the institute, Fell generated funds for the organization the old-fashioned way: he earned them. During the commission's first year, in 1964, citizens in northern Illinois's Boone County voted to establish the state's first conservation district. For guidance, the trustees of the new district turned to the man who had developed the enabling legislation. They hired Fell to conduct a survey of the "wildland and open space resources" of the county, recommend areas for the conservation district to buy, and undertake negotiations for their acquisition.[26] Among the several sites he cultivated for acquisition on behalf of the new conservation district was a rare, dry dolomite prairie remnant where in 1946 his father had collected the state-endangered wooly milkweed. Nearly thirty years later, the ten-acre site was permanently protected as the Flora Prairie Nature Preserve.[27]

Rather than pocketing the money he earned through a small number of these kinds of consulting contracts, Fell directed that 100 percent of all fees be paid directly to the Natural Land Institute. These funds were utilized to offset the direct expenses Fell incurred on behalf of the commission and to instigate another critical component of his natural areas preservation strategy: direct acquisition of natural areas. Fell was well aware that the commission's protection of 4,854 acres during its first twelve months compared favorably with the ten years it took The Nature Conservancy to protect a total of 4,628 acres.[28] Fell also was aware of the critical difference between those two numbers: the dozen sites dedicated as Illinois Nature Preserves were all located on existing public lands, whereas the conservancy's thirty-six sites in fourteen different states had been in private ownership until preserved through fee simple purchase by the conservancy. The several informal surveys Fell had conducted through the Nature Preserves Commission revealed that numerous high-quality Illinois natural areas remained in private ownership and that they continued to be destroyed at a rapid pace. He had pushed for an independent commission empowered to acquire and hold lands, but the Department of Conservation's version of the natural areas bill that passed into law reserved that authority exclusively for itself. While Lodge remained director of the Department of Conservation, Fell had little hope that the agency would acquire much if any land beyond that which could be utilized for recreational pursuits. Once again turning obstacle into opportunity, he turned to the Natural Land Institute to advance his agenda.

Two years before the establishment of the Illinois Nature Preserves Commission, Fell had sought permission from his Natural Land Institute trustees to acquire parcels of land within the Castle Rock area. Located near Oregon, about thirty meandering, Rock River miles southwest of Rockford, Fell knew the area's sandstone cliffs and rugged, lushly forested ravines intimately. After the war, he had helped his father identify and collect specimens there, including twenty-seven different species of ferns and relict boreal plants such as native white pine, bunchberry, hairy woodrush, round-leaved shinleaf, and wild sarsaparilla. In August 1963, the same month that Governor Kerner signed the natural areas bill into law, Fell reported to the institute trustees that with $10 down he had secured a $2,500 option to acquire eleven fern-rich acres in the heart of the Castle Rock area. Little more than a year later, during which time he shepherded the commission in its first year of operation, he reported to his institute trustees that he had secured several more options to acquire an additional 194 prime Castle Rock–area acres for a combined purchase price of $27,624.[29]

To make good on the various land options held by the institute, Fell printed scores of solicitation letters on his old, government-surplus presses and received a little more than six thousand dollars in contributions. Turning to the national office of The Nature Conservancy, he secured a modest loan. However, payout was delayed because of a change in the conservancy's administration. Having relied on the conservancy loan to meet scheduled payments, the Fells loaned the Institute $2,400 out of their personal savings. Still well short of the amount of money needed to pay off the outstanding options, in early 1965 Fell successfully bid on yet more Castle Rock parcels.[30]

Fell considerably overextended the Natural Land Institute to prime the pump, as it were, to encourage the state to join in preserving the exceptional ecological diversity of the Castle Rock area by establishing it as a state park. The idea of a Castle Rock state park was not a new one. The Friends of Our Native Landscape had first raised the idea in its 1921 report recommending the establishment of several state parks: "Few persons who have not visited [Castle Rock] suspect that in the heart of the prairies of Illinois there exists a region of such striking beauty." After delineating the area's many scenic virtues, the report decried the summer cottages popping up like mushrooms along the river's edge and "the crude pavilion for dancing and refreshments, which some misguided mortal has erected in the shadow of Castle Rock. The need for immediate action is apparent."[31] Forty-five years after the report appeared, the need for action was all the more apparent as a number of the area's most ecologically sensitive lands were being subdivided for home sites and others timbered or cleared for agricultural purposes.

At Fell's urging and supported by the extensive botanical surveys he and his father had conducted, in 1965 the state of Illinois recognized the Castle Rock area as one of major scientific importance. Fell then rolled out his maps and explained to the Department of Conservation his strategy for expanding upon the nucleus of more than two hundred acres he already had in hand. The Department of Conservation approved the plan and offered Fell five dollars an hour to assemble a total of at least one thousand contiguous Castle Rock–area acres to establish a new state park. More than anyone else, Fell was aware of the limitations of a state park to provide sufficient protection for natural areas. He accepted the state's offer on the condition that the original eleven-acre Castle Rock tract he had acquired would anchor a dedicated nature preserve within the state park. His terms were accepted, and within five years he had acquired through the institute a total of about 440 acres, which were sold to the state at cost. He negotiated the terms for an additional six hundred acres, which the state acquired outright. On one occasion, when the state was unable to meet a scheduled option payment, Fell raised fifty-five thousand dollars within a few short weeks from Ogle County Bank, commissioner Margery Carlson, and future commissioner Florence Lowden Miller, daughter of the former Illinois governor Lowden Miller, whose sons would later sell to the state about 2,300 acres of the original Lowden estate, located across the river from Castle Rock, to establish the Lowden-Miller State Forest.[32] The Fells also loaned yet more money out of their own savings to meet certain payment obligations. Even before the state park was officially established, in 1978, the Nature Preserves Commission had dedicated 589 acres, more than half of the park's original 1,040 acres, as the Castle Rock Nature Preserve. As the park expanded over time to include more than 2,000 acres, so too did the renamed George B. Fell Nature Preserve within it swell to a total of 685 acres.[33]

With the fees he received to prospect for property in the Castle Rock area, Fell hired staff through the Natural Land Institute to perform similar services in downstate Illinois on behalf of the Nature Preserves Commission. Among those he hired were Max Hutchison and John Schwegman. Schwegman, a former student of commissioner Klimstra, recalled being invited to spend a weekend at the Fell home as part of his new-hire orientation. Most of the two days were spent "just getting to know one another," with Fell wanting to make sure that Schwegman was on board with the spirit as well as the letter of the law establishing the nature preserves system. He need not have worried. Within two years, Schwegman had worn out his new car by logging one hundred thousand miles scouting prospective natural areas as part of his job.[34]

Hutchison, who ended up working as a southern Illinois field representative for the Illinois Nature Preserves Commission and The Nature Conservancy for more than thirty years, recalled Fell as a skilled negotiator.[35] Relying on the reconnaissance and relationship building of his field representatives, Fell had a knack for keying in on strategic parcels and exercising patient persistence with prospective land sellers. In early 1969, the team effort resulted in Fell's signing of a four-thousand-dollar option for the Natural Land Institute to acquire a sixty-five-acre parcel that included Wildcat Bluff and a portion of Heron Pond. Located in the far southern tip of Illinois, Heron Pond is the kind of Cache River wildland that makes visitors think they have been transported to the bayous of Louisiana. Nestled amid sandstone bluffs and dense floodplain forests lies a maze of backwater swamps, out of which rise water tupelo and bald cypress trees. The area is rich with bobcat, river otter, and a startling diversity of birds, including many threatened and endangered species; the only things that seem to be missing in the primeval-looking landscape are alligators and Spanish moss.[36]

Unlike his deal with the state to acquire Castle Rock properties, Fell had no guarantee that the state would buy additional properties from the institute. Yet his Cache River–area acquisition was a calculated risk that eventually paid off. In 1967 Lodge resigned his position and was replaced by an acting director who was decidedly friendlier to the cause of natural areas preservation. A newspaperman by trade, Dan Malkovich—father of the stage and film actor John Malkovich—was editor and publisher of *Outdoor Illinois*, a magazine devoted to conservation and the history of the state. A founder and director of the Rend Lake Association, which promoted the establishment of the Rend Lake reservoir near his hometown of Benton in southern Illinois, Malkovich was also a member of the Sierra Club and a director of the Illinois Nature Conservation Association, a short-lived organization that promoted conservation values.[37]

In the first year of his interim appointment, Malkovich reported that Illinois ranked fourth among all states in the number of visitors to its state parks but dead last in the average number of state park acres per person.[38] The following year, the state's new governor, Richard B. Ogilvie, to his political cost, instituted the state's first income tax to remedy a number of state problems, including its glaring deficit in public lands. Other land acquisition funds were anticipated from the federal Land and Water Conservation Fund, established in 1965 in part to provide matching grants to state and local governments for planning, land acquisition, and recreational development. Aware that the Department of Conservation was set to acquire considerably more acreage, Fell petitioned Malkovich to make sure that a significant percentage of those acres included high-quality natural areas. Malkovich reported in 1969 that the Department of Conservation had acquired 26,000 acres, of which 7,324 acres were dedicated as nature preserve lands.[39] Included were the 65 acres the institute had acquired in the Cache River area and sold to the state at cost, along with an additional 1,046 acres of adjacent land the state had acquired directly. Together, these lands were dedicated as the Heron Pond-Wildcat Bluff Nature Preserve. Expanded eventually to 1,861 acres and renamed the Heron Pond-Little Black Slough Nature Preserve, the state's largest nature preserve today anchors an impressive public–private effort of the Illinois Department of Natural Resources (successor to the Department of Conservation), the US Fish and Wildlife Service, The Nature Conservancy, and Ducks Unlimited to protect and restore a forty-five-thousand-acre wetland corridor along fifty miles of the Cache River.[40]

Fell was fortunate that his quest to acquire natural areas for dedication came at a time when the Department of Conservation possessed both the will and the means to increase its land holdings. From 1971 through 1973, the Department of Conservation spent a total of $52.3 million to add land to existing state parks and recreation areas and to establish thirteen new ones.[41] Under Malkovich's successor, Henry N. Barkhausen, the Department of Conservation continued its evolution beyond its recreation-dominated roots. Barkhausen's number one priority during his two-year tenure was to acquire additional land "as a far-sighted investment in preserving the natural environment for the people of today and generations to come."[42] Serious about advancing a preservation agenda, he created a Natural Areas Section within the Department of Conservation in 1972 and asked John Schwegman, first hired by Fell to conduct a survey of downstate natural areas, to lead it. The Natural Areas Section consolidated all of the Department of Conservation's nature preserves system responsibilities—namely acquiring land for dedication and conducting preserve management—under a single, dedicated administrative body. This gave natural areas preservation institutional standing on a par with traditional hunting, fishing, boating, and other recreational interests for the first time in the Department of Conservation's history.

In spite of the Department of Conservation's growing appreciation for the ecological values of land, Fell rightly perceived that the agency remained under intense popular pressure to acquire and develop land for recreational purposes. By the mid-1970s, more than twenty-five million people annually visited the state's 120 parks and recreation areas.[43] Fell made it his job, therefore, to counter that pressure by setting an aggressive natural areas acquisition agenda. Having resigned his position as commissioner in 1970 in order to staff the commission as its first executive secretary, Fell and three full-time field representatives—all, including Fell, employed through the Natural Land Institute on behalf of the commission—scoured the state for high-quality natural areas to acquire and dedicate. To guide their work, Fell sent his staff into the field with assessment criteria that were significantly more specific than those given to his fellow commissioners during the commission's first few months.

By statute, a nature preserve had to retain some significant degree of its primeval character or have unusual flora, fauna, or geological or archaeological features of scientific or educational value. Additionally, Fell directed his staff to assess the quality of each natural area, the statewide scarcity of the natural type, and its representation in the nature preserves system.[44] This meant that, in general, high-quality sites would be given priority over degraded sites and that prairie remnants—all types of which were exceptionally rare—would rank higher in need of preservation than upland forests, various types of which were found in relative abundance in federal, state, county, and municipal preserves throughout the state. Perhaps most important, to ensure that sufficient representative examples of all types of native Illinois habitat types were included in the nature preserves system, Fell commissioned John Schwegman, before he assumed his position with the Natural Areas Section of the Department of Conservation, to identify the major natural divisions of the state. Combining soils, topography, geology, and the distribution of flora and fauna into a single classification system, Schwegman identified fourteen regions or natural divisions and thirty-three subregions or sections. By far the largest natural division identified in Schwegman's *The Natural Divisions of Illinois* was the Grand Prairie Division, whose five sections in east central and northern Illinois covered nearly half the state. Many of the other divisions were considerably smaller and were named for the portion of river courses they encompassed.[45] Fell directed his staff to search for examples of each distinctive natural community within each division and section.

Through 1974, the Department of Conservation acquired 8,819 acres of the 24,000 recommended by the Nature Preserves Commission for acquisition and dedication as nature preserves.[46] Fell acknowledged the achievement, but for him the disparity between the two numbers was cause for serious concern. Reiterating the mantra he repeated throughout his career—that "this is the last opportunity there will ever be to save natural areas"—he lamented in the commission's biennial report for 1973–74 that the state's land acquisition system was too "slow and cumbersome and severely limits the ability to secure protection for natural areas, especially those that are threatened with imminent destruction."[47] He supported this statement with numerous examples of natural areas that had been identified and recommended by commission staff, only to be destroyed before the state could take action.

In spite of Fell's emphasis on what natural areas remained at risk, the commission's accomplishments during its first decade were considerable. Under Fell's leadership, it had dedicated a total of fifty-two nature preserves, affording the highest level of legal protection to nearly fifteen thousand acres.[48] Of the Department of Conservation's thirty-one nature preserves, twenty-one were composed of land that had been acquired specifically for the purpose of preservation. Perhaps the most personally gratifying to Fell among all the state-owned nature preserves was Harlem Hills Nature Preserve. After twelve years of on-again, off-again negotiations, the Natural Land Institute had finally acquired the fifty-three-acre gravel hill prairie remnant and in turn sold it to the state at cost for dedication as a nature preserve. Thus successfully concluded Fell's multi-year effort to preserve one of his father's favorite natural areas and to honor the passionate physician-botanist who had first sparked in him a love of the natural world.

In addition to nature preserves dedicated on new and existing government land, the commission secured dedications on lands owned by nongovernment agencies. Several came about in part through Fell's active role in other organizations. He remained a board member of the Illinois chapter of The Nature Conservancy through 1968, helping to mold it into the kind of sustained preservation presence he had envisioned in establishing the conservancy's chapter system. By 1974 the Illinois chapter had acquired seven sites, retaining title to some and selling others to the state. Among the latter were portions of the prairie chicken preserves in Jasper and Marion Counties, the first nature preserves dedicated to protecting an endangered animal species. The Natural Land Institute, of course, played an instrumental role in the acquisition of several sites for dedication as nature preserves, all of which were acquired by or sold to the state at cost except Beach Cemetery Prairie Nature Preserve. The institute retained title to this 2.25-acre prairie remnant discovered in an abandoned pioneer cemetery near Rockford. The Vermilion County Conservation District, established in 1968, was the first conservation district to dedicate a site as a nature preserve. Located along the Vermilion River in the Forest Glen Reserve about nine miles southeast of Danville, the 160-acre Russell M. Duffin Nature Preserve is a rare beech-maple forest remnant that supports a particularly rich diversity of animals, including 160 different species of birds.[49]

Protection by Management

As important as acquisition and dedication are, alone they are insufficient to protect the natural features that are the reason nature preserves are designated. "The greatest threat to natural conditions on existing nature preserves," Fell warned in the commission's two-year report for 1973–74, "is not from outside forces or intrusions. It is from the lack of management."[50] Prior to human settlement, Illinois was, in effect, one big natural area, perfectly capable of taking care of itself. Its ecologically rich array of prairies, forests, wetlands, and other community types, which had co-evolved over thousands of years, was resilient and self-sustaining. These topographical features survived and in many instances even required natural disturbances, such as fire. Prairie habitat, for instance, is a fire-dependent community, relying on periodic fires to enrich soils, keep invasive tree species from gaining a toehold, and maintain a balanced composition among a diversity of native plant, animal, insect, and microbial species.[51]

As waves of settlers discovered the rich prairie soils, lumber-rich forests, and bountiful waterways, they and their descendants plowed and harvested and drained the land to such an extent that within 150 years, by Fell's estimate, approximately 75 percent of the state's nearly thirty-six million acres had been cultivated for row crops or converted to urban uses, with a significant portion of the balance in pasture, strip mines, and other high-impact land uses.[52] Most of the natural areas that remained did so in small, isolated pockets, often because they were too difficult to cultivate or otherwise develop. Greatly diminished in size and cut off from other natural areas and the natural processes that sustained them, they became highly susceptible to a number of ills—namely invasive species both native and nonnative—that threatened their biological health.

Even before the first nature preserve was dedicated, Fell anticipated the need for a proactive and consistent system of management for remnant sites, and he developed a draft set of management rules. Refined over the course of several years, they included (1) developing a master plan for each nature preserve; (2) assigning management responsibility to a responsible steward; (3) installing specified fences, barriers, signs, and trails; (4) stopping adverse land use activities; (5) conducting specified land rehabilitation, such as the control of invasive species; and (6) scheduling ongoing surveillance, patrol, and maintenance.[53]

A master plan for each nature preserve was required by statute. The commission took the lead in developing the majority of these plans in consultation with the Department of Conservation, which was responsible for their implementation. The goal of each master plan, inclusive of specific management objectives and procedures, was to ensure the long-term viability of the natural features for which individual nature preserves had been dedicated.

One of the key issues addressed early on by the commission was the use of fire as a management tool. At the time of the commission's establishment, in the early 1960s, a majority of the environmental academic community strongly opposed the manipulation of natural areas. In general, most held that any form of human interference, especially something as drastic as the intentional use of fire, would hurt the ecosystem, not help it. Sparked by an understanding that wildfires, both naturally caused and those set by native Americans for hunting and agricultural purposes, had played a critical role in shaping the Midwestern landscape over the course of millennia, Robert F. Betz, a professor of biology at Northeastern Illinois University, and Ray Schulenberg, a botanist at the Morton Arboretum, had for several years been bucking conventional wisdom by using fire to manage prairie remnants found in several Illinois pioneer cemeteries.

Fell was no stranger to the benefits of fire for certain kinds of natural areas. As an undergraduate student at the University of Illinois, he was familiar with Professor Victor Shelford's monitoring of a railroad prairie that frequently caught fire from sparks emitted by passing trains. Nonetheless, Betz recalled that Fell remained cool to the idea of fire as a management tool until he saw for himself the pioneer cemetery prairie remnants that had flourished under Betz's and Schulenberg's experimental fire regimes.[54] Thereafter, he invited Betz to present his findings to the commission, which endorsed "the principle of preservation of prairie vegetation in pioneer cemeteries and authorizes the Chairman to address a letter to Robert F. Betz expressing the interest of the Commission in his work."[55] Over the course of several years, Fell facilitated a vigorous, ongoing debate among his commissioners—what specific types of habitat should be burned, how often and how intensely, and the benefits and drawbacks of fire compared to other management techniques—which ultimately led the commission to adopt prescribed burns as a management tool in fire-dependent natural communities throughout the entire state.

The breadth of management issues, both general and site specific, that Fell and his commissioners had to address and resolve was staggering. Many nature preserves were plagued by invasive species, including European buckthorn, multiflora rose, Canada thistle, Japanese honeysuckle, Kentucky bluegrass, and Chinese Elm, which threatened to choke out many native species. The long-term ecological integrity of some preserves was threatened by a change in the amount of water flowing into or out of the site, typically caused by dams, drainage ditches, or other water-control structures on adjacent lands. Some preserves were plagued by poachers who targeted species such as black walnut trees for their high commercial value. Many preserves suffered from other kinds of human abuse, including damage caused by motorcycles, snowmobiles, and other off-road vehicles, specimen collectors who snatched up rare and endangered species for the collector trade, and casual visitors who liked to pick flowers or, as Fell complained, host beer parties in the woods.

On these and most issues before the commission, Fell often took the lead in framing the debate. The commission, as John Warnock and almost every other commissioner acknowledged, was "George's baby," and there was a tendency to let him run things, which he did, "but never in an overbearing way." Warnock, a professional field biologist at Western Illinois University who was appointed to the commission in 1972, recalled Fell as "very unassuming" but very thorough. "He would call in advance of the meetings to ask you to get prepared. Afterwards, he'd follow up to clarify something or to get more information or opinions. [At the meetings,] he would sort of control the flow of things but never cut anyone off. He was a bulldog, but he had all the patience in the world. His idea was not to get through the agenda but to discuss everything thoroughly. He didn't leave too many stones unturned."[56]

Fell had come far from his Nature Conservancy days in which his capable but stringent style of administration had alienated certain colleagues and members of the board of governors. He still retained a strong penchant for steering debate in the direction of ideas and principles he believed were right, but he had learned to accept, however begrudgingly, some compromises. For instance, Fell repeatedly pushed to minimize or eliminate all human influences on nature preserves. What few trails might be necessary, he argued, should be restricted to a narrow, unobtrusive width. This ran contrary to the opinions of several commissioners who argued in favor of wider trails and more of them. This, they reasoned, would provide for a more enjoyable visitor experience, which in turn would result in greater public support for the preservation activities of the commission and other environmental agencies and organizations. Fell countered that "wide and unnaturalistic heavy duty trails . . . have the appearance of a permanent road rather than a path [that] is usually out of place in a nature preserve."[57] John Schwegman recalled that Fell's goal in this recurring back and forth was to maximize the land preserved and "if it meant walking single file like the Indians used to do, so be it."[58] In the end, Warnock remembered that on those occasions when commissioners differed with their chief executive, Fell had an adept way of tabling issues "until he got what he wanted in the end. Most of the time, anyway. We got our wider trails."[59]

Conservationists to the Core

As had happened with the board of governors during the earliest years of The Nature Conservancy, the commissioners of the Illinois Nature Preserves Commission afforded Fell a great deal of latitude in his administrative responsibilities. They appreciated his passion, commitment, and skill, not to mention the fact that he fulfilled his responsibilities for little or no pay. Fell served as secretary of the commission from its first meeting in 1964 through 1970. In accordance with his initial conception for the commission, neither he nor any other commissioner received any compensation, even though he effectively served as the commission's full-time executive. During that time, he took on occasional, short-term consulting contracts for entities such as the Boone County Conservation District, the Prairie Chicken Foundation of Illinois, and the Department of Conservation. However, the fees he earned were paid not to him but directly to the Natural Land Institute to support the activities of the Nature Preserves Commission.

In 1970 Fell resigned his position as secretary of the Commission to become, officially, its executive secretary. Although the commission's first staff person, Fell was loath to be a state employee. Instead, he successfully negotiated with the Department of Conservation to pay the Natural Land Institute approximately $12,600 per year for his services to staff the commission. Even then, rather than receive the full amount, Fell opted to draw an annual salary from the institute of only $8,736, an amount he described as "commensurate with [my] personal needs."[60] What he did not share was that this salary level ensured that he paid little or no income tax. In any event, the difference between his salary and the total fees paid to the institute by the Department of Conservation and other parties in exchange for his services was placed in a reserve fund to be used by the institute, primarily in support of the commission.[61] Starting in 1976, Fell reduced his annual salary even further, to four thousand dollars per year, a level that remained fixed until 1983, at which point he returned to working full time for no wage until his death, a little more than a decade later.

More than a few friends and colleagues wondered how the Fells managed to stay afloat on such meager wages. During Fell's first ten years with the commission, his wife, Barbara, was the primary breadwinner, working in her old job as a bacteriologist at the Rockford Public Health Department. In addition to that, they earned a little rental income from subleasing a second house they rented from a Chicago businessman. The Fells may not have earned a lot of money, but they spent even less, which is how they more than made ends meet. Like many children of the Great Depression, they were possessed of a strong sense of economy. In a high school essay, Fell went so far as to express his thankfulness for the lessons the Depression taught him. Their exceptional personal thrift also reflected their conservation values. Fell believed that one of his primary challenges in preserving remnant natural areas stemmed from what he perceived as the wasteful ways of modern American culture: "We just can't seem to, as a society, realize our situation and how urgent the need is to save what we have and to take care of it and to use it moderately to save some for the future."[62]

Living moderately, to the Fells, meant growing much of their own food rather than paying grocery-store prices. A master canner and preserver, Barbara cultivated an extraordinary garden in the yard of the home they rented for many years at 819 North Main Street in Rockford, next door to the Burpee Museum of Natural History. Living moderately meant that Fell performed his own maintenance on his car: he changed the grease and oil, adjusted the brakes, and installed replacement parts such as speedometers, fuel pumps, timing belts, and bearings. Taking care of what they had meant that Fell undertook all of his own household repairs and renovations, including reroofing and residing his house, replacing floors and subfloors, and repairing the furnace and the water heater. In his free time, he built cabinets for his father's extensive herbarium.

Together, the Fells haunted auction houses and thrift shops to furnish their home and office. Schooled by Fell's father, who, when not botanizing, restored antique furniture, the Fells developed a keen eye for antiques that they could repair and restore themselves. When they needed clothes, Goodwill was their first stop. New clothes, when necessary, were bought when on sale. In their lives they never bought a single item on credit. "It would scare me to death to borrow money," Fell confessed during an interview late in life. In the many miles the couple logged in prospecting land deals, Fell regularly avoided the cost of tolls by limiting himself to free highways, even if it meant going out of his way. They saved on meals while traveling by always bringing with them enough sandwiches or baby food—prepackaged jars requiring no refrigeration—to last their trip. Among those who knew the Fells, few would have argued with their self-assessment: "I think we were the original pinch pennies."[63]

What most people did not know is that what little money the Fells earned, they invested expertly. Fell spent countless hours poring over corporate prospectuses and playing the stock market. Ned Garst, Fell's brother-in-law and a Natural Land Institute board member, observed, "I went to Harvard Business School, but I could have taken [investment] lessons from him."[64] And so it was that the Fells managed to earn enough money to splurge on the one thing that mattered most to them: the protection of natural land. In addition to the several land acquisition loans they made to the Natural Land Institute or on behalf of the Illinois Department of Conservation, the Fells acquired an eighty-acre tract of woods for themselves near Fuller Forest Preserve, located six miles southwest of Rockford. They spent countless hours restoring what came to be known as Fell's Woods and relishing the wildflower patches in spring—hepaticas, marsh marigolds, bluebells, spring beauties, dogtooth violet, skunk cabbage, red trilliums, and white trilliums. In summer they picked wild berries, and when the leaves turned color they gathered hickory nuts. In all seasons, with friends, family, or just by themselves, they walked their woods, enjoying the birdsong, the beavers, and the deer. The measure of the Fells' wealth never was how much money they had in the bank but the unassuming pride they enjoyed in the permanent preservation of such refuges.

The Fells' frugality reaped critical benefits for the Natural Land Institute as well as for the Nature Preserves Commission. From year to year, salary and expense reimbursements for Fell's services on behalf of the commission accounted for 50 to 90 percent of the institute's total annual revenues, with Fell accepting only a portion of the salary due him. The balance of the funds was available to support the activities of the institute, which cycled them back to support the commission. In some years, the institute effectively doubled the commission's budget. From time to time, the institute also helped the commission cover shortfalls. In 1972, for instance, the commission was running $7,628 over budget for the first half of its fiscal year. Rather than reduce expenses, which would have resulted in scaling back the commission's activities, the institute trustees voted unanimously to meet the budget overrun from its own reserve fund.[65]

Illinois Natural Areas Inventory and Private Landowner Contact Program

By the late 1970s, the Natural Land Institute was the largest and most influential nonprofit land conservation organization in the state of Illinois. As the de facto staffing arm of the commission, it employed five full-time and several seasonal staff people on an annual operating budget in excess of $250,000. Fell continually pressed the Department of Conservation to increase the commission's annual budget allocation so that the institute could hire yet more commission field representatives. In spite of the commission's considerable achievements, he believed that there remained many natural areas in dire need of preservation. Just how many and how imminent the threats no one knew precisely.

The institute had become adept at conducting land surveys in targeted geographies throughout the state, so much so that it was hired to conduct surveys beyond the borders of Illinois. One example was the natural areas inventory the institute conducted for the Lake Michigan Coastal Zone in Lake, Porter, and LaPorte Counties, Indiana, with special attention given to rare or endangered species of plants and animals.[66] In 1977 the institute received a grant to conduct the Endangered Species Project within its home state. The findings of this project spurred the Illinois Endangered Species Protection Board, established one year before passage of the federal Endangered Species Act in 1973, to adopt an official list of endangered plants and animals.[67] This information was critical in helping the Illinois Nature Preserves Commission fulfill its statutory obligation to protect the habitat of rare and endangered species of plants and animals.

By statute, the Nature Preserves Commission is also charged with maintaining a registry of nature preserves and other natural areas in the state. Since the commission's inception, Fell had pressed for a comprehensive survey to compile such a registry. At the time, the only statewide survey ever conducted was *Proposed Park Areas in the State of Illinois*, published by the Friends of Our Native Landscape in 1921. As useful as it was in guiding some early preservation efforts, including the establishment of several state parks, by the 1970s it was a half century out of date. More important, with a stated emphasis on large areas of a thousand acres or more, it excluded the small remnant natural areas that were the primary focus of the commission.

Fell and the Nature Preserves Commission were not alone in their desire to map all remaining natural areas. Soon after joining the staff of The Nature Conservancy in 1970, Robert E. Jenkins, a Harvard graduate, promoted the idea of a nationwide survey in order to strategically redirect the conservancy's acquisition efforts. Since its inception, driven by the freelance entrepreneurial ways of early leaders such as Richard Pough, the conservancy had employed a largely opportunistic approach to preservation, seizing upon what natural areas were available rather than prioritizing those with the greatest ecological value. Jenkins's push for a more strategic approach to conservation marked a return to what Fell had originally envisioned during his tenure as secretary of the conservancy when he wrote, "we must systematically seek out unchanged remnants of natural features not now preserved and see that they are given perpetual protection."[68]

For people like Fell and Jenkins, the drive to underpin conservation efforts with more detailed and comprehensive surveys had the effect of prioritizing those natural areas with the greatest degree of biological diversity, or what the famed entomologist E. O. Wilson would champion a decade later as "biodiversity." Although there is no single accepted definition of biodiversity, the science writer Boyce Rensberger sums it up pretty well: "The more species of plants, animals, and other life-forms in a given region, the more resistant that region is to destruction and the better it can perform its environmental roles of cleansing water, enriching the soil, maintaining stable climates, even generating the oxygen we breathe."[69]

In his quest to conduct a national survey, Jenkins encountered too many obstacles, not the least of which was cost. Nonetheless, he did manage to initiate a state-by-state conservancy survey effort in 1974 called the Natural Heritage Program.[70] Also in 1974, the Natural Heritage Section of the Illinois Department of Conservation announced a call for proposals to conduct a statewide inventory of natural areas. John Schwegman, who headed up the section, recalled that Henry Barkhausen, director of the Department of Conservation, also wanted to make sure that, since the state was investing so much in land, it was buying the "best of the best."[71] Fell, an ecologist by training and committed to the preservation of the full spectrum of Illinois's native biodiversity, promptly submitted a proposal for the Natural Land Institute to conduct the survey. The proposal ran into several snags, not the least of which was a glaring conflict of interest. The Natural Land Institute was an independent 501(c)(3) nonprofit organization, but everyone knew that it was inextricably tied to the Illinois Nature Preserves Commission, which operated under the umbrella of the Department of Conservation. How would it look, then, if the Department of Conservation, at the recommendation of the commission, of which Fell was the chief executive, awarded a major contract to the institute, of which Fell also was the chief executive?

Meantime, the botanist John White resigned his position as field representative for the commission in order to devote all his time to developing an independent methodology for conducting the inventory. Fell withdrew his proposal and, hoping to mitigate the institute's inherent conflict of interest, teamed with White. Together, they approached the University of Illinois to develop a data processing system, and through the university they ultimately submitted a joint proposal to conduct the survey. The Department of Conservation awarded the approximately $650,000 contract to the University of Illinois, with John White serving as the unofficial principal investigator and the Natural Land Institute providing contractual labor support.

Over the course of three years, White and his staff of five field ecologists, seven field assistants, and a dozen seasonal field assistants conducted the "first inventory project of such magnitude in the country."[72] After reviewing existing data, the survey team conducted aerial surveys to identify potential areas, ground-truthed the data via preliminary field surveys, and finally conducted full field surveys. They searched for wooded sites with a minimum size of twenty acres and, because of their rarity, prairies sites measuring as small as one-quarter of an acre. For sites with rare, endangered, or relict species, there was no minimum acreage requirement. In several instances, the survey teams had a hard time keeping up with the bulldozers. A three-mile stretch that appeared from the air to be good prairie was found to have been plowed up by the time it was visited two weeks later. During another aerial survey of railroad prairies, field staff observed "three stands of prairie grass being bulldozed as they flew over them."[73]

At each of the more than one thousand sites identified, surveyors collected as many as ninety items of information. In addition to listing each site's location; its basic natural characteristics, including topography, geology, and soils; and, of course, its significant natural features, the survey recorded its ownership, surrounding land use, management needs, preservation status, and the level of threat it faced. Finally, each site was graded for its degree of disturbance: Grade A, being "relatively stable or undisturbed . . . example: Old growth, ungrazed forest," through Grade E, representing "very early successional or very severely disturbed . . . example: Cropland."[74] When completed, in 1978, the survey revealed that there remained 25,700 acres of Grade A natural areas, scattered across the state in 1,089 sites as small as one-tenth of an acre. The total represented just seven-hundredths of 1 percent of Illinois's total land and water area of roughly thirty-six million acres.[75] If the state of Illinois were a 2,500-square-foot home, the amount of remaining high-quality natural areas remaining would equal about 1.75 square feet, or the footprint of a small bedside nightstand. However, to put this into truer perspective, one would have to imagine this small nightstand chopped into 1,089 pieces and scattered throughout the house. The inventory further revealed that fully half of the remaining areas were threatened with destruction and that only 20 percent could be considered permanently protected.[76] Although the findings were grim, they served as a spur for Fell and a growing number of professional and amateur interests to redouble their efforts to save what was left of Illinois's natural heritage.

The Illinois Natural Areas Inventory provided the first reliable, comprehensive data about the state's remaining natural areas. What it did not provide was any new strategy or financial support for preserving those areas. Some within the Nature Preserves Commission and the Natural Heritage Section of the Department of Conservation believed the best strategy was to keep the survey results under wraps for fear that landowners might react negatively to the state's eyeing portions of their property. Fell believed otherwise. He believed that if landowners were not made aware of the importance of the high-quality natural areas in their keeping, they might willfully or inadvertently destroy them. He also held fast to the belief, dating back to the pitch he had made to the Ecologists' Union in 1949 to pursue a national preservation organization, that "People *are* . . . sold on 'conservation' in general, and they want to do whatever needs to be done."[77] Nonetheless, to avoid any hint of misperception that the state was gearing up for a land grab, Fell urged that landowners be contacted by a letter from the institute or the University of Illinois — definitely not from the Illinois Department of Conservation — letting them know that their land holdings included some special, high-quality natural areas and offering them additional information and advice if they desired.

Gerald A. Paulson, a Natural Land Institute employee since 1971, recommended a far more ambitious outreach plan. Paulson represented a new generation of preservationists. With a bachelor of science degree in ornamental horticulture and a master of science degree in plant pathology from the University of Illinois, he was well versed in biological science but understood that most of the general public was not. In his view, to preserve a significant percentage of Illinois's remaining natural areas would require more than notification by letter. Paulson envisioned sending teams of people into the field, not to survey plants and animals but rather to cultivate awareness, understanding, and interest about natural areas among people.

With funding provided by a three-year grant of $525,000 from the Joyce Foundation, whose mission at the time included environmental protection in the Great Lakes region, Paulson developed the Private Landowner Contact Program. Among the five full-time staff he hired for the project was Don McFall. Several years earlier, as a young boy born and raised in Fell's hometown of Rockford, McFall and his family had often visited the Burpee Museum of Natural History. In 1968, at the age of fifteen, while thumbing through selections in the museum's bookstore, McFall had come across a copy of *The Flora of Winnebago County, Illinois*, authored by Fell's father, Dr. Egbert W. Fell. Seeing the teenager engrossed in the book, Milton Mahlburg, the museum director and a Natural Land Institute board member, informed him that the man who knew where to find the plants listed in the book lived right next door to the museum. McFall telephoned Fell, who invited him to visit. "George was real open and full of information. I was fascinated." Fell likewise was impressed and offered McFall a seasonal job surveying natural areas. "The summer I received my driver's license, George contracted me to survey Lee County. My salary was a dollar an hour. I was paid once a month and had to front all my own gas and hotel money."[78]

Paulson hired McFall and other staff not only for their botanical skills but also for their people skills. In what was perhaps a first in the environmental movement, Paulson hired a psychologist to hone his staff's interview and active listening skills. After their training, they collectively traveled more than ninety-five thousand miles to make personal visits to more than six hundred individual landowners. What they discovered was both encouraging and troubling. Many landowners were aware that they owned special properties and were taking various steps to preserve them. However, the majority of landowners interviewed were farmers getting on in years without having made any long-term provision for the protection of their natural areas.[79]

The immediate results of the outreach program were that more than twenty natural areas were donated or sold for preservation and about 10 percent of the owners contacted expressed a willingness to preserve their land by some other means.[80] McFall, who went on to work for several years as a full-time employee of the institute before spending the majority of his career with the Illinois Nature Preserves Commission, reported that, more than twenty-five years after what might have been "a one-time, one-hour contact," the commission was still receiving the occasional call: "You said to get in touch with you if I ever considered selling my land. Well, I'm considering it."[81]

With the Landowner Contact Program, the Natural Land Institute further solidified its position as the largest and most accomplished nonprofit preservation organization in the state, but that position did not go unchallenged. At the same time Fell had submitted a grant request to the Joyce Foundation to support the Land Owner Contact Program and other initiatives under the umbrella of what he called the Natural Heritage Program (a name he freely borrowed from The Nature Conservancy), the Midwest office of The Nature Conservancy submitted a proposal to the same foundation to support an expansion of *its* Natural Heritage Program in several Midwestern states, including Illinois. Craig Kennedy, program officer of the Joyce Foundation, astutely observed the overlapping if not competing nature of the two proposals and suggested that the institute and the conservancy meet to discuss their respective roles and then submit a joint proposal. In 1978 the Natural Land Institute was considerably stronger than the Illinois chapter of the conservancy. It had a larger budget, it had acquired more land, and, with its close working relationship with the Nature Preserves Commission, it had significant influence in the acquisition and dedication of natural areas throughout the state. The conservancy's proposed Natural Heritage Program in Illinois—short of staffing the Illinois Nature Preserves

Commission—would have effectively replicated the stated purpose of the institute. In the end, Fell and the conservancy's Midwest regional office director, John Humke, came to an agreement that the institute would operate exclusively in Illinois and the conservancy would focus its efforts in other Midwestern states. This agreement led to the awarding of what was then the largest grant in the Joyce Foundation's history: a three-year, $1.2 million grant, $525,000 of which went to the institute and $675,000 to the Midwest regional office of the conservancy.[82]

At first glance, it may appear that Fell brokered a strict geographic division of labor in order to protect his home state turf from the organization that had effectively fired him twenty years earlier. True, he did co-opt the term "Natural Heritage Program," first employed by the conservancy. Otherwise, the balance of his actions demonstrated nothing but support and cooperation. With a significantly expanded funding capacity, the institute entered into an agreement with the Illinois chapter of the conservancy in 1980 to conduct inventories and assessments of prospective natural area parcels for the conservancy to acquire. The institute further helped the Illinois chapter by undertaking the development of master plans for many of its existing natural areas and performing other management services. To Fell's way of thinking, the Illinois chapter of the conservancy was not a competitor but a key component of the robust, multifaceted statewide preservation effort he had cultivated.

After decades of effort, Fell achieved even more than he initially envisioned. At the state level, he launched the Illinois Nature Preserves Commission. At the national level, he launched The Nature Conservancy. These twin entities— along with forest preserve districts, conservation districts, and a growing number of related conservation interests within and beyond the borders of Illinois— constituted an entire movement of natural areas preservation.

His legacy secured, Fell could have rested. Perhaps he should have rested. He did not. He could not. In his final years, what mattered most to Fell was ensuring that what he had built—primarily, the Illinois Nature Preserves Commission—was strong enough to survive without him. As a result of his efforts to further strengthen the commission, he got the chance to see how it would fare on its own much sooner than he anticipated.

6

Sowing More Acorns, Fighting More Battles

Under George Fell's leadership, the Illinois Nature Preserves Commission came to function very much as the proactive, independent body he initially envisioned. However, his desire to expand and formalize this independence through legislative action placed him at further odds with the Illinois Department of Conservation, which sought to bring the commission more fully under its authority. The ensuing struggle was reminiscent of Fell's unsuccessful effort to wrest control of The Nature Conservancy two decades earlier. The end result was much the same.

It was often said of Fell that he was more adept at sowing acorns than at nurturing oak trees to full maturity. Denied the opportunity to continue with the conservancy and the commission, Fell resorted to exploring yet more ways to preserve natural areas. Some ideas, such as the Natural Areas Association, found fertile ground. Other ideas did not. Whatever the outcomes, Fell never gave up, never slowed down, even during his battle with the cancer that ultimately claimed his life.

Founder's Syndrome Redux

The Illinois Natural Areas Preservation Act was the first of its kind in the nation. Fell described it as "very successful," but—keeping in mind that it was not the one that he had championed for passage—he could not refrain from pointing out that it had many "serious problems."[1] Some problems were decidedly easier to fix than others. For instance, he believed that, with so little virgin prairie remaining in Illinois, it was important to protect even tiny remnants, such as those in pioneer cemeteries. To do so, in 1975 Fell secured passage of the

Cemetery Prairie Nature Preserves Act, which granted county boards the authority to designate abandoned cemeteries containing prairie remnants—especially rare and important for being unplowed and ungrazed—as nature preserves.[2]

Other problems would prove far more challenging, in part because Fell all but stood alone in understanding them as problems. One of his primary concerns was what he described as the unclear "allocation of responsibility" between the commission and the Illinois Department of Conservation.[3] In Fell's twice-vetoed proposed structure for the nature preserves system, the commission would have had powers equal to those of the Department of Conservation and a significant if not unprecedented degree of independence from political and bureaucratic influences. As established by law with the passage of the Illinois Natural Areas Preservation Act, the commission possessed the authority to designate and set policy for nature preserves but could not hire its own staff. The Department of Conservation held the power to acquire and hold land for designation as nature preserves, to manage them in accordance with principles and management plans co-developed with the commission, and to provide support—including the hiring of staff—to allow the commission to function. Aside from a small handful of minor technical issues, the allocation of responsibility between the commission and the Department of Conservation was workably clear. What Fell sought was not to clarify the allocation of responsibility between the commission and the Department of Conservation but to reallocate the responsibility to reflect his desire for a truly independent commission.

Fell had equally strong concerns about the bureaucratic reshuffling the commission endured within the Department of Conservation. In this he stood on firmer ground. In 1972 Department of Conservation director Henry Barkhausen sought to bolster his agency's commitment to natural areas preservation and to integrate the commission more fully into the agency by consolidating all nature preserves responsibilities under a new Natural Areas Section. Although the new administrative section afforded natural areas protection unprecedented stature within the agency, Fell perceived it as an encroachment on the independence he had managed to secure for the commission. He also felt that the new arrangement underscored the destabilizing vagaries inherent in shifting administrative priorities. The Natural Areas Section started out in the Department of Conservation's Division of Long Range Planning but later was placed under the authority of the director's administrative staff. Later it was transferred to the Division of Parks and Memorials and then transferred again to a new Bureau of Public Lands and Historic Sites, where it was dissolved and its natural areas goals merged, along with those of endangered species and nongame wildlife, into a Natural Heritage Section. This new section subsequently was merged into the Division of Forest Resources and Natural Heritage. All of this bureau-cratic reshuffling occurred under three different directors within the span of eight years.[4] To Fell's way of thinking, subjecting the commission to the whims of different politically appointed directors with different perspectives and priorities compromised its effectiveness and threatened its long-term viability.

Fell's solution to these and other issues was as simple as it was astonishing. He crafted a new Natural Heritage Preservation Bill, which, if passed, would have repealed the landmark Illinois Natural Areas Preservation Act and its attendant acts in favor of combining all nature preserves–related provisions in a new, single act. In addition, it would have transferred authority for all rule making, planning, management, protection, and contracting for staff and consultants from the Department of Conservation to the commission.

Some of the provisions of Fell's bill were relatively noncontroversial. For instance, the bill would have provided tax relief for owners of dedicated natural areas on privately owned land. The Landowner Contact Program, conducted by the Natural Land Institute as a follow-up to the Illinois Natural Areas Inventory, revealed that a major barrier keeping private individuals from dedicating their natural areas as nature preserves was the financial penalty inherent in designation. Since lands designated as natural areas could not be developed, their value was decreased, often significantly, in areas of intense development pressure. Accordingly, Fell proposed that dedicated nature preserve lands be assessed at one dollar an acre, which would have effectively rendered them tax exempt.

Other provisions revealed Fell's desire to extend and strengthen the protec-tions afforded dedicated nature preserves and other high-quality natural lands. The bill would have provided for a hefty civil penalty of up to ten thousand dollars to be levied against anyone who removed, damaged, or destroyed any object within a nature preserve and empowered police and sheriffs to enforce the act and make arrests. Fell also proposed a registry program whereby a degree of legal protection would be extended to privately owned natural areas identified in the Illinois Natural Areas Inventory with or without the owner's consent.

Unlike Fell's 1961 and 1963 versions of the natural areas bill, the Natural Heritage Preservation Bill of 1977 never made it to the governor's desk. In fact, it was never brought up for a vote in the legislature. Introduced as Senate Bill 882, it passed from the Agriculture, Conservation, and Energy Committees to a study group "where it was never heard from again," presumably with the blessing of the Department of Conservation director, David Kenney.[5]

At their first meeting, Kenney found Fell possessed of a "very complex personality. His persona displayed an indifference to things other people paid attention to, like appearance. He dressed very simply with almost a genteel shabbiness to him." But when it came to the subject of natural areas protection, Kenney found Fell anything but indifferent. He was struck by Fell's "totally single minded" commitment to the cause and his "determination and bull-doggedness" in his effort to preserve every last acre possible.[6] Kenney was possessed of his own conservation passions. An ecologist himself, Kenney was appointed director of the Department of Conservation in 1977 and at his direction the department made its strongest statements to date in support of natural areas protection. In stark contrast to earlier reports that emphasized the Department of Conservation's commitment to active recreational pursuits, the biennial report for 1979–80 opened with the declaration "The Department is the steward of Illinois' natural and cultural resources." Channeling Aldo Leopold, the report listed among its primary goals "developing in Illinois citizens a conservation ethic emphasizing the value of our natural and cultural heritage for present and future generations."[7]

As strongly as Kenney supported the preservation of natural areas, however, he was equally committed to organizational cohesiveness and accountability. He feared that if Fell were successful in his bid to make the commission an independent entity, other components of the Department of Conservation likewise might clamor for independence, the effect of which, in his opinion, would have been to fragment and weaken statewide preservation efforts.[8] Kenney agreed that some clarifications and improvements were necessary to the existing nature preserves statute but believed that by and large the system worked, as evidenced by the dedication of the commission's eightieth nature preserve, in 1981, which brought the total number of acres afforded the highest degree of legal protection to 18,559.[9]

For Fell, such a milestone was less important than the long-term strength and integrity of the entire nature preserves system. Displaying the tenacity for which he had become well known, in 1981 he advanced yet another bill. The Illinois Natural Areas Preservation Bill was virtually identical to the Natural Heritage Preservation bill that had died in committee four years earlier. He had no illusions that the Department of Conservation would embrace the bill because of a mere name change. Circulating draft copies to cultivate support, he acknowledged, "I suspect [the Department of Conservation] will not find the draft acceptable, but at least we have a clean bill before us and can make another try at getting it into a form [the department] will tolerate."[10]

Under Kenney, the Department of Conservation did support several of the provisions Fell proposed, such as those related to civil penalties for violating any provision of the act and the one that authorized the dedication of "buffer areas," land of lesser ecological quality that nonetheless provided protection for adjacent nature preserves. The Department of Conservation also recommended pursuing in a separate bill the idea of a registry program with certain modifications to address concerns that imposing registry protections on privately held lands would amount to an illegal taking of private property. The agency held fast, however, in opposing any and all measures that would have increased the independence of the commission.[11] In fact, the harder Fell pushed for his agenda, the harder Kenney pushed back. In response to Fell's having resurrected his idea not only to authorize the commission to hire its own staff but to exempt it from the state's personnel code, Kenney pointed out the "blazing conflict of interest" inherent in Fell serving as the chief executive of both the commission and its primary contracted agent, the Natural Land Institute.[12] Fell shot back that the directorship of the Department of Conservation should be an elected rather than an appointed position.[13] Thereafter, Kenney directed the Internal Audit Division of the Department of Conservation to examine the institute's financial records. Only minor irregularities in bookkeeping were found, and these were easily amended, but the larger point was clear to Fell and to nature preserve commissioners alike: the Department of Conservation intended to maintain firm control over the commission.

After several months of stalemated negotiations between Fell and the Department of Conservation, in September 1981 Governor James R. Thompson signed an Illinois Natural Areas Preservation Act. Once again, the bill signed into law was the one advanced by the Department of Conservation, not the one urged by Fell. The new law corrected several shortcomings in the original Illinois Natural Areas Preservation Act and provided some needed clarifications in the relationship between the Department of Conservation and the Nature Preserves Commission. What it did not do was secure for the commission any of the formal independence that Fell had labored endlessly to achieve. In the end, Fell supported the passage of the bill for its many necessary technical improvements and assumed that he would be allowed to continue to direct the commission as he had previously.

Fell's legislative push to establish an independent Nature Preserves Commission was less dramatic than his attempt to take over the board of The Nature Conservancy by advancing an alternate slate of officers with himself as president, but the end result was effectively the same. If Fell had not resigned from the conservancy in the aftermath of the board elections, the board of governors would have terminated his employment. After Governor Thompson signed the Illinois Natural Areas Preservation Act into law, the Department of Conservation overrode an offer by the commissioners for Fell to continue as executive secretary of the commission through the usual contractual agreement with the Natural Land Institute. Instead, the Department of Conservation put forth an agreement that compelled Fell to choose: he could work for the commission or the institute, but not both. Furthermore, if he remained as executive secretary of the commission, he would not be allowed to hire institute staff on a contractual basis without a competitive bidding process.

Several commissioners, placing great value on Fell's leadership, encouraged him to resign his position with the institute and continue as the commission's chief executive. This likely would have required the Fells to move to Springfield and, according to the directive of the Department of Conservation, definitely required Fell to become an employee of the state. Few could imagine that Fell would remain with the commission under those terms. Throughout his career—throughout his life, in fact—he had remained a staunch individualist and was not about to change at the age of sixty-five.

In a last-ditch attempt to remain with the commission and remain true to himself, he proposed continuing as executive secretary of the commission under a contractual arrangement whereby he would remain an employee of the institute but resign his position as its executive director. When this was rejected, he offered to change the name of the Natural Land Institute to the Illinois Nature Preserves Foundation and to amend its bylaws to restrict its activities to supporting work of the commission. This idea, too, was turned down. Finally, in January 1982 the Department of Conservation, the commission, and the Natural Land Institute signed a Memorandum of Agreement that effectively ended Fell's tenure as head of the commission. Article IV of the memorandum stated, "[the Natural Land] Institute shall employ no person representing to other parties that he or she is 'Executive Secretary of the Commission' or 'Executive Director of the Commission,' or any similar title, nor shall the Commission contract for the services of any such executive officer."[14] The commission then initiated a search to hire its first staff person on the state payroll. Unwilling to cede the reins to just anyone—and all the more astonishing in view of his having been effectively let go from the commission—Fell volunteered to serve on the search committee.

No explicit offer ever was made, but Fell apparently hoped to keep an active hand in the commission by filling the new position with a Natural Land Institute employee, Jerry Paulson. Immediately after finishing his graduate studies at the University of Illinois, Paulson had received a deferment from serving in the military during the Vietnam War because of a minor medical condition and had been recommended to Fell, who hired him "on the spot."[15] Paulson was impressed with Fell's many accomplishments but recalled that he provided little guidance to Paulson in his job as a field representative for the Nature Preserves Commission. As exacting as Fell could be, in general he gave his staff a great deal of latitude in the execution of their duties as long as they produced the desired results. Paulson, his own kind of individualist and self-starter, flourished in this environment. Gaining confidence with experience, he advanced a number of innovative ideas such as the Private Landowner Contact Program. He recalled that Fell was seldom one to encourage such new ideas, but neither did he discourage them. In this, Fell was not so much a mentor as one who allowed those who worked for him to succeed or fail on their own merits, just as he had always done. Although Fell might not have said as much to his employee, he had great faith in Paulson, who "was a great influence in our activities . . . and he really ran the staff in the later years."[16] Paulson, after more than ten years as the de facto number two person at the Natural Land Institute, was ready for new challenges but suspected that it would have been difficult if not impossible to be viewed as anything other than Fell's Springfield surrogate and consequently did not pursue the post as the commission's first official staff person.[17]

In August 1982 the Nature Preserves Commission resolved that "the Natural Land Institute be thanked for its long sustained superior service to the Commission over the past many years with special appreciation for the support George Fell has given as Executive Secretary for an even longer period of time; without the assistance of both George and the Natural Land Institute the outstanding record of the Commission would not have been what it is today."[18] The resolution was followed by the hiring of Karen Witter, formerly of the Department of Conservation Division of Planning, to serve as chief administrative officer and spokesperson for the commission. For several commissioners, this marked an inevitable evolution of the commission from a semiautonomous body to one fully within the fold of state government. This, they hoped, would bring with it a larger annual budget allocation, resulting in an expanded programmatic capacity. John White, the driving force behind the Illinois Natural Areas Inventory who was present at the meeting, perceived a less optimistic feeling among the commissioners: "At least several of them looked scared and embarrassed and they acted it all out as if they didn't really want to admit what they were actually doing."[19] What they were doing, although few if any of them knew it, was repeating history. Almost twenty-three years to the day after Fell's last board meeting at The Nature Conservancy, the commission that Fell envisioned, advocated into existence, and directed for nearly two decades determined that it no longer required his services and hired someone else to take his place.

The Aftermath

Years later, Fell could laugh in admitting that he had made "lots of tactical mistakes" in handling certain matters at the Illinois Nature Preserves Commission and The Nature Conservancy.[20] At the time, however, leaving both organizations, especially the commission, was no laughing matter. Fell had devoted his entire career to protecting natural lands. Both he and his wife had made tremendous sacrifices in service to the cause. Fell's acknowledged culpability notwithstanding, he was understandably disappointed, angry, and hurt. More important, with so much conservation work yet to be done, he was at a loss what to do next.

As hard as these transitions were for Fell, they were just as hard on the organizations he had willed into being. The Nature Conservancy had run through several executive directors before an internal management audit, conducted by Alexander Adams, conservancy president from 1960 to 1962, and formerly of Mellon Bank and the FBI, identified numerous management shortcomings, many of which stemmed directly from reforms Richard Goodwin had instituted in moving Fell out of the position of chief executive.[21] Over the next half century, the conservancy passed through an inevitable succession of management challenges in the course of becoming the juggernaut it is today. However, as acknowledged by conservancy president John Sawhill in a letter to Fell in 1994, the bedrock for its growth remained Fell's original vision and the structure he put into place: "The direct action approach that you developed to accomplish the preservation of nature remains the organization's fundamental strength."[22]

Among the challenges faced by the Illinois Nature Preserves Commission after Fell's departure was the drastic reduction in revenue and staff. In its start-up years, the commission squeaked by on an annual budget of about five thousand dollars. In Fell's final year as executive secretary, its budget had swelled to $300,000. Half of its revenues came from the Department of Conservation. The other half was provided by the Natural Land Institute, courtesy of the three-year Joyce Foundation grant awarded in 1980. The institute provided the commission's entire staff of five on a contractual basis. In addition, the institute supported the commission by providing additional programmatic and support services at no cost to the commission. The year following Fell's departure, the absence of institute support, coupled with a 50 percent budget slash by the Department of Conservation (quite the opposite of the hoped-for increase), reduced the commission's total annual operating budget to seventy-five thousand dollars and its staff to one full-time employee.

It would take a number of years before the Commission's budget and staffing regained their 1982 levels. The Commission survived its lean times in part because of a sound structure, but, just as important, because of the institutional culture Fell had cultivated as its leader for nearly twenty years. Bound by statute to consult with the chief of the Illinois Natural History Survey and the director of the Illinois State Museum in the appointment of commissioners, a succession of governors consistently selected well-qualified individuals who had "demonstrated an interest in the preservation of natural areas" rather than ones vested in political agendas or financial gain, because appointments came with no compensation.[23] As commissioners retired or were replaced, Fell took pains to encourage new commissioners to follow the example set by their predecessors. Commissioners devoted two full days to each quarterly meeting. Fell largely drove each meeting's agenda, but he encouraged active participation by all. In between quarterly meetings, he kept in regular contact with commissioners, following through on action items, soliciting their feedback, and generally keeping them up to date on commission affairs. Over the course of nearly two decades, Fell developed the commission into a highly functional deliberative body, in which the commissioners shared a profound sense of ownership, pride, and accomplishment.

Following the hiring of his replacement, Fell continued to earn the respect of commissioners. Kenneth Fiske, who as commission chairman had strongly urged Fell to accept the Springfield-based job in order to establish closer ties with the Department of Conservation, recalled that after Fell's departure he had taken to monitoring a number of nature preserves on his own and pressed the commission to improve their management. "George would go to Busse Woods, for instance, and report the damaging effects inflicted by an overpopulation of deer. He essentially moved from being executive secretary of the Commission, which he did for practically nothing, to the self-appointed overseer of existing preserves [which he did for absolutely nothing]. He became the watchdog and I loved him for that."[24]

The Natural Land Institute weathered its divorce from the commission decidedly less well. Over the course of twenty years, Fell had built up the institute primarily to serve the commission. In his final year as its executive secretary, he calculated that 86 percent of the institute's $288,000 annual operating budget was directly related to activities performed on its behalf. With the end of the institute's contractual relationship with the commission, so, too, ended the financial support of the Department of Conservation, which amounted to about half of the institute's annual revenues. That same year, the institute received its final installment of the three-year Joyce grant. After that, its revenues were reduced to a trickle. Fell picked up the occasional contract to conduct a natural areas inventory or develop a natural areas management plan for organizations including the Indiana Division of Nature Preserves, the Arkansas Natural Heritage Commission, and the Illinois chapter of The Nature Conservancy. The commission employed the institute on a minor contractual basis to index commission minutes and resolutions, prepare biennial reports, and develop preserve management plans for select nature preserves. The combined fees afforded by these contracts seldom amounted to more than twenty thousand dollars a year.

As the financial fortunes of the Natural Land Institute waned, those of the Illinois chapter of The Nature Conservancy improved significantly. One of the purposes of the three-year Joyce Foundation grant was to challenge both organizations to cultivate additional, ongoing sources of support by matching a portion of their respective allocations dollar for dollar. The institute successfully raised the match amount, but, because Fell had no interest in building up an organization, the support came from a small number of sources that turned out to be mainly one-time contributors. The Illinois chapter, on the other hand, utilized the challenge to sustainably expand its membership and donor base. Additionally, while Fell insisted that the institute board of trustees remain restricted to a small number of trusted colleagues, the Illinois chapter cultivated a large and diversified board that included prominent conservationists such as William Beecher, director of the Chicago Academy of Sciences, and Dan Malkovich, former director of the Department of Conservation. Perhaps even more important, the Illinois chapter opened the doors to numerous private and institutional funding sources by bringing onto the board business and civic leaders including Charles C. Haffner, treasurer of R. R. Donnelley Corporation; Frederick C. Pullman, vice president of Northern Trust Bank; and Waid R. Vanderpoel, vice president of the First National Bank of Chicago.

With its increased capacity, the Illinois chapter was able to take on some of the programs and staff that the Natural Land Institute no longer could afford. In order to keep the successful Private Landowner Contact Program up and running, institute staff members Don McFall and Lydia Meyer went to work for the Illinois chapter before eventually transferring the program and themselves to the Illinois Nature Preserves Commission. Max Hutchison, working out of his home in downstate Illinois, managed to hang on as a part-time employee of the institute for a few years but eventually hired on at the Illinois chapter, as well. John White left the institute to join the science staff at the national office of The Nature Conservancy. As the conservancy's chief ecologist, he went on to oversee Natural Heritage Programs in all fifty states and nine foreign countries. Stephen Packard, who quickly advanced from commission field representative to the institute's director of public information, signed on with the Illinois chapter, where he developed his ideas about citizen participation in restoration into the Volunteer Stewardship Network. Jerry Paulson took a different route. After declining to pursue the position with the Illinois Nature Preserves Commission, he signed on with the Lake Michigan Federation, today the Alliance for the Great Lakes, to focus on wetland research and restoration before eventually returning to the institute many years later.

Within a year of the cutting of the cord with the commission, the institute had reduced its staff to a couple of part-time employees, including longtime administrative assistant Gladys Campbell. Having worked for Fell for twenty years, Campbell attempted several times to retire, but Fell always replied that he was older than she and still working.[25] She stayed on, working two days per week due to limited funding. Fell continued working his accustomed more-than-full-time schedule, once again for no salary. "He'd spend hours at his desk just reading," Campbell recalled admiringly. But sometimes his working silently and alone was too much for her to take: "Sometimes I tried to start an argument just to get him to talk."[26]

To a person, former institute staff expressed both joys and challenges in working for Fell. Along with Paulson, they recalled a general lack of communication and encouragement from their boss. To work for Fell, McFall remembered, you had to be a "self-starter. You had to be entirely self-motivated and self-critiquing. Each of us had a long leash but no feedback from George. You never quite knew how you stood with him."[27] Packard, with the experience of having launched a pioneering volunteer restoration project along the North Branch of the Chicago River, tried several times to get Fell to sign off on a new newsletter to build a more active constituency for nature preserves stewardship. Receiving no response, one way or the other, he finally printed and mailed the first issue of *Natural Area Notes*, using his own money. Only afterward did Fell send a note to Packard that read, "Congratulations, I knew you could do it."[28]

Campbell, her manufactured argument strategy having failed to break the office quietude, one day had suggested that that it might be nice for everyone in the office to take a coffee break every day and talk, just for fifteen minutes or so. To her astonishment, Fell agreed. Packard recalled that during one of the coffee breaks someone asked what everyone did for fun. When it was Fell's turn, he said he was disappointed that no one had answered that they considered work to be fun. "I can't imagine that people could live a life and not devote oneself to one's work."[29] John Alesandrini, a field representative for the Illinois Nature Preserves Commission, had not known much about George Fell before setting up a field office at the Natural Land Institute in 1989. His first impression was of "this cranky old guy who couldn't understand that not everyone wanted to work sixty, seventy, a hundred hours a week."[30] Over time, over many coffee breaks, Alesandrini, like many others, came to see Fell in a very different light. Fran Harty, a longtime natural areas biologist for the Illinois Department of Natural Resources before becoming the director of land conservation for the

Illinois chapter of The Nature Conservancy, recalled that once you sat down with Fell, "He had this low-key fire and brimstone that burned right through. And once he had you, then you were done. He put you under a spell. You helped save the land."[31]

The Natural Areas Association

The Natural Land Institute's sharp reduction in staff and revenues coincided with Fell's having achieved retirement age. The timing would have been perfect for him to dissolve the institute. The "shell corporation" had served its purpose of incubating and supporting the Illinois Nature Preserves Commission. The effort required to reimagine and rebuild the institute's capacity would have been a mighty struggle for anyone, let alone a man approaching seventy years of age. Yet, never did Fell allow a lack of resources or any other reason hold him back, not when there remained more natural areas in need of protection.

The minutes of the Natural Land Institute during the 1980s reveal that Fell explored a range of additional initiatives, most with limited success. In January 1983 he launched the Illinois Natural Heritage Foundation. Modeled after the Iowa Natural Heritage Foundation, the Illinois version was to be a member-supported, nonprofit organization that championed the statewide protection of prairies, wetlands, and woodlands but also greenways, trails, and river corridors.[32] A Natural Land Institute survey indicated support for the concept of an Illinois Natural Heritage Foundation, yet it never achieved more than a hundred or so members, and its few programmatic initiatives were modest in scope and limited in success. Fell followed up with a comprehensive investigation into starting a new community foundation to raise money for preservation organizations, but the idea never advanced to the implementation phase. For several years the institute continued its support of Robert Mohlenbrock's planned forty-volume *Illustrated Flora of Illinois* (an effort that remained in process in 2016), but Fell's idea to write a book of his own on the natural history of Illinois never came to pass.

Ultimately, the idea that took root was one he had sowed twenty years earlier. In November 1964, on the heels of the passage of the Illinois Natural Areas Preservation Act, Fell co-organized the first conference on state natural areas systems, held in Madison, Wisconsin. His co-organizer was Bruce Dowling of the Natural Area Council, a group founded by Richard Pough, Fell's colleague from The Nature Conservancy, to support small groups interested in preserving natural areas. Over the next ten years, Fell was too enmeshed in his Illinois work to organize additional conferences. By 1974, however, the number of state natural areas program had grown to twenty-five, most clustered in Midwestern states that scarce could afford to lose what little natural land they had left. Iowa,

Illinois, and Indiana, for instance, ranked one, two, and three, respectively, in surveys of which states had the least amount of land remaining in a seminatural state.[33] And so, Fell, along with others working in the burgeoning field of natural areas preservation, began meeting informally on an annual basis in what came to be known as the Midwest Natural Areas Workshops. At the fourth workshop, a committee was formed to explore the possibility of creating a formal association. At the sixth workshop, held in Minneapolis in 1979, bylaws were adopted and the Natural Areas Association was established. The mission of the association was and is to support the community of natural area professionals.

When asked about his role in the launch of the association, Fell characteristically and inaccurately deflected any credit: "I didn't start it. In fact, I turned my nose up at the idea."[34] In point of fact, he assumed his accustomed role as the association's first secretary-treasurer and de facto unpaid administrator. Among the first things he did was propose that the Natural Land Institute serve as fiscal agent for the association and provide administrative support services, office space, and facilities at no cost. Yet his most valuable contributions were to play the role of elder statesman and to recruit new members. Drawing on more than thirty years of experience, including the establishment of The Nature Conservancy and the Illinois Nature Preserves Commission, he barnstormed countless environmental conferences, preaching the gospel of natural areas preservation. Robert McCance Jr., director of the Kentucky State Nature Preserves Commission, was among those who were deeply impressed: "He gave the most emotional and personally stirring talk I have ever heard at the 1981 Kentucky Natural Areas workshop."[35] John Humke, who worked for The Nature Conservancy for more than thirty years, acknowledged that Fell was not the easiest person with whom to have a relationship but also noted that he "had so much commitment that when you hung around him some always rubbed off on you. You didn't really have any choice in the matter; you just came away a better person."[36]

Fell inspired many in the cause of natural areas preservation but went out of his way to gloss over his seminal role in sparking the movement. Others, however, knew where credit was due. At the Natural Areas Association's board of directors meeting on October 21, 1986, Glenn Juday, the board president, asked Fell to step out of the meeting temporarily. Juday then related that several current and former board members had "suggested establishing an award for those working in the natural areas profession, and that George Fell was widely acknowledged as the founder of our profession in its modern form."[37] In Fell's absence, the board members voted to create the George B. Fell award to honor those who exemplify lifelong dedication to the preservation and stewardship of natural areas.

Among the first individuals nominated for the George B. Fell Award was Richard Goodwin, who had "volunteered his services in the cause of natural areas protection for more than 40 years and is widely known and appreciated within the New England States conservation community."[38] What the award nominating committee had not realized was that thirty-five years earlier it was Goodwin who had been instrumental in Fell's controversial leave-taking from The Nature Conservancy. Association vice president, John Humke, a career conservancy staff member who knew of the earlier rift between Goodwin and Fell, felt obliged to inform Fell in advance of the nomination becoming public. "I called George, who didn't exactly let me off the hook, but he said, 'It's fine with me, but call Dick Goodwin and see how he feels.' I called Dick and he just laughed. 'George and I talk all the time, we get along fine.' Dick gave a wonderful talk about George and really brought public closure to the public split we insiders knew about."[39]

Fell never was one to let public recognition go to his head. If anything, having an award named in his honor caused him to work harder. He redoubled his efforts to recruit new members to the Natural Areas Association and steadily surpassed successive goals of 500, 1,000, and 1,500 new members. Unfortunately, the increase in membership did not generate enough money to allow the association to hire staff and undertake its own administrative responsibilities. At its October 1987 board of directors meeting, Fell surprised everyone by reporting that he had been in negotiations with an anonymous donor.[40] Two months later, the association received a no-interest loan of nearly $150,000. Several board members suspected that Fell was the anonymous donor, but Fell refused to say.

The financial windfall allowed the association to advertise for a paid executive director. It also spurred considerable discussion about the future direction of the association. Fell pressed the association to aggressively pursue on-the-ground natural areas preservation efforts throughout the country. He also envisioned the Natural Land Institute—still struggling in the aftermath of its separation from the Illinois Nature Preserves Commission—serving as the association's permanent headquarters. A number of fellow board members felt just as strongly that the kind of activist role Fell suggested would inappropriately compete with the work of The Nature Conservancy, which, by 1986, had established field or chapter offices in forty-six states.[41] The majority of board members voted to continue the association as a conventional professional association, providing a medium of exchange and coordination for information of relevance to its membership. They also decided to keep their options open regarding a permanent headquarters.[42] In September 1991 the association hired David N. Paddock as its first executive director. Within a year, the association moved its offices to

Mukwonago, Wisconsin, where Paddock had continued to reside. Soon thereafter, the association assumed responsibility for all of its own administrative and fiduciary functions.

Fell had fought mightily, at times questionably, to conform both The Nature Conservancy and the Illinois Nature Preserves Commission to his singular vision. Not so with the Natural Areas Association. He abided by the decision of his fellow board members without a challenge. Over the course of a lifetime, he had wrestled with "his worst shortcoming," a "quite unreasonable" irritation with those with whom he disagreed. In his seventh decade, he was no less passionate about the cause of natural areas preservation, but he managed to reconcile himself to the fact that others could, in fact, do things "just as good" as he.[43] Also, as it turned out, there were more important battles to be fought.

In 1990 Barbara became severely ill. Throughout their lives, both of the Fells had been blessed with good health, and visits to doctors were rare. But when Barbara could not shake a persistent feeling of fatigue and other symptoms, she broke down and saw a physician. The diagnosis was advanced lymphoma. Her physician admitted her immediately and started her on an aggressive course of chemotherapy and radiation treatment.

Barbara was one of five charter members of the Natural Land Institute, yet, unlike with The Nature Conservancy, she had played no formal role in its administration. Neither did she hold any position with the Illinois Nature Preserves Commission. Nonetheless, she was critical to her husband's success in these endeavors. For the many years Fell earned little or no pay, she provided modest but steady income as a medical technician. She managed their household. She grew, prepared, and preserved much of their food. She loved to entertain and often hosted teas for Rockford society members, which provided her husband with introductions to people of influence and means. To balance his workaholic ways and provide further introductions to Rockford society, she insisted that they be season subscribers to the Rockford Symphony, Rockford's New American Theatre, and the Starlight Theatre at Rock Valley College. They scouted natural areas together, and when Barbara was unable to accompany him, she made sure he had enough food for the trip. In short, as several close colleagues observed, Barbara's job, her mission, was to support, promote, and protect her husband.[44]

When Barbara became ill, Fell dropped everything. He took the first days off from work that any of his staff could recall and all but locked himself in the University of Illinois School of Medicine library. He read up on everything related to his wife's illness and the available courses of treatment. He made copies of everything he believed was relevant and shared it with Barbara's doctor. "His theory," according to a longtime institute staff member, Jill Kennay, "was that no doctor could possibly be up to speed on every disease. Barbara needed an advocate and that's what he could do to help his wife."[45] It is impossible to know what, if any, impact Fell's advocacy had on his wife's treatment, but in spite of the odds she eventually made a full recovery. According to several staff members, the prospect of losing her brought out a tender, sensitive side of Fell they had never seen before, along with a hint of humor. Even before her hair had grown fully back, Barbara returned to her perpetually energetic ways as if to make up for lost time. Asked how his wife was recovering, Fell deadpanned, "I could do without the vacuuming at two in the morning."[46]

The Last Battles

George Fell played a direct role in preserving more natural land than any other individual in Illinois history. During his tenure with the Illinois Nature Preserves Commission, he led the charge to designate nearly one hundred preserves, totaling twenty-one thousand acres.[47] Between 1958 and 1992, through the Natural Land Institute alone, he acquired or negotiated the acquisition of at least ninety-seven parcels of land in twenty Illinois counties comprising 5,148 acres. On behalf of the Illinois Department of Conservation, The Nature Conservancy, and several other groups, he negotiated at least forty-four additional land deals.[48] The largest deal he put together was the 1,040 acres that made up the core unit of Castle Rock State Park. Just as important were the small parcels, such as the 1.5-acre addition to the Rockton Nature Preserve Fell had the institute pre-acquire at the request of the Department of Conservation.[49] In 1986 Fell negotiated a five-acre addition to the conservancy's Cedar Glen preserve, which provides a critical winter roost along the Mississippi River for the then federally endangered bald eagles. In that same year, he had the Natural Land Institute enter into the initial contract to acquire 115 acres of Nachusa Grasslands, the core unit of one of the state's largest remaining prairie remnants, located in the north-central village of Franklin Grove and today one of the crown jewels of The Nature Conservancy's holdings in Illinois.[50]

Fell protected an additional 551 acres in six counties by negotiating conservation easements held by the Natural Land Institute.[51] An alternative and increasingly popular tool in the arsenal of land protection, a conservation easement, according to the Land Trust Alliance, is a "voluntary legal agreement between a landowner and a land trust or government agency that permanently limits uses of the land in order to protect its conservation values." In addition to providing permanent protection for lands that afford distinct public benefit, conservation easements tend to provide a little more flexibility than nature preserves designation and also may yield certain tax benefits for private landowners.[52]

Beyond the sheer number of acres Fell protected by nature preserves designation, acquisition, and easement, he singled out lands of particular strategic
significance. On the surface, his acquisition through the Natural Land Institute
of small vacant lots adjacent to the Gensburg-Markham Nature Preserve might
have seemed no more than an incremental means to expand an existing nature
preserve. For Fell, however, these lots represented ground zero in a purposeful
test of the legal strength of the Illinois Natural Areas Preservation Act.

Gensburg-Markham Prairie Nature Preserve is the largest of four prairie remnants, collectively known as Indian Boundary Prairies. Located in the
densely developed inner ring of south suburban Chicago, Gensburg's 167 acres
represent an unusual kind of tallgrass prairie that originally existed along the
western shore of Lake Michigan in the lake bed of its ancient predecessor, Lake
Chicago. A combination of black silt loam and true sand prairie types supports
a remarkably rich diversity of plant species, including rare specimens such as
grape fern, sundrop, narrow-leaved sundew, and grass pink orchid. It supports
nesting populations of imperiled short-billed marsh wrens, bobolinks, swamp
sparrows, and Henslow's sparrows.[53] In an ongoing attempt to restore the full
complement of original flora and fauna, the conservation biologist Ron Panzer
of Northeastern Illinois University successfully reintroduced to the site three
former native residents: the rattlesnake master borer moth, the rare Franklin's
ground squirrel, and the state-endangered prairie white-fringed orchid.[54]

Gensburg-Markham and its three companion prairies—Dropseed, Paint-
brush, and Sundrop—are all the more remarkable for being failed subdivisions.
In the 1920s, the site was platted for new homes, but a bust in the housing market doomed the planned development. By the time better economic times returned, "greenfields" further from the urban core had become more attractive
to developers. The site sat neglected until the 1960s, when Robert Betz, who
first came to Fell's attention as one of the pioneers using fire as a management
tool to restore native prairie habitat, discovered the abandoned development
and suspected a prairie remnant lurked beneath the weed trees, brush, and trash.
With support from the Markham Garden Club and Openlands, a Chicago-
based land trust dedicated to natural land protection in northeastern Illinois,
he convinced three brothers, Louis, David and Myer Gensburg, to donate their
lots within the site to the Illinois chapter of The Nature Conservancy in 1971.

Upon securing title to an initial sixty acres, Betz and a team of volunteers
began restoration of the degraded site. Within a decade, once impenetrable
thickets of nonnative buckthorn and multiflora rose had given way to a rich
tapestry of indigenous grasses and flowers. The reward for all the hard work
came with the dedication of the site as an Illinois Nature Preserve in 1980, followed by its designation in 1987 as a National Natural Landmark. (Established

in 1962 by the Secretary of the Interior under the authority of the Historic Sites Act of 1935 and administered by the National Park Service, the National Natural Landmark program has as its purpose to encourage and support the voluntary preservation of outstanding examples of the nation's natural history.)[55]

The year after the dedication of the Gensburg-Markham Prairie Nature Preserve, Fell began securing title, through tax sales and by donation, to more than 120 individual lots within the failed development and immediately adjacent to the nature preserve. Among the lots he acquired were several targeted because they lay within the boundaries of a Tax Increment Financing (TIF) District established by the City of Markham to encourage the development of a truck stop. Fell knew it was just a matter of time before the development plans of the City of Markham advanced. He had to move quickly to get his TIF lots designated as an addition to the existing nature preserve to see whether the Illinois Natural Areas Preservation Act and those charged with enforcing it were strong enough to withstand political, economic, and legal pressures.[56]

In 1993 Fell petitioned the Illinois Nature Preserves Commission to dedicate a total of 10.56 acres as an addition to the Gensburg-Markham Prairie Nature Preserve. The petition did not hide the fact that most of the lots were, in fact, within the boundaries of the TIF and targeted for development as a truck stop. A consultant hired by the City of Markham identified the land in question as "blighted and vacant." Commission staff reviewing Fell's petition pointed out that the Illinois Natural Areas Inventory identified them as high-quality prairie.[57]

Clearly, the prospect of having any land within the TIF boundaries dedicated as an addition to an existing nature preserve conflicted with the city's desire for development. At the March 3, 1993, meeting of the Illinois Nature Preserves Commission, the Markham TIF site's developer, parroting the same arguments that have been used to promote economic development over natural areas preservation since John Muir first sought to protect Yosemite from commercial exploitation, "expressed the view that not only endangered species deserve protection, but also human beings." The mayor of Markham adopted a more diplomatic tone, expressing "his long-standing support of the nature preserve," but asked the commission "to give some consideration to economic development of the area." However, a local resident and board member of Friends of the Indian Boundary Prairies questioned the mayor's sincerity by pointing out that he had initiated condemnation proceedings against the Natural Land Institute without the requisite forty-eight-hour public notification and that he also had released $2.1 million in TIF funding to the developer without city approval. The meeting minutes record that "a heated discussion ensued," at the end of which the commission voted to grant preliminary approval of the proposed additions to the Gensburg-Markham Prairie Nature Preserve.[58]

Up to that point, there had been no legal challenge to any dedicated nature preserve. In the well-established pecking order of government, federal law trumps state law, which in turn trumps local law. In theory, therefore, neither Markham nor any other municipality could, by any legal means, seize land dedicated by the state as a nature preserve. But that did not stop Markham from moving forward with its condemnation proceedings against the Natural Land Institute. With the theory of law on his side, Fell recommended to his institute board that an attorney be retained to fight the City of Markham. In the absence of established case law, especially since the institute parcels had been only preliminarily approved as an addition to the existing nature preserve, the institute board wavered. In a rare demonstration of independence, Fell's fellow trustees proved less concerned about setting a precedent than about the cost-benefit of defending small parcels. They rejected Fell's recommendation. Instead, they took the more conservative route of first authorizing an appraisal of the lands in question.[59]

In April 1993 the City of Markham's developer attempted to flout the legal process by commencing the bulldozing of the institute lots within the TIF boundary. Fell notified the US Army Corps of Engineers, which put an immediate halt to the illegal action. Prior to the 2001 US Supreme Court ruling in *Solid Waste Agency of Northern Cook County vs. Army Corps of Engineers*, 531 U.S. 159, which had the effect of removing certain wetland areas from of the Corps' jurisdiction, the Corps was empowered to regulate actions that affected virtually any wetland areas. The Corps' cease-and-desist order encouraged the developer and the City of Markham to consider a proposal by the Nature Preserves Commission to scale back the size of the proposed truck stop to take up no more than half the site and to allow the balance of the site to be dedicated as an addition to the existing nature preserve. Displaying an uncharacteristic willingness to compromise, Fell agreed to the proposal, which would have required the institute to relinquish title to two parcels within the footprint of the proposed truck stop.

Upon further investigation, the Corps determined that any development would need to be restricted to a mere 25 percent of the TIF site in order to avoid an adverse impact on the existing wetland areas. This determination left the city and the developer with two undesirable options: scale back the proposed truck stop even further or abandon the project altogether. Fell reported to his Natural Land Institute trustees in June 1993 that the developer had recommended abandoning the project and selling the land for preservation purposes.[60] Stung by the defeat, the City of Markham left on the table the prospect of taking legal action to condemn the institute parcels within the TIF district, but in time the controversy faded, and in 1998 the Nature Preserves

Commission approved adding the 10.56 acres owned by the Natural Land Institute to the Gensburg-Markham Prairie Nature Preserve.

For Fell, this victory came just in time. He had spent nearly a half century in pursuit of a strong, systematic approach to protecting natural lands. The Markham affair gave him the assurance he sought that the Illinois Natural Areas Preservation Act did, in fact, provide solid protection for Illinois's natural lands. This must have been some comfort when soon thereafter he was diagnosed with malignant melanoma.

During Barbara's cancer scare, Fell had all but ignored his work responsibilities as he learned everything he could to help aid his wife's recovery. When his own illness struck, he again hit the medical library, leading to his enrollment in a clinical trial program at the John Wayne Cancer Institute in Santa Monica, California. Otherwise, he strove to maintain as regular a work schedule as possible. Several times he took an early-morning flight to California to receive an experimental vaccine but insisted upon taking a red-eye flight home the same day, in part to save the expense of a hotel but also to miss less work. Among his priorities at the time was negotiating on behalf of the Department of Conservation for the acquisition of three tracts of land to expand and buffer Harlem Hills Nature Preserve, the site he had personally dedicated to the memory of his father.

In addition to the clinical trial, Fell underwent an aggressive course of chemotherapy and interferon injections administered by a clinic in Rockford. In November 1993 he wrote to his attending physicians at the John Wayne Cancer Institute of his "excellent progress under the present course of treatment." But the letter also revealed that he suffered severely from the typical array of adverse side effects.[61] Still, Fell kept busy. An inveterate tinkerer with all things mechanical, he found that working on computers took on the added benefit of distracting him from his symptoms. A month after providing his doctors with the update on his health, he sent a letter to Intuit, recommending "a simple way to eliminate [an] annoying mistake" in its accounting software program. He ended the letter, "I hope you find these suggestions of some use. The problem seems so obvious that I expect you have . . . taken care of it already. If you do find the suggestions useful, and if you have any way of providing any kind of compensation, that could be directed to the Natural Land Institute, a nonprofit organization devoted to preserving natural areas."[62]

A short while later, as it became clear that his treatments were failing to reverse the course of his illness, Fell ran through several drafts of another letter, this one to the membership of the Natural Land Institute. "I'm quitting," he began. "At least I'm retiring from my occupation of 44 years." At the age of seventy-seven, after seven years heading up The Nature Conservancy, nineteen years leading the Illinois Nature Preserves Commission, thirty-five years as the executive director of the Natural Land Institute, and a lifetime of never shying away from a fight, Fell resigned himself to the one battle he knew he could not win. With only a few months to live, he added optimistically, "I hope to be devoting some of my time to the large accumulation of papers documenting the progress of the natural areas preservation movement since Barbara Fell and I first became involved in it in 1948. . . . I've done the things of which I'm most capable. I've helped develop a strong and sound organization with very good attributes of staff, files, computer system, physical plant, and reputation. We've accomplished a prodigious amount of work over the years."[63] He closed the letter with a reminder to all to renew their institute memberships for the coming year.

At the December 16, 1993, meeting of the institute's board of trustees, Bill Jacobs was introduced as the new executive director. The trustees voted unanimously to grant Fell the title of executive director emeritus. Two months later, for the first time in thirty-six years, he missed a meeting of the Natural Land Institute. On March 5, 1994, he passed away, with his wife, Barbara, by his side.

Among the many lands that George Fell helped protect, directly and indirectly, there is one that best encapsulates his life: a gravel hill prairie overlooking the Rock River. As a young boy, he shared in a school essay his love for this "bare desolate hill [that] becomes a beautiful flower garden" teeming with native pasque flowers, goldenrods, and asters.[64] He later revealed to a classmate, "'You know, this is one of the very few pieces of natural, unplowed prairie left in Winnebago County, and it ought to be preserved.'"[65] When he married, he and his new bride and conservation partner for life spent their honeymoon night camping on its bed of wildflowers and native grasses. It took Fell many years to figure out the best form and structure for preserving such lands, but once he did he returned to his gravel hill prairie and patiently negotiated with its owner to buy the land and designate it as an Illinois Nature Preserve. Although its official name is the Harlem Hills Nature Preserve, unbeknownst to anyone beyond a small handful of trusted friends, in his heart he dedicated it to the co-author of *The Gravel-Hill Prairies of Rock River Valley in Illinois*, the man who first inspired his love of nature: his father.

For Fell, every last patch of natural land was important. Each one was personal. And the fact that he spent the final months of his life negotiating the acquisition of yet more land to expand and buffer the preserve he loved, perhaps, most of all reminds us that the work of protecting natural land is never done. But George Fell has left us with the inspiration, the tools, the institutions to carry on this work. "What nobler cause can there possibly be?"

Epilogue

I met a traveller from an antique land,
Who said   "Two vast and trunkless legs of stone
Stand in the desert. . . . Near them, on the sand,
Half sunk a shattered visage lies, whose frown,
And wrinkled lip, and sneer of cold command,
Tell that its sculptor well those passions read
Which yet survive, stamped on these lifeless things,
The hand that mocked them, and the heart that fed;
And on the pedestal, these words appear:
My name is Ozymandias, King of Kings;
Look on my Works, ye Mighty, and despair!
Nothing beside remains. Round the decay
Of that colossal Wreck, boundless and bare
The lone and level sands stretch far away.

Percy Bysshe Shelley

I̶n his *Natural Areas Journal* article "The Natural Areas Movement in the United States, Its Past and Its Future," George Fell provided a detailed comparison between IBM and The Nature Conservancy. Being a self-taught and highly successful investor, he knew "Big Blue" nearly as well as he did "Big Oak Leaf." Referencing a series of logarithmic graphs that he had plotted, he calculated that between 1962 and 1988 IBM's accumulated earnings (with dividends re-invested) had grown at an annual rate of 18.5 percent. "Quite a phenomenal record of consistent sustained growth through good times and bad," he observed by way of teeing up the even more impressive growth numbers of the conservancy. In truth, Fell's comparison was apples to oranges: it compared the most recent third of a mature, seventy-five-year-old corporation to the entire life-span of a nonprofit organization half its age. Nonetheless, his fundamental point stands on its own merit: the conservancy's growth from its inception in 1951 through 1988 was indeed impressive. Its membership base had increased by an average of 21.5 percent per year. The total number of conservation projects and total acres protected had grown by annual average rates of 29 percent and 39 percent, respectively. Total operating revenues and total fund balances had expanded on average by 33 percent and 47 percent, respectively, year after year after year.[1]

In the article, Fell took not the least credit for the conservancy's "remarkable growth history." In fact, he dismissed the very idea that this history had any-thing to do with its organizational concept and structure. Rather, he chalked it all up to "the determined efforts of a growing band of dedicated believers." Fell went further still in quoting in its entirety Shelley's most frequently antholo-gized poem, "Ozymandias," and then opining, "We [in the conservation field] have an advantage over the builders of structural monuments" in our knowl-edge that nature will, in the end, outlast both us and our creations.[2] Fell was no Ozymandias. He took pains not to call attention to himself. But, in his own summary history of the natural areas movement, he considerably undervalued himself and the importance of the institutions he had built. As much as the natu-ral lands he protected, they are—for more than half a century and still going strong—living monuments to his legacy.

The Nature Conservancy

Were George Fell still with us today, he would have enjoyed continuing to chart the logarithmic ascendancy of The Nature Conservancy. By several mea-sures, it has become the largest environmental organization in the world. Fell once envied European conservation organizations for having membership rolls numbering "in the thousands!" Today, the conservancy boasts a million mem-bers worldwide. Fell once chided his trustees for not investing in staff capacity. The conservancy currently employs 600 scientists and a total staff numbering more than 2,500.[3] Fell envisioned a robust chapter system coordinating conser-vation efforts throughout the country. The conservancy's reach now extends beyond its fifty state chapters to efforts in sixty-eight countries besides the United States. The conservancy was birthed with three hundred dollars in its bank account. Over the course of 2014 and 2015, its average annual revenues exceeded $1 billion, with total net assets of nearly $6 billion.[4] Following its launch, in 1950, it took nearly five years for the conservancy to protect its first parcel of land, totaling sixty acres. Worldwide, the conservancy has increased the number of acres it has helped protect to nearly 120 million and counting.

The Illinois chapter of the conservancy, with which Fell remained involved for many years, is one of the largest and most active chapters, with seven major ongoing project areas throughout the state. These range from a cluster of four globally rare prairie remnants a mere twenty-five miles from downtown Chicago to major floodplain river restorations in central Illinois and the far southern tip of the state. Together, TNC Illinois and its partners have protected more than ninety thousand acres and orchestrated the first bison reintroduction effort in the Prairie State at Nachusa Grasslands, a 3,500-acre preserve less than an hour's drive from Troy Grove, where the last known wild bison in Illinois was shot in 1837.[5] The conservancy recently reintroduced a second bison herd in the Kankakee Sands, a complex of ten thousand acres held by the conservancy that straddles the Illinois–Indiana state line about ninety minutes south of Chicago.[6]

The Illinois Nature Preserves Commission

Within a decade of Fell's passing, in 1994, the annual operating budget of the commission had recovered to nearly $1.2 million. It employed thirteen full-time and four part-time staff. In 2001 it celebrated the dedication of the three-hundredth Illinois Nature Preserve, a forty-three-acre parcel within White Pines Forest State Park, fittingly where the Fells spent a portion of their honeymoon. Asked what she thought her husband would have had to say about the milestone achievement, Barbara Fell responded without a moment's hesitation: "He'd say dedicate more."[7]

The commission would need every ounce of the strength it had rebuilt to deal with a fundamental issue Fell had foreseen but had been unable to address to his satisfaction. As the state of Illinois's financial problems increased throughout the 1990s and into the 2000s, governors of both political parties regularly swept the state budget for dollars to fill gaps, with conservation-related line items being a frequent target. In 2004, for example, the year after the Nature Preserves Commission celebrated its fortieth anniversary, Governor Rod Blagojevich recommended the diversion of $34 million in dedicated real estate transfer tax revenues from the Natural Areas Acquisition Fund and the Open Space Land Acquisition and Development program to the General Revenue Fund. Not only would this have deprived local governments of funding to acquire more natural lands, but it also would have zeroed out the budget line for the entire staff of the Illinois Nature Preserves Commission.[8] At the time of this writing, the state budget crisis, under the administration of Governor Bruce Rauner, who took office in 2015, had grown considerably worse, resulting in several key staff positions within the commission remaining unfulfilled.

Fell feared such assaults on the commission's funding and staffing, which was why he had fought so stubbornly to structure the Illinois Nature Preserves Commission in a way that insulated it from the inevitable ups and downs of government finances and politics. Although he fell short in securing the degree of independence he felt was necessary, the structure he did manage to put into place, coupled with the strong culture of conservation he had inspired within the commission and more broadly throughout the state, is among the reasons that, time and again, a diverse coalition of conservation interests has beaten back the most draconian of proposed budget cuts to the commission and the Illinois Department of Natural Resources.

In spite of its challenges, the nation's first state nature preserves commission remains an acknowledged leader in the field. To date, the number of dedicated nature preserves has risen to 392, encompassing more than fifty-eight thousand acres in 85 out of Illinois's 102 counties. To broaden the scope of preservation further still, in 1991 the commission established a slightly less restrictive covenant known as a Land and Water Reserve. Currently, there are 191 such reserves, which, combined with dedicated nature preserves, has raised the total number of acres afforded legally binding protection under the Illinois Nature Preserves system to nearly 109,000.[9]

Beyond the mere tally of acres protected is the critical nature of the acres. While the total number of nature preserve acres equals 0.3 percent of Illinois's thirty-six million total acres, they harbor 33 percent of all state-listed threatened and endangered mammals and 48 percent of all T&E plants. In fact, Illinois nature preserves are the last refugia in the entire state for ten animal species, including the Mississippi green water snake, and forty plant species, including Kankakee mallow. Remnants of eighteen entire natural communities survive only in Illinois nature preserves.[10] One such community is algific talus slope. Confined to unglaciated areas in the extreme northwest corner of Illinois, algific talus slopes commonly form at the base of north-facing cliffs and retain subsurface ice throughout the summer. The ice creates a microclimate that supports a range of plants and animals that typically are found in the Upper Great Lakes Region, Canada, and upper elevations of the northeastern Appalachian Mountains. Of particular note is the Iowa Pleistocene snail, which was thought to be extinct until living specimens were found in 1955 in a small handful of algific talus slope sites in Illinois and Iowa.[11]

The Natural Areas Association

The value of the Illinois Nature Preserves Commission, of course, extends far beyond the boundaries of the Prairie State. As Fell anticipated, its enabling legislation—the Illinois Natural Areas Preservation Act—served as the template for other states to follow in using dedications as a tool to protect natural land. These include Iowa (1965), Indiana (1967), Ohio (1970), Tennessee (1971), Arkansas (1973), Kansas (1974), North Dakota (1975), Kentucky and South Carolina (1976), Delaware and Mississippi (1978), and Oregon (1981.) Such is the strength of these programs that not a single one of them nor a single one of the nature preserves they dedicated has been challenged in court.[12] The legal protections they afford are rock solid.

In turn, these programs sparked the passage of related programs in other states. All in all, forty states have some kind of statutory mechanisms in place for the protection and management of natural areas.[13] In turn, the establishment of these statewide natural areas programs helped fuel an exponential increase in the number of nongovernment, nonprofit land trusts. In 1982 there were four hundred land trusts operating throughout the country. Today, there are more than 1,700. Together, they have conserved more than forty-seven million acres—an area about 30 percent larger than the state of Illinois, ground zero for the natural areas preservation movement.[14]

The Natural Areas Association, relocated to Bend, Oregon, has expanded beyond its initial emphasis on state programs to include land trusts, federal programs, and other conservation interests. Through its annual conference and quarterly, peer-reviewed *Natural Areas Journal*, the alliance is the go-to resource for the latest research findings, management practices, and related developments in the natural areas field. The alliance is supported by a growing membership base in all fifty states. Incidentally, to this day the association retains the anonymous donation received in 1987, arranged by Fell, as a quasi-endowment, drawing upon it for special projects. As many suspected but Fell himself never confirmed, he was the anonymous donor.[15]

The Natural Land Institute

It is never easy to follow in the footsteps of a dynamic founder. True to form, the Natural Land Institute—akin to The Nature Conservancy and the Illinois Nature Preserves Commission before it—initially struggled following Fell's departure. It cycled through a couple of leaders before Jerry Paulson returned to head up the institute in July 2000. In the intervening years, Paulson had greatly expanded his skills and experiences through extended stints with the Lake Michigan Federation, McHenry County Defenders, and The Wetlands

Initiative. Under his leadership, the institute made significant strides in establishing an institutional presence independent of the personality of its founder. Paulson recruited a stronger board, reenergized its membership base, doubled the institute's annual operating budget, and grew the endowment from $75,000 to nearly $2 million.

With this expanded capacity, Paulson led the institute in protecting an additional five thousand acres of land, nearly a third of the total sixteen thousand acres the institute has protected across twelve Illinois counties and one in Wisconsin. Paulson also led the institute through a signature restoration effort: the Carl and Myrna Nygren Wetland Preserve. Named for its principal donors, the preserve represents a next wave in the natural areas movement: reclaiming large-scale agricultural and other lands for nature. Prior to its restoration, the 720-acre preserve at the confluence of the Pecatonica and Rock Rivers, north of Rockford, was farmed for a century or so. Restoration included removing agricultural drain tiles, reestablishing the original meander in a creek that had been straightened and ditched, and returning corn and soybean fields to a richly diverse complex of prairie, wetland, and oak woodland.[16]

A Growing Band of Dedicated Believers

The current executive director of the Natural Land Institute, Kerry Leigh, never met George Fell, but she is committed to carrying on his work. "Our challenge now," she stated at an annual dinner for the institute, "is to transform George Fell's legacy for a new generation."[17] In the course of building institutions, Fell left an equally important legacy in the people he hired, the people he inspired, the people who found not only a career but a life calling in the natural areas field he functionally pioneered.

Leigh is among the next generation of conservation leaders who are forging new partnerships and expanded collaborations to achieve even greater natural areas gains. Chicago Wilderness, for instance, founded in 1996, is a regional alliance of two hundred public and private groups that seeks to expand upon the greater Chicago region's five hundred thousand acres of protected lands to create an even larger, sustainable network of natural areas. Initiated by the Grand Victoria Foundation in 2007, Vital Lands Illinois is a diverse and expanding network of conservation interests with "an overall goal of creating a statewide, connected system of natural lands, ensuring their permanent protection and long-term stewardship, and building public support for conservation."[18]

And it is not just hard-core conservationists marshalling resources to protect and steward land. Citizens throughout northeastern Illinois have voted overwhelmingly with their pocketbooks. Over the past twenty-five years, people from all walks of life have passed thirty-four bond referenda — effectively voting a tax upon themselves—for the protection of open space. The $1.3 billion raised through these referenda has allowed forest preserve districts, conservation districts, municipalities, and park districts to protect an additional forty thousand acres of land.[19] One by one, homeowners, too, are jumping on the bandwagon. In 2005 The Conservation Foundation, a land trust serving Will, Kane, DuPage, and Kendall Counties, launched Conservation@Home. This program encourages homeowners to replace conventional turf grass in their yards with native plants, install rain gardens, and reduce the use of fertilizers and pesticides. Recently expanded into Cook, Lake, and McHenry Counties, the program now has certified more than 150,000 homes, which are individually and collectively saving water, reducing pollutant runoff into streams and lakes, and creating buffer habitat for the region's protected lands and the critters that depend on them.[20]

In the end, perhaps we should take Fell at his word, but with a caveat. There is no doubt that the conservation successes during his lifetime and after can be ascribed in part to "the determined efforts of a growing band of dedicated believers," as he proclaimed in his *Natural Areas Journal* article. But it is important to remember that the inspiration for a lot of those successes traces back to Fell. "George was the stone that started a lot of ripples," recalled Fran Harty, a 2013 recipient of the Natural Areas Association's George B. Fell Award.[21] At a time when there were few models sufficient to the task at hand, Fell had the persistence to build new, innovative institutions. The very act of building those institutions galvanized a lot of people, offering them mechanisms within which to focus and realize their own conservation passions. The fact that Fell was not the one to nurture the institutions he built to maturity ultimately is immaterial. George Fell was a stone, a rock, a force of nature, whose legacy lives with us still: in the institutions he built, in the people he inspired, in the natural lands he loved and protected forever.

Notes

Prologue

1. Leslie Ann Epperson, Saving Nature, WILL-TV, Urbana, IL, 1989, documentary film.

2. George B. Fell, "We Strive for Beauty," single-page manuscript, December 14, 1993, George Fell Papers, University of Illinois Archives (hereafter cited as Fell Papers). Fell kept copies of minutes, memos, correspondence, and other materials from his time with various organizations. When he died, all of these materials were in the possession of the Natural Land Institute but were later transferred to the University of Illinois Archives.

3. George B. Fell, "The Natural Areas Preservation Movement in the United States, Its Past and Future," *Natural Areas Journal* 3, no. 4 (October 1983): 51.

Chapter 1. From the Bend of a Beautiful River to the Alcatraz of Conscientious Objector Camps

1. *Rockford 1912* (Rockford, IL: Rockford Morning Star, 1912), 43.

2. Elizabeth Carter, interview with author, December 19, 2002, tape recording.

3. George and Barbara Fell, interview with Brian Anderson, November 4, 1993, transcript, 35, Fell Papers.

4. Ibid.

5. Olive Brady Fell to George Fell, March 17, 1935, Fell Papers.

6. Carter, interview with author.

7. "Dr. Egbert Fell Dies at Age 82," *Rockford Register Star*, July 17, 1960.

8. *McCoy's Rockford City Directory 1922* (Rockford, IL: McCoy Directory Company, 1922), 163.

9. Carter, interview with author.

10. George and Barbara Fell, Anderson interview, 36.

11. Egbert W. Fell, M.D., "Illinois Physician-Botanists," *Illinois Medical Journal* 109, no. 5 (May 1956): 1.

12. "Dr. Egbert Fell Dies," *Rockford Register Star*.

13. C. Hal Nelson, ed., *Sinnissippi Saga* (Mendota, IL: Wayside Press, 1968), 516.

14. "Doctor's Hobby Becomes Area Plant Life Crusade," *Rockford Register Star*, May 6, 1956.

15. Elizabeth Carter, letter to author, January 9, 2003.

16. Stephen Fox, *The American Conservation Movement: John Muir and His Legacy* (Madison: University of Wisconsin Press, 1985), 333.

17. Ibid., 121–30.

18. Oliver H. Orr Jr., *Saving American Birds: T. Gilbert Pearson and the Founding of the Audubon Movement* (Gainesville: University Press of Florida, 1992), 8–34.

19. Fox, *The American Conservation Movement*, 274.

20. Ibid., 275–77.

21. Alden C. Hayes to Barbara Fell, December 18, 1994, Fell Papers.

22. George B. Fell, high school botany workbooks (Fall Semester, 1931, and Spring Semester, 1932), Fell Papers.

23. Minutes of Third Meeting of Board of Trustees, Natural Land Institute, December 30, 1960, 3.

24. George B. Fell, "A Hilltop" (student paper, Keith Country Day School, September 22, 1932), Fell Papers.

25. George B. Fell, "A Storm on the Water" (student paper, Keith Country Day School, September 30, 1932), Fell Papers.

26. George B. Fell, "The Depression and I" (student paper, Keith Country Day School, circa 1932), Fell Papers.

27. "The Morrow Plots: A Century of Learning," University of Illinois at Urbana-Champaign, http://cropsci.illinois.edu/research/morrow (accessed May 27, 2016).

28. Illinois Department of Agriculture, "Facts about Illinois Agriculture," https://www.agr.state.il.us/facts-about-illinois-agriculture (accessed May 27, 2016).

29. Maynard Brichford, "A Brief History of the University of Illinois," University of Illinois Archives, 1971 (rev. June 1, 1983), www.library.illinois.edu/archives/features/history.php (accessed May 27, 2016).

30. Greg Mitman, *The State of Nature: Ecology, Community, and American Social Thought, 1900–1950* (Chicago: University of Chicago Press, 1992), 16–18.

31. Robert A. Croker, *Pioneer Ecologist: The Life and Work of Victor Ernest Shelford, 1877–1968* (Washington, DC: Smithsonian Institution Press, 1991), 64.

32. William Temple Hornaday and Frederic Collin Walcott, *Wildlife Conservation in Theory and Practice* (New Haven: Yale University Press, 1914), 184.

33. Croker, *Pioneer Ecologist*, 121.

34. George B. Fell, "What I Think of College Profs" (loose-leaf paper, circa 1938), Fell Papers.

35. Croker, *Pioneer Ecologist*, 49.

36. Ibid., xvii.

37. George Fell to Egbert Fell, October 11, 1940, Fell Papers.

38. Egbert Fell to George Fell, September 21, 1934, Fell Papers.

39. George Fell to Egbert Fell, February 10, 1937, Fell Papers.

40. *Illio* (yearbook for the class of 1938), University of Illinois, 465.

41. George Fell to Olive Brady Fell, October 13, 1936, Fell Papers.

42. George Fell to Olive Brady Fell, October 19, 1936, Fell Papers.

43. George Fell to Olive Brady Fell, June 13, 1937, Fell Papers.

44. George Fell to Olive Brady Fell, October 19, 1936, Fell Papers.

45. "Ramsar Convention Country Profiles," http://www.ramsar.org/country-profiles (accessed May 27, 2016).

46. Alden C. Hayes to Barbara Fell, December 16, 1984, Fell Papers.

47. Peter Aleshire, *Deserts: The Extreme Earth* (New York: Chelsea House, 2008), 85.

48. George Fell to Olive Brady Fell, July 17, 1937, Fell Papers.

49. Alden C. Hayes to Barbara Fell, December 16, 1984, Fell Papers.

50. George and Barbara Fell, Anderson interview, 35.

51. George Fell to Olive Brady Fell, November 17, 1935, Fell Papers.

52. Frank Bellrose, telephone interview with author, March 26, 2004.

53. Frank Bellrose to George B. Fell, July 22, 1938, Fell Papers.

54. Curt Meine, *Aldo Leopold: His Life and Work* (Madison: University of Wisconsin Press, 1988), 430–31.

55. Aldo Leopold, "The Farmer as a Conservationist," *American Forests* 45, no. 6 (June 1939): 1.

56. Ibid.

57. George Fell to Olive Brady Fell, April 22, 1940, Fell Papers.

58. George Fell to Egbert Fell, March 6, 1940, Fell Papers.

59. Stephen J. Norling, *Necedah National Wildlife Refuge: Past, Present and Future* (n.p.: Rocky Ridge Enterprise Publishing, 2008), 4–5.

60. Helen McGavran Corneli, *Mice in the Freezer, Owls on the Porch: The Lives of Naturalists Frederick and Frances Hamerstrom* (Madison: University of Wisconsin Press, 2002), 71.

61. Ibid., 86.

62. George Fell to Olive Brady Fell, August 3, 1939, Fell Papers.

63. George Fell to Olive Brady Fell, April 22, 1940, Fell Papers.

64. George B. Fell, résumé (circa 1940), Fell Papers.

65. George Fell to Olive Brady Fell, May 8, 1940, Fell Papers.

66. George Fell to Olive Brady Fell, August 19, 1940, Fell Papers.

67. "Conscientious Objection in America," Swarthmore College, https://www.swarthmore.edu/library/peace/conscientiousobjection/co%20website/pages/HistoryNew.htm (accessed June 26, 2016).

68. Neil M. Maher, *Nature's New Deal* (New York: Oxford University Press, 2008), 3–15.

69. Carter, interview with author.

70. George Fell to Olive Brady Fell, July 4, 1941, Fell Papers.

71. George Fell to Olive Brady Fell, September 7, 1941, Fell Papers.

72. Judith Ehrlich and Rick Tejada-Flores, *The Good War and Those Who Refused to Fight It*, Paradigm Productions, Berkeley, CA, 1993, documentary film.

73. George Fell, application for transfer to mental hospital unit (Brethren Service Committee, December 18, 1941), Fell Papers.

74. "Won't Use Objectors at Elgin Institution" (unnamed newspaper clipping, January 21, 1946), Fell Papers.

75. George Fell to Olive Brady Fell, May 19, 1942, Fell Papers.

76. Matthew C. Perry, "The Evolution of Patuxent as a Research Refuge and a Wildlife Research Center" (sixty-fifth anniversary publication, circa 2004), 3.

77. George Fell to Olive Brady Fell, August 17, 1942, Fell Papers.

78. George Fell to Olive Brady Fell, March 6, 1943, Fell Papers.

79. George Fell to Olive Brady Fell, March 11, 1942, Fell Papers.

80. George B. Fell to To Whom It May Concern, Civilian Public Service Camp No. 34, May 24, 1943, Fell Papers.

81. Marvel R. Garner, "Fell, George" (addendum to transfer request, n.d.), Fell Papers.

82. George Fell to Olive Brady Fell, September 21, 1943, Fell Papers.

83. George Fell to Olive Brady Fell, June 1, 1943, Fell Papers.

84. George Fell to Olive Brady Fell, September 21, 1943, Fell Papers.

85. Ibid.

86. Antonio Thompson, *Men in German Uniform: POWs in America during World War II* (Knoxville: University of Tennessee Press, 2010), 84.

87. V. H. Whitney, "C.O.'s: Second-Class Citizens," *Nation* (December 29, 1945): 736.

88. Brethren Service Committee, George Fell personnel record (December 12, 1942), Fell Papers.

89. George Fell to Egbert Fell, November 28, 1944, Fell Papers.

90. Carter, interview with author.

91. George and Barbara Fell, Anderson interview, 41.

92. George Fell to Egbert Fell, January 18, 1945, Fell Papers.

93. Shirley Carlson, "A Two Hundred Year History of Learning Disabilities," research document, Regis University, November 17, 2005, 5.

94. George Fell to Olive Brady Fell, November 22, 1944, Fell Papers.

95. George Fell to Olive Brady Fell, November 15, 1945, Fell Papers.

96. Untitled, sung to the tune of "Over There" (lyrics to be sung to popular song tunes in CPS camps, circa 1941–45), Fell Papers.

97. George Fell to Egbert Fell, November 28, 1944, Fell Papers.

98. George Fell to Egbert Fell, November 15, 1944, Fell Papers.

99. Ibid.

100. George Fell to Olive Brady Fell, October 25, 1945, Fell Papers.

101. George Fell to Olive Brady Fell, July 13, 1944, Fell Papers.

102. George Fell to Olive Brady Fell, December 4, 1944, Fell Papers.

103. James Tracey, *Direct Action: Radical Pacifism from the Union Eight to the Chicago Seven* (Chicago: University of Chicago Press, 1996), 42–43.

104. George Fell to Olive Brady Fell, December 16, 1945, Fell Papers.

Chapter 2. Threatened Lands, Living Museums

1. C. Hal Nelson, ed., *Sinnissippi Saga* (Mendota, IL: Wayside Press, 1968), 16.

2. George B. Fell to Arthur G. Vestal, January 21, 1946, Fell Papers.

3. Arthur G. Vestal to George Fell, January 22, 1946, Fell Papers.

4. John Ripley Forbes to George Fell, April 22, 1946, Fell Papers.

5. George and Barbara Fell, interview with Brian Anderson, November 4, 1993, transcript, 17.

6. Ibid., 16.

7. Barbara Fell, interview with author, December 19, 2003, tape recording.

8. George and Barbara Fell, Anderson interview, 17.

9. Elizabeth Carter, interview with author, December 19, 2002, tape recording.

10. John Strohm, "Why Is U.S. Far Ahead of Russia in Farming? Mr. K Seeks the Answer," *Kingsport Times*, September 21, 1959, 2.

11. Richard Wilson, "'Highlight of the Trip,' Lodge Tells Garst," *Des Moines Register*, September 22, 1959, 6.

12. Harold Lee, *Roswell Garst: A Biography* (Ames: Iowa State University Press, 1984), 23.

13. George and Barbara Fell, Anderson interview, 36.

14. Edward Charles (Ned) Garst, "Early Memories of Family Life" (personal reminiscence, October 1, 2000), Natural Land Institute, 3.

15. Roy Ginstrom to Barbara Garst, June 14, 1945, Fell Papers.

16. Garst, "Early Memories," 3.

17. Harlow B. Mills, "Report of Chairman," Conservation Committee, Illinois State Academy of Science, May 7, 1948, Fell Papers.

18. George B. Fell to Harlow B. Mills, April 26, 1948, Fell Papers.

19. George B. Fell, "Examples of Small Natural Areas in the Vicinity of Rockford, Illinois Worthy of Preservation" (white paper, circa 1948), Fell Papers.

20. Resolution, Illinois State Academy of Science, May 7, 1948, Fell Papers.

21. George B. Fell to Fellow Conservationists, November 30, 1948, Fell Papers.

22. Ibid.

23. Ibid.

24. Ibid.

25. Daryl D. Smith, "Iowa Prairie: Original Extent and Loss, Preservation and Recovery Attempts," *Journal of the Iowa Academy of Science* 105, no. 3 (1998): 94–108.

26. Friends of Our Native Landscape, *Proposed Park Areas in the State of Illinois—A Report with Recommendations* (Chicago: Friends of Our Native Landscape, 1921), 10.

27. Forest Preserves of Cook County, "Next Century Conservation Plan for the Forest Preserve District of Cook County, Illinois," http://www.nextcenturyconservation plan.org/forest-preserves-history (accessed May 27, 2016).

28. Trustees of Reservations, "Historical Origins of the Trustees of Reservations," http://www.thetrustees.org/pages/89_historical_origins.cfm (accessed May 27, 2016).

29. George B. Fell, "Memorandum Concerning Establishment of a Nature Protection 'Foundation,' 'Trust,' or 'Association'" (white paper, December 6, 1949), Fell Papers.

30. George and Barbara Fell Journal, October 1, 1948, Fell Papers.

31. Robert A. Croker, *Pioneer Ecologist: The Life and Work of Victor Ernest Shelford, 1877–1968* (Washington, DC: Smithsonian Institution Press, 1991), 144–45.

32. Ibid.

33. Smith, "Iowa Prairie," 94–108.

34. Curtis L. Newcombe to W. C. Alee, December 16, 1948, Fell Papers.

35. George B. Fell, "A Proposal for a System of State Natural Area Preserves" (outline, circa March 1949), Fell Papers.

36. George B. Fell, "Living Museums for Illinois" (white paper, circa March 1949, 3–4), Fell Papers.

37. Illinois Natural History Survey, "About Us," http://wwx.inhs.illinois.edu /organization (accessed May 27, 2016).

38. George B. Fell to Barbara Garst, circa 1947, Fell Papers.

39. Fell, "A Proposal for a System of State Natural Area Preserves."

40. George and Barbara Fell Journal, May 2, 1949.

41. Richard W. Westwood, editorial, *Nature* magazine, February 1949, 63.

42. George and Barbara Fell Journal, February 2, 1949.

43. S. Charles Kendeigh, unpublished memoirs, 32, Fell Papers.

44. Request for Personnel Action, Soil Conservation Service, May 4, 1949, National Personnel Records Center, St. Louis, MO, photocopy, Fell Papers.

45. Report of Efficiency Rating, US Civil Service Commission, March 31, 1949, National Personnel Records Center, St. Louis, MO, photocopy, Fell Papers.

46. O. A. Potts to B. B. Clark, May 2, 1949, National Personnel Records Center, St. Louis, MO, photocopy, Fell Papers.

47. Ibid.

48. George and Barbara Fell Journal, May 10, 1949.

49. George B. Fell, questionnaire for client farmers, May 4, 1949, Fell Papers.

50. Fell to Garst, circa 1947, Fell Papers.

51. C. E. Swain to George Fell, May 26, 1949, Fell Papers.

52. George B. Fell, "Progress Report on the Illinois Natural Area Preservation Plan" (white paper, May 5, 1949), Fell Papers.

53. Richard W. Westwood to George B. Fell, September 27, 1949, Fell Papers.

54. George and Barbara Fell, interview with John "Jack" White, November 22, 1993, transcript, 36, Fell Papers.

55. George and Barbara Fell, Anderson interview, 38.

56. George and Barbara Fell Journal, November 23, 1949.

57. George and Barbara Fell, Anderson interview, 10.

58. Ibid., 17.

59. Stephen Fox, *The American Conservation Movement: John Muir and His Legacy* (Madison: University of Wisconsin Press, 1985), 262–64.

60. Ibid., 266.

61. Ibid., 252–53.

62. Fell, "Memorandum Concerning Establishment of a Nature Protection 'Foundation.'"

63. Ibid.

64. Kendeigh, unpublished memoirs, 32.

65. Richard Pough, telephone interview with author, February 20, 2002.

66. George B. Fell to William D. Blair, Jr., December 4, 1981, Fell Papers.

67. Barbara Fell, interview.

Chapter 3. The Nature Conservancy

1. Richard Pough, telephone interview with author, February 20, 2002.

2. George B. Fell, "Memorandum Concerning Establishment of a Nature Protection 'Foundation,' 'Trust,' or 'Association'" (white paper, December 6, 1949), Fell Papers.

3. S. Charles Kendeigh to George B. Fell, March 10, 1950, Fell Papers.

4. Ibid.

5. George and Barbara Fell Journal, January 18, 1950, Fell Papers.

6. Barbara Fell, interview with author, December 19, 2003, tape recording.

7. Elizabeth D. Mulloy, *The History of the National Trust for Historic Preservation* (Washington, DC: Preservation Press, 1976), 3.

8. National Trust for Historic Preservation in the United States, Public Law 408, 81st Cong, 1st sess. (October 26, 1949), 1.

9. Pough, interview.

10. "The History of Conservation Legislation in the U.K.," Naturenet, http://www.naturenet.net/status/history.html (accessed May 29, 2016).

11. Mulloy, *History of the National Trust*, 10.

12. Bill Providing for a Nature Conservancy, H.R. 8513, 81st Cong., 1st sess.

13. George and Barbara Fell Journal, March 8, 1950.

14. George B. Fell to Russell Lord, June 13, 1950, Fell Papers.

15. George B. Fell to Jeff McCord, president, board of directors of the Fernbank Children's Nature Museum, December 28, 1950, Fell Papers.

16. George B. Fell, John Simon Guggenheim Memorial Foundation Fellowship Application (circa fall 1950, photocopy), Fell Papers.

17. George and Barbara Fell Journal, September 11, 1950.

18. The Nature Conservancy, Certificate of Incorporation (October 22, 1951, photocopy), Fell Papers.

19. George and Barbara Fell Journal, August 21, 1951.

20. Minutes of Nature Conservancy Board of Governors, Executive Director's Report, December 4, 1954, 5.

21. *Nature Conservation News* 1, no. 8 (May 1951).

22. George and Barbara Fell, interview with John "Jack" White, November 22, 1993, transcript, 5, Fell Papers.

23. Fell, "Memorandum Concerning Establishment of a Nature Protection 'Foundation.'"

24. John Bertram, "Conservation: Wilds, Group Is Formed to Preserve the Typical Unspoiled Areas throughout the Nation," *New York Times*, July 1, 1951.

25. *Nature Conservation News* 2, no. 4 (November 1952): 5.

26. Fell, "Memorandum Concerning Establishment of a Nature Protection 'Foundation,'" 1–2.

27. *Nature Conservation News* 2, no. 1 (March 1952): 3.

28. Stephen Fox, *The American Conservation Movement: John Muir and His Legacy* (Madison: University of Wisconsin Press, 1985), 264.

29. Richard H. Goodwin, *A Botanist's Window on the Twentieth Century* (Perersham, MA: Harvard Forest, 2002), 166.

30. Ibid., 262–63.

31. Foster Rhea Dulles, *The American Red Cross: A History* (New York: Harper and Brothers, 1950), 331.

32. George B. Fell, "The Nature Conservancy Chapter System," August 16, 1958, 1–2, Fell Papers.

33. Ibid., 1.

34. George B. Fell, "Living Museums of Primeval America" (brochure, October 1950), Fell Papers.

35. Dyana Z. Furmansky, *Rosalie Edge: Hawk of Mercy* (Athens: University of Georgia Press, 2010), 157–59.

36. Frank Graham Jr., "In Memoriam: Richard H. Pough 1904–2003," *The Auk*, July 2004.

37. Ibid.

38. Pough, interview.

39. "Preserves Aided Legally and/or Financially by The Nature Conservancy," *American Institute of Biological Sciences Bulletin* (February 1961): 20.

40. Minutes of Nature Conservancy Board of Governors, December 4, 1954, 5.

41. Robert H. Boyle, "An Earth-Saving Bulldozer That Runs on Money," *Sports Illustrated*, May 28, 1973, 42.

42. An Act to Establish the Fire Island National Seashore and for Other Purposes, Public Law 88-587, 88th Cong. (September 11, 1964), 4.

43. George B. Fell to Richard H. Pough and select, unnamed members of the Nature Conservancy board of governors, July 25, 1955, Fell Papers.

44. George B. Fell to Joseph J. Hickey, January 6, 1955, Fell Papers.

45. George B. Fell to Richard H. Pough, July 24, 1954, Fell Papers.

46. Barbara Fell to Richard H. Pough, January 3, 1955, Fell Papers.

47. Richard H. Pough to Robert W. Schery, December 15, 1955, Fell Papers.

48. George B. Fell to Herbert A. McCollough, December 19, 1955, Fell Papers.

49. Richard H. Pough to George B. Fell, August 15, 1955, Fell Papers.

50. Dorothy Behlen, "The First Acre," *Nature Conservation News* 31, no. 4 (July–August 1981).

51. George B. Fell, "Proposed General Policies of Nature Conservancy," August 24, 1955, Fell Papers.

52. E. Laurence Palmer to Richard H. Pough, August 9, 1955, Fell Papers.

53. Fell, "Proposed General Policies of Nature Conservancy."

54. Richard H. Pough, "Reorganization of the Nature Conservancy," December 9, 1955, Fell Papers.

55. Fox, *The American Conservation Movement*, 285.

56. Ibid.

57. Herbert A. McCollough to George B. Fell, December 14, 1955, Fell Papers.

58. Robert W. Schery to Richard H. Pough, December 12, 1955, Fell Papers.

59. S. Charles Kendeigh to George B. Fell, September 14, 1954, Fell Papers.

60. Frank Engler to Richard H. Pough, May 7, 1956, Fell Papers.

61. Kendeigh, unpublished memoirs, 34, Fell Papers.

62. Fell to Pough et al., July 25, 1955, Fell Papers.

63. Pough, interview.

64. Bill Birchard, *Nature's Keepers: The Remarkable Story of How The Nature Conservancy Became the Largest Environmental Organization in the World* (San Francisco: Jossey-Bass, 2005), 10–11.

65. Goodwin, *A Botanist's Window*, 161-65.

66. George B. Fell, "Memorandum on Nature Conservancy Management," December 1957, Fell Papers.

67. George B. Fell, "Summary of Nature Conservancy Policies and Actions," August 15, 1958, Fell Papers.

68. Fell, "Memorandum on Nature Conservancy Management."

69. Richard Goodwin, telephone interview with author, October 21, 2002.

70. George and Barbara Fell, interview with Brian Anderson, November 4, 1993, transcript, 24–26.

71. Goodwin, *A Botanist's Window*, 166.

72. Birchard, *Nature's Keepers*, 10.

73. Minutes of Board of Governors Meeting, June 18, 1957, 8.

74. Goodwin, interview.

75. Minutes of Board of Governors Meeting, June 18, 1957, 1–2.

76. Goodwin, *A Botanist's Window*, 163–65.

77. *Nature Conservation News* 7, no. 4 (August 1957): 1.

78. *Nature Conservation News* 7, no. 1 (February 1957): 2.

79. Ibid., 5.

80. Fell, "Summary of Nature Conservancy Policies and Actions."

81. *Nature Conservation News* 4, no. 3 (June 1954): 24.

82. Fell, "Memorandum on Nature Conservancy Management."

83. Elizabeth Carter, interview with author, December 19, 2002, tape recording.

84. D. Louis Steinberg to George Fell, October 24, 1947, Fell Papers.

85. George B. Fell to Dr. P. S. Waters, June 4, 1948, Fell Papers.

86. Fell, "Memorandum on Nature Conservancy Management," 3.

87. Minutes of Executive Session Held in Conjunction with Meeting of The Nature Conservancy Board of Governors, December 7, 1957.

88. Executive Session Held in Conjunction with Meeting of The Nature Conservancy Board of Governors, March 1, 1958.

89. Goodwin, interview.

90. George and Barbara Fell, Anderson interview, 24.

91. George B. Fell to Barbara Garst, circa 1947, Fell Papers.

92. George and Barbara Fell, Anderson interview, 31.

93. William R. Huntington to F. R. Fosberg (Chairman, Nominating Committee, The Nature Conservancy), August 8, 1958, Fell Papers.

94. George B. Fell to William R. Huntington, August 10, 1958, Fell Papers.

95. Birchard, *Nature's Keepers*, 19.

96. Goodwin, *A Botanist's Window*, 167.

97. Minutes of the Executive Session of Board of Governors of The Nature Conservancy, August 28, 1958.

98. Fox, *The American Conservation Movement*, 319.

99. Ibid., 321.

100. Fell, "Memorandum on Nature Conservancy Management."

101. *Nature Conservation News* 8, no. 1 (April 1958): 2.

102. *Nature Conservation News* 8, no. 2 (May 1958): 3.

103. Fell, "Summary of Nature Conservancy Policies and Actions."

104. *Nature Conservancy News* 9, no. 1 (January 1959): 3.

105. Fell, "Memorandum on Nature Conservancy Management."

106. George Fell to Alton A. Lindsey, November 28, 1958, Fell Papers.

Chapter 4. The Illinois Natural Areas Preservation Act

1. Aldo Leopold, *A Sand County Almanac* (New York: Oxford University Press, 1949), 212–13.

2. George and Barbara Fell, interview with John "Jack" White, November 22, 1993, transcript, 6–7, Fell Papers.

3. Ruth Little, telephone interview with author, March 27, 2003.

4. Edward C. Garst, telephone interview with author, April 13, 2003.

5. George and Barbara Fell, interview with Brian Anderson, November 4, 1993, transcript, 34.

6. George and Barbara Fell, White interview, 11.

7. "Wild Flower Preservation Society Records," New York Botanical Garden, Mertz Library, http://www.nybg.org/library/finding_guide/archv/WFPSb.html (accessed May 30, 2016).

8. Jim Lockhart, "The Prairie Boomer," *Outdoors in Illinois* 7, no. 2 (Fall and Winter 1960): n.p.

9. Ibid.

10. Hugh Moore Fund Collection, Princeton University Library, http://finding aids.princeton.edu/collections/MC153#description (accessed May 30, 2016).

11. *Nature Conservation News* 3, no. 34 (May 1, 1953).

12. George and Barbara Fell, Anderson interview, 40.

13. George B. Fell, fund-raising solicitation, Prairie Chicken Foundation of Illinois (January 1962), Fell Papers.

14. Minutes of Third Meeting of Board of Trustees, Natural Land Institute, December 30, 1960, 3.

15. Egbert W. and Olive B. Fell, "Bell Bowl Prairie," *Audubon Bulletin* 106 (June 1958): 7.

16. Egbert W. Fell, *Flora of Winnebago County* (Washington, DC: Nature Conservancy, 1955), preface.

17. Roderick Frazier Nash, *Wilderness and the American Mind* (New Haven: Yale University Press, 1982), 220–22.

18. Susan Lukowski, ed., *Preserving Our Natural Heritage*, vol. 2, *State Activities* (Washington, DC: US Government Printing Office, 1977), 628.

19. "Policies and Standards for Natural Areas," Michigan Natural Areas Council, April 1951, 2.

20. George B. Fell, "Draft of a Bill to Create a State System of Nature Preserves," November 5, 1960, 4, Fell Papers.

21. Robert V. Percival and Dorothy C. Alevizatos, *Law and the Environment* (Philadelphia: Temple University Press, 1997), 193.

22. George and Barbara Fell Journal, January 18, 1961, Fell Papers.

23. Edward M. Levin, "A Remembrance of George Fell and the Creation of the Illinois Nature Preserves Commission" (reminiscence sent to author, August 31, 2002).

24. Illinois Natural Areas Preservation Act, 1961, SB 465.

25. George and Barbara Fell Journal, April 20, 1961.

26. Dale Birkenholz, interview with author, April 2, 2003.

27. Editorial, *Chicago Daily Tribune*, May 1, 1960, 12.

28. George and Barbara Fell Journal, February 23, 1961.

29. George and Barbara Fell Journal, April 11, 1961.

30. Otto Kerner, *Veto Messages on Senate and House Bills Passed by the 72nd General Assembly of Illinois* (Springfield: State of Illinois, 1961), 27.

31. Ibid., 28.

32. Paul Powell, ed., *Illinois Blue Book, 1967–68* (Springfield: State of Illinois), 626.

33. S. Charles Kendeigh, unpublished memoirs, 42, Fell Papers.

34. Lewis Stannard to George Fell, March 22, 1960, Fell Papers.

35. *Nature Conservation News* 7, no. 4 (August 1957): 1.

36. Minutes, Executive Meeting of the Illinois Nature Conservancy, November 9, 1958, 2.

37. Lewis J. Stannard to George B. Fell, March 29, 1960, Fell Papers.

38. Minutes of Meeting of the Board of Trustees, Illinois Chapter of The Nature Conservancy, December 10, 1961.

39. George B. Fell to Lewis J. Stannard, March 27, 1961, Fell Papers.

40. George B. Fell, "Proposed Agreement between The Nature Conservancy, the Illinois Chapter of The Nature Conservancy, and the Illinois Nature Conservancy," George B. Fell, April 1962, 1.

41. Kendeigh, unpublished memoirs, 40.

42. Friends of Our Native Landscape, *Proposed Park Areas in the State of Illinois*, 1921, 98.

43. George B. Fell, "Wilderness Remnants for Illinois," circa 1963, Fell Papers.

44. Levin, "A Remembrance of George Fell."

45. George and Barbara Fell Journal, May 1, 1963.

46. Otto Kerner, *Veto Messages on Senate and House Bills Passed by the 73rd General Assembly of Illinois* (Springfield: State of Illinois, 1963), 22.

47. George and Barbara Fell Journal, June 17, 1963.

48. Natalie Bump Vena, "Preservation's Loss: The Statutory Construction of Forests in Cook County, IL," Anthropology and Environment Society, http://ae .americananthro.org/index.php/preservations-loss-the-statutory-construction-of-forests-in-cook-county-il (accessed May 30, 2016).

49. Louisa County Conservation Board, "About Us," http://louisacounty conservation.org/index.php?option=com_content&view=category&layout=blog&id= 84&Itemid=506 (accessed May 30, 2016).

50. "A Resolution to Recognize the 50th Anniversary of the Creation of County Conservation Boards," Iowa State Senate Resolution 28 (2005), http://coolice.legis .state.ia.us/Legislation%5CResolutions%5CIntroduced%5CSR28.html (accessed May 30, 2016).

51. George B. Fell, "The Illinois Conservation District Act" (draft language for bill), 1964, 4, Fell Papers.

52. Ibid., 2.

53. Ibid., 4.

54. Bill Birchard, *Nature's Keepers: The Remarkable Story of How The Nature Conservancy Became the Largest Environmental Organization in the World* (San Francisco: Jossey-Bass, 2005), 21.

55. Richard Goodwin, telephone interview with author, October 21, 2002.

56. Kerner, *Veto Messages* (1963), 22–23.

Chapter 5. The Illinois Nature Preserves Commission

1. George B. Fell, "The Natural Areas Movement in the United States, Its Past and Its Future," *Natural Areas Journal* 3, no. 4 (October 1983): 49.

2. S. Charles Kendeigh, unpublished memoirs, 44, Fell Papers.

3. Edward M. Levin, "A Remembrance of George Fell and the Creation of the Illinois Nature Preserves Commission" (reminiscence sent to author, August 31, 2002).

4. Kendeigh, unpublished memoirs, 44.

5. "Lake County, Illinois History," http://lakecountyhistory.blogspot .com/2011/05 /robert-douglas-horticultural-heritage.html (accessed June 4, 2016).

6. Illinois Department of Natural Resources, "Illinois Beach State Park," http:// dnr.state.il.us/lands/landmgt/PARKS/R2/ILBEACH.HTM (accessed June 4, 2016).

7. Illinois Nature Preserves Commission, "Illinois Beach Nature Preserve," http:// www.dnr.illinois.gov/INPC/Pages/Area2LakeIllinoisBeach.aspx (accessed June 4, 2016).

8. US Constitution, art. 6.

9. Illinois Natural Areas Preservation Act (1963), sec. 14.

10. Sam Pearsall, "Public Dedication of Nature Preserves," *Natural Areas Journal* 4, no. 1 (1984): 11.

11. Ibid.

12. Illinois Natural Areas Preservation Act, sec. 3.06.

13. Pearsall, "Public Dedication of Nature Preserves," 12.

14. Ibid.

15. William H. Chamberlain, ed., *Illinois Blue Book, 1963–64* (Springfield: State of Illinois), 617.

16. Illinois Nature Preserves Commission, *Illinois Nature Preserves Three-Year Report, 1964–1966* (Rockford: The Commission, 1967), 13.

17. Minutes of Seventh Meeting, Illinois Nature Preserves Commission, May 20, 1965, 3–4.

18. Dwight H. Perkins, *The Metropolitan Park System, Report of the Special Commission to the City of Chicago—1904* (Chicago, 1905), 63.

19. Minutes of Fourth Meeting, Illinois Nature Preserves Commission, May 2, 1964, 3.

20. Illinois Nature Preserves Commission, *Illinois Nature Preserves Two-Year Report, 1967–1968* (Rockford: The Commission, 1969), 7.

21. Minutes of Fourth Meeting, Illinois Nature Preserves Commission, May 2, 1964, 3.

22. Paul Powell, ed., *Illinois Blue Book, 1967–68* (Springfield: State of Illinois), 627.

23. Roderick Frazier Nash, *Wilderness and the American Mind* (New Haven: Yale University Press, 1982), 129.

24. Stephen Fox, *The American Conservation Movement: John Muir and His Legacy* (Madison: University of Wisconsin Press, 1985), 111.

25. Minutes of the Fifth Meeting of Board of Trustees, Natural Land Institute, March 10, 1964.

26. Ibid.

27. Don McFall and Jean Kearnes, eds., *A Directory of Illinois Nature Preserves*, vol. 2 (Springfield: State of Illinois, 1995), 60.

28. "Preserves Now Owned by The Nature Conservancy or under Purchase Contract," *American Institute of Biological Sciences Bulletin* (February 1961): 18–19.

29. Minutes of the Sixth Meeting of Board of Trustees, Natural Land Institute, June 9, 1964, 1–2.

30. Minutes of the Eighth Meeting of Board of Trustees, Natural Land Institute, November 3, 1965, 4.

31. Friends of Our Native Landscape, *Proposed Park Areas in the State of Illinois*, 1921, 37–42.

32. Phillip Miller, telephone interview with author, December 13, 2005.

33. McFall and Karnes, *Directory of Illinois Nature Preserves*, 2:56.

34. John E. Schwegman, telephone interview with author, March 31, 2003.

35. Max Hutchison, telephone interview with author, March 28, 2003.

36. McFall and Karnes, *Directory of Illinois Nature Preserves*, 2:89.

37. Paul Powell, ed., *Illinois Blue Book, 1969–70* (Springfield: State of Illinois), 626.

38. Ibid., 627.

39. Illinois Nature Preserves Commission, *Illinois Nature Preserves Two-Year Report, 1971–1972* (Rockford: The Commission, 1973), 14.

40. Illinois Chapter of The Nature Conservancy, "Grassy Slough Preserve in the Cache River Wetlands," http://www.nature.org/ourinitiatives/regions/northamerica/unitedstates/illinois/placesweprotect/the-cache-river-wetlands-grassy-slough.xml (accessed June 4, 2016).

41. John W. Lewis, ed., *Illinois Blue Book 1971–72* (Springfield: State of Illinois), 438.

42. Ibid.

43. Michael J. Howlett, ed., *Illinois Blue Book 1975–76* (Springfield: State of Illinois), 339.

44. Illinois Nature Preserves Commission, *Illinois Nature Preserves Two-Year Report, 1971–1972*, 6.

45. Illinois Nature Preserves Commission, *Illinois Nature Preserves Two-Year Report, 1973–1974* (Rockford: The Commission, 1975), 66–69.

46. Ibid., 5.

47. Ibid., 1.

48. Ibid., 5.

49. Ibid., 42.

50. Ibid., 9.

51. Chris Helzer, *The Ecology and Management of Prairies* (Iowa City: University of Iowa Press, 2010), 13–18.

52. Illinois Nature Preserves Commission, *Illinois Nature Preserves Two-Year Report, 1973–1974*, 7.

53. Ibid., 11.

54. Robert Betz, telephone interview with author, August 23, 2004.

55. Minutes of the Seventh Meeting, Illinois Nature Preserves Commission, May 20, 1965, 6.

56. John Warnock, telephone interview with author, April 22, 2003.

57. Illinois Nature Preserves Commission, *Illinois Nature Preserves Two-Year Report, 1973–1974*, 10.

58. Schwegman, interview.

59. Warnock, interview.

60. Minutes of the Sixteenth Meeting of Board of Trustees, Natural Land Institute, October 5, 1970, 1.

61. George B. Fell, memorandum to members, Illinois Nature Preserves Commission, June 21, 1971, Fell Papers.

62. Leslie Ann Epperson, *Saving Nature*, WILL-TV, Urbana, IL, 1989, documentary film.

63. George and Barbara Fell, interview with John "Jack" White, November 22, 1993, transcript, 36, Fell Papers.

64. Edward C. Garst, telephone interview with author, April 13, 2003.

65. Minutes of the Nineteenth Meeting of Board of Trustees, Natural Land Institute, February 4, 1972, 1.

66. Natural Land Institute, "Program and Accomplishments," December 31, 1978.

67. John White, *Summary Report Illinois Natural Areas Inventory*, Department of Conservation, November 1978, 11.

68. Bill Birchard, *Nature's Keepers: The Remarkable Story of How The Nature Conservancy Became the Largest Environmental Organization in the World* (San Francisco: Jossey-Bass, 2005), 37.

69. Boyce Rensberger, "Biodiversity: The Final Countdown," *Audubon* 101, no. 6 (November/December 1999): 64–69.

70. Birchard, *Nature's Keepers*, 30–52.

71. Schwegman, interview.

72. Susan Lukowski, ed., *Preserving Our Natural Heritage*, vol. 2, *State Activities* (Washington, DC: US Government Printing Office, 1977), 180.

73. White, *Summary Report*, 20.

74. Ibid., 2–4.

75. Ibid., summary page.

76. Ibid.

77. George B. Fell, "Memorandum Concerning Establishment of a Nature Protection 'Foundation,' 'Trust,' or 'Association'" (white paper, December 6, 1949), Fell Papers.

78. Don McFall, telephone interview with author, April 1, 2003.

79. Gerald A. Paulson, "The Illinois Landowner Contact Program—Revisited," *Journal of the Natural Areas Association* 1, no. 1 (January 1981): 2–4.

80. Ibid.

81. McFall, interview.

82. Minutes of the Forty-Second Meeting of Board of Trustees, Natural Land Institute, December 11, 1979, 3.

Chapter 6. Sowing More Acorns, Fighting More Battles

1. George Fell, "Senate Bill 1124 Illinois Natural Areas Preservation Bill Summary," April 29, 1981, Fell Papers.

2. Susan Lukowski, ed., *Preserving Our Natural Heritage*, vol. 2, *State Activities* (Washington, DC: US Government Printing Office, 1977), 171.

3. Fell, "Senate Bill 1124 Summary."

4. George B. Fell, "A Message to Persons Interested in Saving Illinois' Natural Heritage" (draft position paper), June 3, 1982, 11–12, Fell Papers.

5. Mary Lou Marzuki to Liz Hollander, September 25, 1979, Fell Papers.

6. David Kenney, telephone interview with author, May 21, 2003.

7. Alan J. Dixon, ed., *Illinois Blue Book, 1979–80* (Springfield: State of Illinois), 349.

8. Kenney, interview.

9. Fell, "Senate Bill 1124 Summary."

10. George B. Fell to Roger Findley, January 23, 1981, Fell Papers.

11. Glenn Harper to David Kenney, "Proposed Illinois Natural Areas Preservation Act," February 3, 1981, Fell Papers.

12. Kenney, interview.

13. Kenneth Fiske, telephone interview with author, April 1, 2003.

14. Minutes of Eighty-Seventh Meeting, Illinois Nature Preserves Commission, January 25, 1982, 3.

15. Jerry Paulson, e-mail message to author, May 25, 2011.

16. George and Barbara Fell, interview with John "Jack" White, November 22, 1993, transcript, 25, Fell Papers.

17. Jerry Paulson, telephone interview with author, December 3, 2005.

18. Minutes of Ninetieth Meeting, Illinois Nature Preserves Commission, August 23, 1982, 2.

19. John White to author, July 1, 2003.

20. George and Barbara Fell, White interview, 6.

21. Bill Birchard, *Nature's Keepers: The Remarkable Story of How The Nature Conservancy Became the Largest Environmental Organization in the World* (San Francisco: Jossey-Bass, 2005), 22–23.

22. John C. Sawhill to George B. Fell, January 24, 1994, Fell Papers.

23. Illinois Natural Areas Preservation Act, 1963, sec. 4.

24. Fiske, interview.

25. Gladys Campbell, telephone interview with author, March 31, 2003.

26. Ibid.

27. Don McFall, telephone interview with author, April 1, 2003.

28. Stephen Packard, telephone interview with author, April 14, 2003.

29. Ibid.

30. John Alesandrini, telephone interview with author, April 1, 2003.

31. Fran Harty, telephone interview with author, March 16, 2016.

32. George B. Fell, "Illinois Natural Heritage Foundation By-laws," January 13, 1983, Fell Papers.

33. Glenn Patrick Juday, "State Legislative Initiatives on Natural Areas," *Natural Areas Journal* 8, no. 2 (1988): 107.

34. David N. Paddock, "George B. Fell," *Natural Areas Journal* 14, no. 2 (April 1994): 86.

35. Robert McCance Jr. to Barbara Fell, December 13, 1994, Fell Papers.

36. John Humke, "Letter from the President," *Natural Areas Journal* 14, no. 2 (April 1994): 85.

37. Minutes of Twenty-Fourth Meeting of Board of Directors, Natural Areas Association, October 21, 1986, 4.

38. Minutes of the Forty-Second Meeting of the Board of Directors, Natural Areas Association, October 26, 1992, 4.

39. John Humke, telephone interview with author, April 16, 2003.

40. Minutes of Twenty-Seventh Meeting of Board of Directors, Natural Areas Association, October 13, 1987, 4.

41. Juday, "State Legislative Initiatives on Natural Areas," 107.

42. Humke, interview.

43. Fell to Garst, circa 1947, Fell Papers.

44. Jerry Paulson, Suzette Merchant, and Jill Kennay, interview with author, May 22, 2016.

45. Jill Kennay, telephone interview with author, August 9, 2005.

46. Ibid.

47. *The Illinois Nature Preserves System 1981–1982 Report,* Illinois Nature Preserves Commission, September 1983, foreword.

48. George B. Fell, "Program and Accomplishments of the Natural Land Institute 1958–1992," 2–4, Fell Papers.

49. Minutes of the Sixtieth Meeting of Board of Trustees, Natural Land Institute, July 19, 1993, 3.

50. Minutes of the Sixty-Third Meeting of Board of Trustees, Natural Land Institute, March 20, 1986, 3; Minutes of the Sixty-Fifth Meeting of Board of Trustees, Natural Land Institute, December 11, 1986, 5.

51. Minutes of the Sixty-Third Meeting of Board of Trustees, Natural Land Institute, March 20, 1986, 3; Minutes of the Sixty-Fifth Meeting of Board of Trustees, Natural Land Institute, December 11, 1986, 5.

52. Land Trust Alliance, "What You Can Do," http://www.landtrustalliance.org/what-you-can-do/conserve-your-land/questions (accessed June 11, 2016).

53. Don McFall and Jean Kearnes, eds., *A Directory of Illinois Nature Preserves,* vol. 1 (Springfield: State of Illinois, 1995), n.p.

54. Ray Wiggers, "Gensburg-Markham Prairie," *Chicago Wilderness Magazine,* Summer 2000, 5–6.

55. National Park Service, "National Natural Landmarks Program," http://www.nature.nps.gov/nnl (accessed June 14, 2016).

56. John E. Schwegman, telephone interview with author, March 31, 2003.

57. Stephen Byers and Loretta Arient, "Proposal for Dedication of an Addition to Gensburg-Markham Prairie Nature Preserve," July 1998, photocopy sent to author.

58. Minutes of One Hundred Thirty-Eighth Meeting, Re-convened, Illinois Nature Preserves Commission, March 3, 1993, 3–5.

59. Minutes of the Ninety-Seventh Meeting of Board of Trustees, Natural Land Institute, April 8, 1993, 2.

60. Minutes of the Ninety-Eighth Meeting of Board of Trustees, Natural Land Institute, June 10, 1993, 2.

61. George B. Fell to Dr. Leland J. Foshag and J. Anne Nizze, November 24, 1993, Fell Papers.

62. George B. Fell to Intuit, December 8, 1993, Fell Papers.

63. George B. Fell to members of the Natural Land Institute, December 20, 1993, Fell Papers.

64. George B. Fell, "A Hilltop" (student paper, Keith Country Day School, September 22, 1932), Fell Papers.

65. Alden C. Hayes to Barbara Fell, December 16, 1984, Fell Papers.

Epilogue

1. George B. Fell, "The Natural Areas Preservation Movement in the United States, Its Past and Future," *Natural Areas Journal* 3, no. 4 (October 1983): 49–51.

2. Ibid., 53.

3. The Nature Conservancy, "About Us," http://www.nature.org/about-us /index.htm?intc=nature.tnav.about (accessed March 19, 2016).

4. The Nature Conservancy, "Annual Report," http://www.nature.org/media /annualreport/2015-annual-report.pdf (accessed March 19, 2016).

5. Chris Wigda and John White, "An Ecological History of Bison in Illinois over the Last 9,000 Years" (poster presented at the Wild Things Conference, University of Illinois at Chicago, January 31, 2015).

6. The Nature Conservancy Illinois, "Kankakee Sands," http://www.nature.org /ourinitiatives/regions/northamerica/unitedstates/illinois/placesweprotect/kankakee-sands-in-il.xml (accessed May 26, 2016).

7. Barbara Fell, interview with author, September 5, 2001, tape recording.

8. Public Relations Society of America, "Saving Illinois Parks and Wildlife," Partners for Parks and Wildlife, Public Communications, 2005.

9. Randy Heidorn, e-mail message to author, June 22, 2016.

10. John Wilker, "An Exploration of the Relationship between EOs, INAIs, and INPC" (PowerPoint presentation), Special Meeting of the Illinois Nature Preserves Commission, January 25, 2016.

11. John E. Ebinger and William E. McClain, "Algific Slopes," *Outdoor Illinois* (January 2007): 23.

12. Sam Pearsall, "Public Dedication of Nature Preserves," *Natural Areas Journal* 4, no. 1 (1984): 11.

13. Richard Thom and Mike Leahy, *Status of State Natural Area Programs 2015* (Bend, OR: Natural Areas Association, 2015), 16.

14. Katie Chang, "2010 National Land Trust Census Report," ed. Rob Aldrich and Christina Soto (Land Trust Alliance, November 16, 2011), 5.

15. Randy Heidorn, telephone interview with author, March 23, 2016.

16. Jerry Paulson, interview with author, March 21, 2016.

17. Kerry Leigh, "Transforming George Fell's Legacy for a New Generation" (advance copy of remarks for March 29, 2016, Natural Land Institute Annual Dinner, sent to author, March 25, 2016).

18. Grand Victoria Foundation, "Vital Lands Illinois," http://www.grandvictoria fdn.org/grant-programs/guidelines/vital-lands-illinois (accessed March 31, 2016).

19. Arthur Melville Pearson, "10 Years, 10 Trends," *Chicago Wilderness* (Winter 2008): 33.

20. The Conservation Foundation, "Conservation@Home," http://theconservation foundation.org/page.php?PageID=82 (accessed April 1, 2016).

21. Fran Harty, telephone interview with author, March 16, 2016.

Index

Page numbers in italics indicate illustrations.

conservation: Ansel Adams's photographs and, 10; awareness raising about, 138; bond referenda for, 167 68; conservation easements and, 156; county conservation districts and, 109 11; environmental conferences and, 152 53; federal-state cooperation in, 118 19; historical purposes of, 121; at home, 168; institutions appropriate for preservation work and, 42; land surveys and, 135 36; living museums and, 39, 41; management of nature preserves and, 129 32; Massachusetts Trustees of Public Reservations and, 39; origins of, in United States, 4; permanence of nature preserves and, 116 17; popularity of, 138; preservation of small nature areas and, 36, 37, 39, 41 42, 118; public-private partnerships in, 122, 126; for recreational purposes, 4, 37, 42 43, 49, 100, 109 10, 115 16, 117, 121, 126 27, 144; taxation and, 126; utilitarian versus conservationist land management and, 20, 43
Conservation Foundation, 168
Corkscrew Swamp, 65
Cowles, Henry C., 13 14, 17, 38, 107 8
Cranberry Slough Nature Preserve, 120

Davis, Richard G., 78
DDT, 25, 60, 64
Dilg, Will H., 79
Dinosaur National Monument, 70, 99
Douglas, Paul, 57
Douglas, Robert, 115
Dowling, Bruce, 152
Dropseed Prairie, 157
Ducks Unlimited, 126
Dutcher, William E., 79

Echo Park dam project, 69 70, 99
Ecological Society of America, 15, 39, 40, 51, 58, 60
Ecologists' Union: affiliations of, 51, 54; agencies appropriate for preservation work and, 42; Committee on Preservation of Natural Conditions and, 40; Committee on the Study of Plant and Animal Communities and, 60; Fell invited to join, 39, 40; Fell's

leadership in, 41, 43, 51; Fell's 1949 proposal to, 49 51, 61, 138; The Nature Conservancy and, 44, 51, 53, 55, 58, 64, 113; Richard H. Pough's leadership in, 43 44
Edge, Rosalie, 64
Edison, Theodore, 65
Elgin Botanical Garden, 107
Elgin State Hospital, 8, 24
Eliot, Charles, 39
Emerson, Ralph Waldo, 3
endangered species, 60, 118, 125, 129, 135, 142, 158, 165
Engler, Frank, 71
Evelyn I. Fernald Memorial Herbarium, 9

Farm Security Administration, 24
Fawks, Elton, 114, 115
Fell, Barbara Garst, *87, 88, 90*; background and family of, 34 35; career of, 46, 55, 133, 155; dedication of White Pines Forest State Park and, 164; gardening and, 133, 155; lymphoma and, 155 56, 160; pregnancy and miscarriage and, 96 97. *See also* marriage of George and Barbara Fell
Fell, Egbert W., *82, 89*; botanical work of, 5, 8 9, 30, 98, 123; career of, 7 8, 12; death of, 97; George Fell as adult and, 29 30, 97 98, 133; George Fell's childhood and, 5, 6, 8, 9, 97-98; George Fell's correspondence with, 16, 21, 28, 29-30; George Fell's preservationist tributes to, 128, 160, 161; publications of, 97, 98; war service and, 29 30; writing and publishing and, 11, 138, 161
Fell, Ella, 75 76
Fell, George, *81, 83 90*; adult relationship with father and, 29 30, 97-98, 133; alcoholism in family of, 76; Aldo Leopold's land ethic and, 92; American Motors Conservation Award and, 77; antipathy toward government and, 21 22, 27-28, 42, 45, 47, 111; as autodidact, 26, 29; avoidance of limelight by, 4; botanical work of, 10 11, 30, 123; childhood of, 6-12, 97-98, 161; Civilian Public Service camp governance and, 25 27, 29-30, 40, 50; civil service examination and, 22; as conscientious objector,